SURVIVING THE STORMS OF CHANGE

BY JOHN WADDEY

Copyright 2004 by John Waddey
All rights reserved

*Other books by John Waddey are
listed inside the back cover.*

On the cover:
Rembrandt's *Christ in a Storm on the Sea of Galilee*, 1633

ISBN # 1-56794-292-X
Star Book # C-4011

Published by Star Bible Publications
P.O. Box 821220, Fort Worth, Texas, 76182
1-800-433-7507   www.starbible.com

Dedication

This book is dedicated to that illustrious band of elders and gospel preachers who led Christ's church through the 20th century. They struggled to recover from the devastating losses inflicted by the change agents of a century past and successfully built up the church at home and abroad. To them we are indebted. May they not be ashamed of or disappointed in us as we face a departure, similar in every way to that which they faced.

- The Author

Introduction

This book is published to address the challenges facing churches of Christ in the 21st century. These challenges are coming from those among us who have grown weary of the task of restoring Christianity to its original basis. They long for more excitement, more freedom in what they believe and do in worship and more liberty to fellowship with those of other religious bodies. They are working to change the faith, worship and practice of our people. In days past, men with similar desires left us for the denominational bodies they admired. Today, rather than leave, those we identify as agents of change prefer to stay and work to subvert and capture the thinking of the entire brotherhood. A careful reading of their literature reveals that they no longer believe that churches of Christ are Christ's church, nor do they subscribe to the basic doctrinal principles of New Testament Christianity. We are left to wonder why they are so desirous of staying with a body of people they hold in contempt.

This volume is but one facet of a strategy designed to confront, combat and defeat the change movement.
* Each month we publish and mail a gospel journal entitled **Christianity: Then and Now** to the leaders of several thousand of our congregations.
* Each week we send out an email lesson addressing some aspect of this movement.
* We maintain a website at www.christianity-then-and-now.com that has all previous issues of the paper plus scores of additional articles on the various aspects of the change agenda. Also, it includes our answers to Bible Questions related to the issue before us.
* We read and review all the books being published that promote the program of change. We also review and recommend those books written by faithful men in response to the change movement. The reviews are also published in the paper and on the website. This helps brethren know what is being taught and

what materials are available to combat the error. The reviews are available in a book entitled, **"Books About the Change Movement; Reviews and Recommendations."** It may be ordered from the author.

* We send forth occasional papers suggesting strategies that will help preachers and elders in dealing with this heresy so they can keep their congregations from being harmed by it.
* We engage in extensive correspondence with fellow-Christians across the nation who are standing strong and resisting this heresy in their local settings. In this we answer their questions, provide helpful information and suggest effective ways to counter the false teachers and strengthen the faith of their brethren. We encourage everyone who is fighting the good fight of the faith.

The many articles of this book have been selected from those the author has written in response to the promoters of change. They have been sorted and arranged into categories that give them progression and continuity and cover the entire spectrum of the change movement. Since we live in an age where most people are not inclined to read lengthy articles and books, each article has been written as concisely as possible. That feature means that the information herein is not exhaustive. We need entire books devoted to different dimensions of this new doctrinal departure. Hopefully they will be forthcoming.

We encourage readers to feel free to copy, use and distribute any or all of these lessons in gospel papers, church bulletins, Bible classes or for general distribution. One of the most pressing matters before us today is saving the church from apostasy. We must never forget that a century ago a similar change movement swept through our brotherhood and took away some 85 per cent of our people. Those who left are known as Disciples of Christ and Christian Churches. Our agents of change are all pursuing fellowship with the Christian Churches. Abandoning their Biblical roots, they have come to see things just as they do.

The day a congregation ceases to be a church of Christ such as the Bible describes, it might as well cease to operate because it no longer is part of the family of God. We send forth this book with the fervent prayer that we may help some individual Christian or congregation avoid being caught up in the maelstrom of change.

John Waddey
12630 W. Foxfire Dr.
Sun City West, AZ 85375
e:mail: johnwaddey@aol.com

CONTENTS

I. The Situation We Are Up Against
1. A Dreary Picture Of A Sad Scene — 17
2. Do You Remember? — 19
3. A Generation That Knows Not — 22
4. Dangerous Thinking — 24
5. How It All Began — 26
6. Facts We Must Face — 27
7. What Would It Take To Convince You? — 29

II. To Help Us Understand Our Problem
8. Liberalism And Conservatism: The Mortal Struggle — 31
9. Why We Have Problems That Other Churches Do Not — 35
10. Secularization Of The Church — 37
11. Apostasy: Is It A Possibility? — 41
12. Change Yes: Apostasy No! — 43
13. There Are Schisms And There Are Schisms — 45

III. What It Is They Wish To Change
14. When Is A Church Of Christ Not A Church Of Christ? — 49
15. Community Churches And Churches Of Christ — 51
16. Those Who Criticize The Church — 54
17. Two Kinds Of Critics — 55
18. Faulty Assumptions Of Change Agents — 57
19. Seeing The End From The Beginning — 59

IV. How We Got To This Point
20. How We Got Into This Situation — 63
21. Finding The Source — 65
22. A Self-caused Disaster — 67
23. Sound Men Who Help Make Apostasy Possible — 70
24. Enablers: Good People Who Help Others Do Bad Things — 72

25.	The Lure Of The New	74

V. Our History Is Being Repeated
26.	*Deja Vu* All Over Again	77
27.	Valuable Lessons From The Past	78
28.	Our Past Is The Key To Our Present Problems	80
29.	What If "Change Agents" Had Been Our Leaders	82
30.	Standing At The Crossroads	84
31.	Poor Benjamin's Almanac	86
32.	A Mystery And A Marvel	87
33.	The Slippery Slope	87
34.	The Way Error Gains Entrance Into A Congregation	89
35.	Full Circle	91

VI. A Profile Of Those These Promoting Changes
36.	Change Agents: A Biblical Profile	93
37.	Varieties Of Change Agents	94
38.	Getting Acquainted With A Liberal	96
39.	Deluded Disciples Who Loath The Lord's Church	98
40.	Unworthy Children	100
41.	Some Things An Agent Of Change Cannot Do	101
42.	Are They Truly Christ's Disciples?	103
43.	They Must Be Different Kinds Of Churches	105
44.	Church Of Christ Number III	107
45.	Spiritual LSD	109
46.	Confession Is Good For The Soul	111
47.	Some Incomprehensible Things	113
48.	Powerless Preaching	114
49.	Political And Religious Liberals	117
50.	Some Observations Regarding Christians Who Work In The Billy Graham Crusades	118
51.	Two Kinds Of Heretics	120

VII. The Strategy The Promoters of Change Are Using
52.	To Destroy A People	123
53.	Destroying Our History	125

54.	Beware The Revisionists	127
55.	Games That Liberals Play	128
56.	Lurking In The Shadows	130
57.	Congregational Autonomy: What It Does Not Mean	132
58.	Extremists And Alarmists	133
59.	Isn't It Strange	135
60.	A Felt Needs Ministry	136
61.	Those Infamous 28 Divisions In The Church	138
62.	Incrementalism: One Of Satan's Devices	142
63.	"Let Me Fix Your Problems"	144
64.	Strange Logic Of Change Agents	145

VIII. The Fundamentals They Are Attacking

65.	Changes Do Make A Difference	149
66.	Things Most Commonly Believed And Now Disbelieved Among Us	151
67.	The Fundamental Issue	153
68.	The Bible Must Be Rightly Divided	155
69.	Is Truth Relative Or Absolute?	157
70.	The Law Of Christ	159
71.	The Pattern Of Christianity	160
72.	Leadership By Consensus	162
73.	The Silence Of The Scriptures	163
74.	Believing The Premillennial Lie	166
75.	Man, The Worshiping Creature	170
76.	Information For Those Determined To Spice-up Our Worship	172
77.	Dimensions Of Worship	174
78.	New Songs And Old Songs	175
79.	Praise Teams For Worship: Are They Wrong?	178
80.	The Christmas Holy Day: A Biblical View	180
81.	Traditions	183
82.	More About Traditions	184
83.	Observations On Traditions	186
84.	False Equations	187
85.	I'm Not Ashamed	189

86.	Profaning The Holy	191
87.	Can You See The Wolf?	194
88.	When The Walls Came Down	196
89.	Heroes Who Paved The Way For Us	199
90.	More Heroes Who Paved The Way	202

IX. If We Are To Survive This Assault

91.	Clarion Call To The Soldiers Of Christ	205
92.	How Important Is The Preservation Of Christ's Church To You?	207
93.	A Necessary Ingredient Of Victory	209
94.	Brotherhood	210
95.	Love The Brotherhood	213
96.	God's Remnant	215
97.	Who Will Lead The Remnant?	217
98.	An Appeal To Preachers And Elders	220
99.	Wise Leadership Needed In The Current Conflict	222
100.	Fighting The Good Fight Of Faith With A Proper Attitude	224
101.	Let's Disarm The Enemy	225
102.	If We Are To Win	227
103.	The Conviction It Takes To Win	230
104.	Discerning The Issues	231
105.	Dangers Conservatives Must Avoid	236
106.	Misplaced Loyalty	239
107.	Concessions We Must Make	241
108.	Some Things We Cannot Afford	243
109.	Our Challenge	246
110.	Principles For Christian Soldiers	248
111.	An Appeal To The Administrators Of Our Christian Schools	250
112.	Handmaiden Or Mistress	252
113.	Inoculating Your Congregation Against The Change Disease	254
114.	Unpleasant Truths	256
115.	Painful And Unpleasant, But Necessary	258

116.	Preventive Medicine For Your Congregation	259
117.	Lessons From Our Southern Baptist Neighbors	262
118.	Good Riddance	263
119.	Our Post War Strategy	264
120.	We Beseech You On Behalf Of Christ	266

X. We Must Avoid Both Extremes

121.	Avoiding The Ditches	271
122.	Labels	273
123.	Deadly Enemies Of The Church	276

XI. If Change Agents Surface In Your Congregation

124.	Options Facing Kingdom Citizens	279
125.	When The Enemy Appears At Your Door	281
126.	When The Agents Of Change Come To Your Congregation	284
127.	Before You Invest In A New Thing, Check It Out	286
128.	If Your Church Leaves You	288

XII. Those Who Fail To Defend Christ's Sacred Cause

129.	Have You Kept The Faith?	291
130.	Dangerous Assumptions Can Be Disastrous	293
131.	Some Questions For Preachers And Elders	296
132.	If We Do Nothing	297
133.	Seeds Of Self-destruction	299

XIII. Parables For A Day Of Change

134.	Parable Of The Christian Family	301
135.	Parable Of The Unhappy Husband	303
136.	Parable Of The Firefighters	304
137.	Those Negative Firefighters	305
138.	Parable Of Jack The Firefighter	307
139.	Parable Of The Birds	308
140.	Parable Of The Mosquito	310
141.	Parable Of The Dinosaur Dog	312

142.	Parable Of The Changed Car	313
143.	Parable Of The "Vincible" Army Of Christ	315
144.	A Lesson From Nature In A Day Of Change	317

XIV. Some Basic Truths That Need To Be Re-Emphasized

145.	Knowing And Doing God's Will In Our Postmodern Age	319
146.	Attributes Of Christ's Church	320
147.	Must I Be In The Church To Be Saved?	324
148.	What The Church Is And Is Not	325
149.	Things Not Found In Churches Of Christ	326
150.	The Church And Denominationalism	327
151.	Christ's Church And Men's Churches	328
152.	Is One Church As Good As Another?	329
153.	Restoring A Thing Of Value	330
154.	Back To The Fountain Head	331
155.	A Name Of Which We Should Never Be Ashamed	333
156.	Does It Make Any Difference?	334
157.	"And This Is How Thou Shalt Make It"	336
158.	Women And Leadership	337
159.	The Fine Art Of Worship	338
160.	Worship Is Not Entertainment	339
161.	Unacceptable Worship	340
162.	Sacred Music 101	341
163.	Sing And Be Happy	345
164.	Easter: Did You Know?	346
165.	The Language Of Salvation	348
166.	How God Justifies Sinners	350
167.	Saving Faith	352
168.	Your Free Gift From God	353
169.	The Day You Were Baptized	354
170.	Is Baptism A Work Of Man?	355
171.	What Baptism Is Not	356
172.	Blessings Of The Holy Spirit	357

XV. What The Future Holds
    173. Imagine The Future Of The Church   359
    174. Looking Ahead To The Year 2050   361

XVI. Our Plea And Prayer For Our Departing Brethren
    175. Return O Backsliding Israel   365
    176. A Prayer For Christ's Church   366

XVII. Are You Willing To Help?
    177. Needed: A Thousand Faithful Helpers   371

I.
THE SITUATION WE ARE UP AGAINST

1. A DREARY PICTURE OF A SAD SCENE

Dear Reader:

Regarding the success of the change agents, I personally believe that they will succeed in sweeping a significant portion of our congregations into their apostasy. When they have reached their goal, the churches in fellowship with them will for all intents and purposes be Christian Churches or even more like the Independent denominational churches. They will have a Baptist (Calvinistic) theology and (Charismatic)worship, while maintaining congregational independence.

Already this movement is ensconced in our two largest and most influential universities, Abilene Christian and Pepperdine. Change agents have a strong presence in several others and will likely eventually win control of them. They have already taken scores of congregations, generally our largest, most influential churches in the large metropolitan centers. This gives them wealth and influence. They are already entrenched in churches throughout the country. They are aggressive and evangelistic. They are producing books that promote their new doctrines at an astonishing rate. They have the means to promote and circulate them aggressively.

Although they are still a minority of the whole, most of our brethren are standing by, either totally unaware of the problem, or unsure what to do. Others are totally indifferent to the problem, not wishing to be involved in controversy. While the agents of change have produced 25 or more well done volumes promoting their agenda, we have had only a half dozen or so published in response and not all of them of the best quality. To my knowledge, none of our schools that are yet conservative have taken an militant stand against the change movement.

We have a small, aggressive number among us who are actively at war with the change movement but also against everyone else in the church except their handful of co-workers. Their spirit, attitude and approach are so negative and hateful that they drive many weaker brethren to the liberal camp.

I hate to be so pessimistic, but that is the way I see the picture. We must find a way to rally faithful brethren to stand strong against this apostasy. That is the purpose of my little paper, **Christianity: Then and Now**, my website @ www.christianity-then-and-now.com and this book.

You can help us. If we are to save the Lord's church from being swept away by the agents of change, those of us who love her must go to work immediately to fortify and preserve the hearts of those within our sphere of influence and to establish an effective blockade that will keep the error from spreading.

We must establish a network of men who will stand with us in defense of the faith once delivered and then coordinate our efforts for maximum benefit. Each man needs to do the following:
1. Resolve to take a pro-active role by actively working to protect the church by specific actions that are calculated to educate, inform, fortify the faith of brethren and block the spread of the error.
2. Select an area that he will personally be responsible for "protecting." By this I mean, a brother could say, "I will personally provide a steady flow of information to the leaders of every congregation in my city, or county or even state, (depending on the size and number of the congregations in that area)." Once a month he would mail the churches in his chosen field, a newsletter or bulletin of helpful information on the change movement. He could copy and mail my little paper or, raise the funds and I will mail it. He

could prepare his own. He could collect good materials from many sources, copy and forward them to his neighbors. He could recommend useful papers or books on the topics under attack. He could invite those in his area for occasional get togethers where they could discuss the problem we face. He would go to work at once to educate and inform his elders and members and try to involve them in the project. He would lend aid and encouragement to every faithful brother and cause in his area and similarly refuse to lend such to the promoters of unscriptural change.

3. He should also establish a broader network with other good men across the country and share pertinent information with them as well as receiving it. He needs to be a source of information and help to those who are under attack or who need information.

I am praying that God will raise up 1,000 good men who love Christ, his church and his word. Working together we can quarantine and eventually neutralize this movement that threatens to destroy us. While one man cannot do it, a thousand of us, with God's help and guidance, can. Soon, God willing, there will be many. Would you want to help in this worthy effort? I pray you will.

Yours in Christ,
John Waddey

2. DO YOU REMEMBER?

Several years back a pop song asked, "Do You Remember the Days of Our Lives?" Moses encourage his Hebrew brethren to "Remember the days of old, Consider the years of many generations" (Deut. 32:7).

Living in an era of change when many despise the things of the past and where moral and spiritual confusion prevail, many younger Christians have never known those wonderful days when God's

blessings rested upon his church and she prospered greatly. From 1900 to 1970:
* All of our brethren loved the Church of Christ and gave themselves without stint or reservation to her service. They believed in the church, not as their savior, but as God's saved people.
* There was a holy pride of membership in the church. We had confidence in our faith. We were growing. We were building. Our champions met and routed those of the sectarian world.
* Our preachers and our members knew what they believed and why. Most members were Bible readers and knew enough to give an account their faith to any who asked them about it (I Pet. 3:15).
* Our brethren were not ashamed of their faith or their church. They were not apologetic of the sacred truths they professed. They stood up for the church and bravely defended her against her enemies.
* All congregations had at least one, often two, evangelistic programs each year. We called them gospel meetings. Capable preachers who knew how to lead sinners to Christ were invited to come and preach. We knew how to knock on the doors of our neighbors homes inviting them to come and hear the gospel, and we did so. Usually there would be a harvest of souls. It was not uncommon for many to respond.
* Frequently, all the congregations in a city or a county would pool their resources and combine their efforts in great city-wide gospel campaigns. Those efforts had a great impact on all the community. Brethren worked togther in love and harmony. They got to know each other more intimately. Christ and his church were exalted and glorified.
* Back then thousands of average Christians learned how to be effective soul-winners. They used charts and filmstrips developed by skilled brethren and went forth teaching their neighbors. Many of those soul-winners who were not preachers, won as many or more disciples as did their ministers.
* We sent out hundreds of missionaries to plant the Lord's church in new communities at home and abroad. We sent them not to dig

wells or teach farming techniques, but to preach the gospel and save lost souls. Churches were planted in over 100 nations of the world.
* Our preaching brethren were Bible men. They were full of scripture. They clearly understood why we worshipped and served as we did and they were not ashamed nor afraid to teach those Biblical truths in any forum or circumstance (Rom.1:16).
* Our preachers were admired and respected for their Bible knowledge and their skill in wielding the sword of the Spirit (Eph. 6:10), rather than for their attainments in education and their interaction in community civic associations.
* Our preachers generally spoke with one voice in proclaiming the blessed gospel of Christ.
* They could disagree about minor matters and opinions without being disagreeable.
* They directed their arrows at the enemies of Christ and his church rather than at each other.
* Our Christian schools were bastions of truth and served the church rather than trying to change her into a human denomination. When our young people who attended them came forth they were stronger in faith and more useful to the kingdom, rather than confused and weakened in their commitment.
* Teachers in our schools were chosen because of their Bible knowledge and loyalty to Christ and the church rather than on the basis of higher education gained in secular and denominational schools.
* Back then false teachers were promptly rejected.
* Apostates felt so out of place that they soon left us for other bodies of people.

Tragically things have changed. I pity those younger Christians who were not privileged to see the church in those wonderful days of old. May God in his mercy bring his people to repentance, purify his church and restore to her the happiness she once knew. Let the renewal begin with each of us personally.

3. A GENERATION THAT KNOWS NOT

Following the successful invasion and occupation of Canaan, and the death of Joshua, a generation of Hebrews arose, "that knew not Jehovah, nor yet the work which he had wrought for Israel" (Judg. 2:10). Sad to say, they were not the last generation who knew not their past spiritual history. Today, among our brethren, there is a generation which knows not.

I. Some don't know, understand or appreciate the plea to restore New Testament Christianity. They know little or nothing of those noble patriarchs of the 19th century, who abandoned sectarianism and human doctrines and struggled to find their way back to the faith and practice of the apostolic church. They cannot visualize nondenominational, Biblical Christianity.

II. Some do not know or understand the apostasy that occurred in our ranks following the Civil War. A generation arose then that no longer felt the need for Bible authority in matters of faith and practice. They surrendered congregational autonomy for a national organization that began with the American Christian Missionary Society and later blossomed into the denominational machinery of the Disciples of Christ. They adopted open membership. They ignored the apostolic restrictions on women preachers and elders (I Tim. 2:11-12). Their preachers evolved into pastors. They rushed to embrace denominational churches in fellowship. Most of our generation doesn't know that 85 percent of our congregations and all of our schools were lost in that apostasy. They evidently don't know of the hardships and struggles of our forefathers to rebuild the shattered walls of Zion and to reestablish congregations that had been lost to apostasy. They know nothing of the insults, taunts and ridicule heaped upon them as they struggled to hold on and survive.

III. A generation has arisen that does not know or care about the battles fought to plant the Lord's church in every state and hundreds of foreign fields. They do not appreciate the courage of those who labored to clear the ground, or the grueling work and sacrifices of those who labored to win lost souls and lead churches to maturity.

IV. They know not the roll call of heroes of the past; men who were not ashamed to proclaim the gospel (Rom. 1:16) without apology and with no uncertain sound (I Cor. 14:8). They know little or nothing about such men such as David Lipscomb, James A. Harding; H. Leo Boles, N. B. Hardeman, A. G. Freed, R. L. Whiteside, Austin McGary, C. R. Nichol, Gus Nichols, Otis Gatewood, Roy Lanier, Sr., Guy N. Woods, B. C. Goodpasture, Batsell B. Baxter, to name just a handful out of hundreds.

V. A generation of preachers now exists who enjoy well-paying jobs in numerically strong churches that others established and nourished to strength and stability. They preach in fine meeting houses built by those who sacrificed for a cause they loved. These who have made no sacrifices and fought no battles are now inclined to surrender all the ground others have won. Now we see men who preach a different gospel. They poke fun at the preaching of those who went before them. Their preaching is hard to distinguish from that of our Protestant neighbors. Baptism for remission of sins is almost an embarrassment to them. They want a different kind of worship. To sing psalms hymns and spiritual songs does not satisfy their spiritual appetites. Their hearts incline toward the use of instrumental music. They resent those who ask for scriptural authority for such things. They wish for a choir and see just how close they can get to having one. They crave entertainment. They look with longing admiration at those who use showmanship and entertainment to attract large crowds. They crave to be recognized and accepted by their clergy peers in their communities. They yearn for others to think we really aren't so different from them. Some wish to be seen as thoroughly modern on "women's issues" and are willing to move ladies into leadership roles in the church. Much of our preaching has lost its distinctiveness. There was a time when a gospel preacher of the Church of Christ could easily be identified by his knowledge of Scripture, his citing of verses to establish his points, his boldness in proclaiming the whole counsel of God (Acts 20:28). But now a generation exists whose concept of preaching is vague and generic. One must be told that he is employed by a Church of Christ.

In ancient Israel that generation that knew not Jehovah and what he had done for the Hebrews soon drifted away into idolatry and moral wickedness. They were swallowed up by their heathen enemies. Those who are younger will live to see many of our current congregations and preachers abandon the Christianity of the Bible and slip into the apostasy of denominationalism. We can only pity those of this generation who know not. As in days past, the faithful remnant will cling to the precious Word of God and pass the faith of Jesus on to future generations.

4. DANGEROUS THINKING

As the post-Christian world rushes by us on its way to oblivion, many church leaders are being tempted to abandon the worship and practice of the church which Christ ordained. They are exploring a new, modern version that they hope will help them survive in the 21st century. Those who succumb to these Satanic wiles are not wicked men who want to destroy the churches they lead, but they are misguided and disaster will be the end if they take their eyes off the directions Christ has given us.

Among the excuses being offered are the following. Very likely you have heard some or all of them for they are now commonplace.
* "If we are going to keep our young people, we must make some changes that will please them."
* "If we are going to survive in this modern society, we have got to make some adjustments."
* "If it brings us new members and more interest, it must be OK."
* "Our people really like the changes we have made and we all feel

good about it."
* "We are getting more non-members to come to our services."
* "Many of our Christian College professors have encouraged this approach."

All of these justifications for changing the worship and message and emphasis of the church are faulty because they place the opinions and judgement of human beings above the revealed will of Christ. Jesus is the head of the church (Eph. 1:22). He has all authority in heaven and on earth (Matt. 28:18). We are to teach those converted to Christ to observe all things whatsoever Jesus commanded (Matt. 28:20). Whosoever goes beyond the teaching of Christ and thus fails to abide within its limitations, has not God (II John 9-11).

If we modify each of the above excuses as follows they would then be worthy of our attention.
* We must teach our children from their earliest years that we must always respect and observe the authority of the New Testament of Christ (Heb. 5:8-9).
* To survive in our modern society, we must preach the everlasting gospel, for it is the only power of God for the salvation of mankind (Rom. 1:16).
* We must get the gospel of Christ to those who do not presently attend our services. Only then can they learn the truth that will make them free and bring them into the church (John 8:32).
*When our members have been properly taught and indoctrinated in the principles of New Testament Christianity, they will like our simple and ancient way of worship and feel good about being a part of it, knowing it is pleasing to Christ.
* When our Christian schools only employ and retain men of unquestioned soundness in the Scriptures, they will encourage us to be faithful and loyal to the New Testament in our congregational teaching, worship and service.

Every elder and preacher among us, I exhort. "Be ye steadfast, unmoveable, always abounding in the work of the Lord" (I Cor. 15:58).

5. HOW IT ALL BEGAN

It was in 1984 that Bro. Rubel Shelly publish his book, **I Just Want To Be A Christian**. Its issuance created a sensation throughout the brotherhood. There were those disgruntled members who had long been waiting for a strong voice to articulate their desires for changing the faith, worship, practice and thinking of the church. They rejoiced at the boldness of Bro. Shelly's message and rallied around their new leader. On the other hand, those with deep roots in the church, with faith anchored to the solid rock of Scripture, were shocked at Bro. Shelly's abandonment of truths long held by himself and our people. His book was like a bomb that pierced the dam that had held back the discontent of many of our academics and younger preachers. Since that time, a flood of books have poured forth questioning and challenging virtually every aspect of New Testament Christianity.

Out of this literary ferment sprouted and blossomed what we now call "The Change Movement" among churches of Christ. In a very few years, throughout the nation, there appeared a demand for significant changes in the faith, worship and practice of our congregations. Flowing primarily from the Bible Departments of some of our largest Christian Universities, it soon was manifest throughout the nation. In virtually every large city one or more preachers and congregations were clamoring for change in the church. By change we do not speak of simple cosmetic changes of unimportant features of the church. We speak of profound changes in the way we worship; how sinners are saved; the Biblical definition of who is a Christian; the authority of the Scriptures, how we determine what is right and wrong; the role of women in the leadership of the church, the very nature and identity of the church.

When the author came face to face with this movement he determined to read what the promoters of change were saying. So he set out on a mission to read their books. Along the way, he saw the need for writing reviews of them and passing them along to others who needed to know what was happening. To that list he added those books written to respond to the assertions and claims of the promoters of change. These reviews were published first by email, then in the pages of **Christianity: Then and Now**. They are also posted on his website @ www.christianity-then-and-now.com . This task is opened-ended, for as more books are issued they too will be read and reviewed.

It is hoped that those who are too busy to read such books, and those not inclined to do so, will take the time to read these brief reviews and inform themselves of the danger that confronts us. Those who are just now realizing the extent of our problem could benefit by reading them and seeing just what the missionaries of change are saying. This would bring them "up to speed."

Should God provide the means, there will be a series of additional books. These will reaffirm the essentials of New Testament Christianity, address the many facets of the agenda for change and practical matters that will help the church resist and overcome this destructive movement. Those wishing to be involved in this effort are urged to contact the author.

6. FACTS WE MUST FACE

Apostasy is upon us. The change movement is not a passing fad; it is not a small inconvenience. Not since the defection of the Disciples of Christ and Christian Churches at the beginning of the 20th Century has such a wide-spread malignancy threatened our brotherhood. Back then we lost some 85 percent of our congregations and people. The issues being raised by today's agents of change are virtually identical to those of last century.

We have already lost a significant number of preachers and congregations throughout the nation. Many of our largest congregations have already fallen victim to the allurements of the change agents.

Already at least two of our major universities are squarely in the camp of the change movement and several others have clusters of change agents in their faculty and administration.

The momentum is currently with those promoting the change agenda. They have a network that stretches across the nation. They are producing several new books each year promoting their agenda. Lectureships, workshops, forums and seminars are featuring their champions. Every day they grow bolder in their proposals and in challenging the things most surely believed and practiced among our churches. Many faithful brethren seem unaware of that a serious problem is upon us. Others who see the danger are content to do nothing so long as their home congregations are not affected. They are not interested in addressing the dangers that extend beyond their walls. Even month we hear of new losses as congregations embrace this heresy.

Lethergy and indifference are still prevailing amongst majority of our people. The church is no longer growing and, missions efforts are slacking. Many are weak, ambivalent and uncommitted about their faith. Many preachers and elders are unwilling to engage the enemy. They hope everything will work out without their having to get involved.

A religious movement can be overrun by teachings that are foreign to its original faith and practice. Look about you at what has happened to other bodies of people. The Disciples of Christ were once part of our brotherhood. Today they bear little or no resemblance to churches seeking to restore New Testament Christianity. The United Methodist Church is a totally different kind of church than that founded by John and Charles Wesley. The liberal Presbyterians bodies are a pale shadow of the church founded by John Calvin and John Knox. Martin Luther would not recognize the liberal branches of the Lutheran church. Although theses churches still wear the name of their spiritual ancestors, their original faith and worship has been excised and replaced with something new and different. The same thing can and will happen to churches of Christ if this change movement is allowed to proceed unchallenged.

I plead with all who love the Lord Jesus, his Word and his church to resolve this day that they will never be party to the unbiblical changes being proposed for the faith, worship and practice of the Master's church. I beg all to stand firm in their commitment to the old paths of truth. I implore each and all that they will not yield to pressure or persuasion to compromise those sacred principles they have learned from God's Word. I appeal to every brother and sister to make any sacrifice and pay any price to maintain the true faith and worship ordained by Christ. Such, and such alone, is the faith that saves and that will avail in the day of judgement.

7. WHAT WOULD IT TAKE TO CONVINCE YOU?

Many brethren are like the man from Missouri: They won't believe a report until they have seen with their own eyes. When we warn brethren that apostasy is sweeping our brotherhood under the guise of changing us, many folks just can't believe it. I sometimes wonder just what it would take to persuade them. You who doubt the report, I ask to consider the following:

* If you knew for a fact that some preachers are teaching that sinners can be saved by grace before and even without baptism for forgiveness of sins;
* If you visited congregations of our people who are using women to lead in public worship, teach adult classes with men present and even preach from their pulpits;
* If you observed congregations of the Church of Christ participating Billy Graham Crusades;
* If you could see congregations mixing the Lord's Supper with a common meal;

* If you visited a sister congregation engaged in special Easter and Christmas services;
* If you attended a class or service in a church of Christ where instrumental music accompanied the singing of hymns;
* If you heard with your own ears gospel preachers teaching that the Churches of Christ are really just another denominational body, that we were founded by Alexander Campbell;
* If you could read the words of Christian teachers advocating that we should fellowship denominational churches since they are acceptable to Christ;
* If you heard preachers ridicule and reproach the deceased great heroes of our brotherhood and downplay their achievements:
* If you saw with your own eyes congregations torn asunder by promoters of change and houses of worship built and paid for by brethren who opposed all of the above stealthily taken by false brethren;
* If you knew that some Christian Universities founded and funded by our people are now promoting all of the above;

Would you be convinced that great and serious problems have befallen the Lord's Church in our day? With deep regret I must tell you that such is in fact the case. Furthermore unless we act quickly and decisively the tidal wave of error may well sweep everything before it. I implore you not to stop your ears and close your eyes to the dangers we face. Every faithful man and woman is needed to help preserve the blessed church of our Lord Jesus.

II.
TO HELP US UNDERSTAND OUR PROBLEM

8. LIBERALISM AND CONSERVATISM: THE MORTAL STRUGGLE

There was a time (ca. 1945-1965) when the church heard lessons warning of encroaching liberalism and looked about, trying to find such a problem. Liberals were scarce and unwelcome intruders among us. Generally they left our ranks for the friendly fields of the Disciples of Christ and other denominational bodies. There was a time (ca. 1965-1984) when liberals were able to bother the church only with occasional skirmishes on our borders. A withering line of scriptural missals kept the liberals from making overt inroads. During that period the strategy of these malcontents preceded in two directions.

1. Unable to boldly reach their goals, they were contented to keep a relatively low profile. They stayed in our midst and gradually won the hearts and confidence of their congregations.
2. They surfaced as professors in Christian colleges. They quietly circulated their thoughts and ideas through books and the pages of a few willing journals. They devoted themselves to influencing young and unsuspecting disciples with their errant views. They delighted in scoffing at every conservative brother, paper or school. They championed every brother that challenged long-held views of the faith. They successfully convinced many that advanced education was essential to true usefulness in the church. Those without it were stereotyped as inferior and reactionary.

There came a time (ca. 1984-present) when the forces of liberalism were prepared to make a bold thrust. This was seen in the formation of a new journal **(Image)** which provided a forum for writers whose trumpets gave uncertain sounds and to spokesmen of the Christian Churches. Following Image came **Wineskins** whose writers grew ever bolder. Their new boldness was further manifested in the new unity movement with the Christian Churches and the speeches and literature produced in support of that cause.

It is seen in the acceptance given to apostate brethren and splinter groups that entertain themselves by their slashing attacks against the "mainstream" church. The more bizarre and damaging their attack, the more newsworthy are such men and groups. They are given prominence, recognition and respectability on some college lectureships, soul-winning workshops and journals. Soundness just does not matter to the liberal soul.

It is seen in speeches at lectureships which pronounce the old conservatism dead and declare that a new generation of younger men have now taken the leadership. Past preachers are discredited as not understanding the Restoration Plea and it is asserted that a new wave of young preachers are correctly articulating the message. Past preaching is condemned as flawed since men relied upon the Bible for proof of their propositions. They are scorned as "proof-text" preachers. Liberals insist that "expository preaching" based on historical/literary criticism is the only valid and beneficial method of preaching. While it is no surprise that liberals hold such views, it is noteworthy that they now feel safe in publicly articulating them. Fifteen years ago the first round of a major assault upon those who yet hold a strong conservative loyalty to God's book was launched. Today a full frontal attack is underway. Their real objective is hidden behind a call for "change." The survival of the Lord's church in America will depend on how we respond to this and other barrages that will surely follow.

For twenty years we read of the intestine struggles within the Southern Baptist Church as liberals and conservatives fought for control of that organization. We are now experiencing the same internal struggle within our own brotherhood. A major difference being that we have no convention to conduct business and set policy and no delegates to elect. The battle will be fought in the pages of our journals, in the pulpits of local churches, the governing boards of our Christian Schools and in our mission outposts. Having no central government to capture, ten thousand battles will be fought for the hearts and loyalties of brethren around the world. Whether or not the Churches of Christ will move into the ranks of the Protestant denominations depends upon which of the two contending armies has the most conviction and staying power.

At this point in time liberalism already controls a sizeable number of the large congregations of the major cities of our country. Conservatives find their strength mainly in the small towns and rural congregations.

What Must We Do?

Survival depends on intelligent and courageous response on the part of every faithful brother.

1. We must renew our efforts to indoctrinate the members of our flocks in the sound doctrine of God's word (Titus 2:1). We must preach the word of God (II Timothy 4:2). We must preach on the fundamentals of the faith. They must be taught in our classes. We must supply our brethren with good tracts that set forth God's word on vital spiritual themes and urge them to read them and share them.
2. Preachers must deliver lessons that educate and inform the brethren of the problems we face. Knowledge afore hand helps us avoid a thousand mistakes. Lack of knowledge is disastrous (Hosea 4:6).
3. Preachers need to sit down and discuss current situations with their elders and the men of the congregation. Each must have a strategy for arming, defending and saving his congregation from the invading enemy of liberalism.
4. Leaders must inform themselves regarding this great contest. Preachers and elders need to read a broad sampling of gospel papers, and attend lectureships, both of conservative and liberal

variety. Painful as this may be, we must know what is going on, lest we lose the battle by default.

5. We must read the history of the Restoration Movement in America. From Earl West's **Search for the Ancient Order**, Homer Hailey's **Attitudes and Consequences of the Restoration Movement**, and J.D. Murch's **Christian Only**, we will be able to see how the mistakes made a century ago are being repeated in our day. The apostasy that devastated us then is bound to follow today if we do not turn the tide.

6. We absolutely must close ranks and stand as one man against this onslaught. We cannot afford the luxury of shooting at each other. No fellow conservative is perfect, neither are you. If in matters of faith we agree, then let there be unity. In matters of opinion and judgment we must exhibit liberty and charity. Too long the conservative voice has been muffled by discord and infighting. We need to rally around journals, colleges and schools of preaching that hold fast the faithful word (Titus 1:9). Should we sink or abandon every vessel that has a little rust or barnacles, we will find ourselves undone in the day of battle.

7. We need to patiently reach out to fellow preachers who are wavering in commitment and pull them back to solid ground. There is the temptation to shoot them. Far better it is to salvage them. Talk to them. Pray for them. Encourage them. Help them to find the courage to fight the good fight (I Timothy 6:12).

8. We need to take a special interest in young people in general and young preachers in particular. First, the church of the future rests with them, for good or bad. Secondly, the liberals are definitely courting the young adults of the church. The young are by nature more receptive to voices of change that challenge the leaders and thoughts of the past. When thoughtless conservatives pounce on the young preacher who makes a mistake, the shrewd liberal extends a sympathetic hand. Another soldier who might have been brought into useful services is lost to the cunning enemy.

9. We must add some works to our faith (James 2:26). A chief criticism of conservatives by the liberals is that they are not

evangelistic, not mission minded. We fail our Lord if we allow all of our energies to be expended in only defensive action. Our commission still says go preach the gospel (Mark 16:15). Let us get on with training, sending forth and supporting faithful men for the mission fields of the world. Other good works likewise need our attention.

10. We must move beyond a negative, rear-guard defensive action and boldly provide the spiritual leadership for God's people in these troublesome times. "A strong offense is the best defense" in the fight of faith as well as in carnal war.

11. Let us one and all devote ourselves to penitence and prayer that God will smile on us and help us overcome our problems and rally our scattered troops for a successful battle. Pride, arrogance and indifference have made it possible for Satan to gain the advantage over us (II Corinthians 2:11). God can do little with a proud people, but he gives grace to the humble (I Peter 5:5). When we draw near to God he will draw near to us (James 4:8) and righteous men will more readily follow our leadership. He that ruleth nations and raiseth up kings, can surely give victory to his saints. If not a sparrow can fall to the earth without his divine attention, surely he will aid his people if they call upon him.

12. We must never surrender, never give up. The most precious cause in the world is at stake. Souls hang in the balance (I Timothy 4:16); ours and those of our brethren, our children and grandchildren and a lost world whose hope of hearing the saving gospel hinges on the survival of a faithful church.

9. WHY WE HAVE PROBLEMS THAT OTHERS CHURCHES DO NOT

Those familiar with our brotherhood history and those widely traveled among our churches know that we had have had a number of divisions among our brethren. Enemies of Christ often cite this problem to discredit our plea. While all division involves sin on the part of one or both parties involved, there are some significant factors that contribute to our struggle with this problem (Rom. 16:17).

I. Satan hates Christ's true church and makes continual warfare against her (Rev. 12:13-17). She is the one church founded by the Redeemer (Matt. 16:18). It is to her the Savior adds the saved (Acts 2:47). She alone is charged with seeking and saving the lost. She is the kingdom that Christ will deliver up to the Father in the last day (I Cor. 15:24). All other churches are man-made facsimiles, counterfeits with no spiritual worth or standing. Satan has no interest in wrecking them. They are unwitting supporters of his cause. But the church of Christ he is determined to destroy. Persecution failed, but division has done its destructive work (Matt. 12:25).

II. Members of churches of Christ strongly believe that what one believes and how he worships and serves God is important. For most denominationalists, what one believes is of little consequence, just so long as he loves Jesus. They have little reason to quarrel over doctrine or practice, since such does not matter in their church. John taught that whosoever abandons the doctrine of Christ also leaves God and the Son (II John 9). Paul urges us to "speak...the things that befit the sound doctrine" (Tit. 2:1). Because of our love for Christ and his will we cannot stand by idly when someone seeks to corrupt the faith we hold.

III. Churches of Christ have no pope, president or primate to rule over them and declare the terms of their faith. Jesus in heaven is head over all things to the church (Eph. 1:22). His will is expressed in the New Testament. When our religious neighbors disagree they look to their human head for answers. We look to the New Covenant and try to understand it. Being fallible, we sometimes see matters differently.

IV. Other churches have their faith and practice spelled out in a creedal statement or denominational manual. The individual is not to question the creed. We have no such book, only our Bibles. We must rely on our human intelligence and judgement to understand it.

V. Many churches claim God speaks directly to their preachers so that when their clergyman tells them what to believe or not to believe it is to be taken as the final word from heaven. We reject such unfounded claims and know that God only speaks to us through his written word (Rev. 2:29). Again we must depend on our finite knowledge and ability to correctly interpret that message.

VI. The church of Christ is not a democracy where beliefs and practices are determined by majority vote. The church is a monarchy. Christ has all the authority (Matt. 28:18). He is king (I Tim. 6:15). Our job is to listen to and obey the divine King (Matt. 17:5; Heb. 5:9). Other churches simply take a vote and live with the decision.

VII. God has made every Christian a member of his royal priesthood (I Pet. 2:5,9). To each of us he has given intelligence, volition and autonomy. We are all responsible to search the Scriptures (Acts 17:11). We all must give account for our personal faith and conduct as Christians (Rom. 14:12). For this and the other reasons listed above, we sometimes find ourselves in disagreement with other brethren. We in no way excuse division, we simply point out reasons why the problem might be more frequently seen among us than some other groups.

When we reach the point that what we believe and how we worship and serve God does not matter, then we might as well disband, close our doors and hand a sign up saying "Gone Out of Business."

10. SECULARIZATION OF THE CHURCH

Perhaps the greatest threat to the church of the twenty-first century is secularization. Many will blink as ask what is that?

Webster defines **secular** as, "a. Of or relating to the worldly or temporal concerns; b. not overtly or specifically religious." **Secularism** is defined as, "indifference to or rejection or exclusion of religion and religious considerations." Vergillius Ferm defines **secularization** as, "The taking over of church property by the state for secular purposes..." (**Dictionary of Religion**). Under secularism, **Baker's Dictionary of Theology** says, "Today secularism is the integration of life around the spirit of a specific age, rather than around God. It is living as if the material order were supreme and as if God did not exist...Secularism places the emphasis on temporal social enjoyment rather than on eternal spiritual values."

Secularization is not being forced upon the church by the state or by any mortal enemy from without. Rather it is a matter of the church gradually absorbing the spirit of the age and forgetting its mission and purpose under Christ.

Given the sinful nature of a world in rebellion to heaven and a church designed to "be holy and without blemish" (Eph. 5:27), God expects his church to be different. We are said to be "a holy nation" (I Pet. 2:9). The word holy is from *hagios*, the basic meaning of which is different (Wm. Barclay). Concerning the sinful world we are commanded to come ye out from among them and be ye separate saith the Lord" (II Cor. 6:17). While we must live in a wicked world, we must not be "of the world" (John 17:16). The world will "think it strange that (we) run not with them..." (I Pet. 4:4).

Twenty years ago, Michael Weed wrote in the **Christian Chronicle** that, "many church leaders are actually cooperating with and even accelerating the process of secularization within the church." He points out five prominent areas where this process is visible.

1. It is seen in the attempt to be up-to-date and effective; infatuation

with modern communication; and the use of advertising techniques in their attempt to promote or "sell" Christianity to the world. This often results in "cutting the product to fit the market." They reduce the Christian message to "flashy advertising slogans and catchy cliches...which substitutes for basic Christian beliefs."

2. It is evident in the pursuit of an empty, hollow unity with other bodies of people. In the words of Malcom Muggeridge, "It is the ecumenicity of those who, believing less and less, disagree about very little."
3. It is seen in "the production and sale of Christian literature whose basic quality is not that it is biblical, but that it is innocuous. Bible teaching and traditional Christian views are so diluted that these materials can be marketed to the broadest possible clientele.
4. It is demonstrated in the determined efforts of congregations "to prove (themselves) useful and relevant and to 'meet needs'..." Many of those laboring under this obsession are meeting needs in terms of society's own values and standards rather than God's. Thus this has become a substitute for meeting the spiritual needs of lost men and struggling saints. Health spas and lawyers meet needs but not those the church should be supplying. Some of the needs set forth are trivial and others are no business of the church at all.
5. The education program of some congregations reflects a confusion about the church's mission. When class discussion centers on things of "the world;" when the greater emphasis is on recreation and social activities rather than searching the Scriptures, the progress is at work. Bro. Weed well says, "The education ministry of the church should not be a vestibule through which Christians are comfortably ushered into the secular world views . . . of modern society.

In this writer's judgement, the trend toward secularism is further seen in the following cases:
1. Declining interest in and emphasis on the public proclamation of the Word.

2. A disproportionate emphasis on social activities and recreation in the life of the church.
3. The trend of congregations toward providing schools for general education, with only token spiritual training.
4. The willingness of our churches and Christian Schools to allow the worldly attitudes and practices of members to go unchallenged, thus lending tacit approval thereof.
5. Loss of interest in evangelism to win souls and the substitution of programs of social service.
7. A movement away from serious study of the Scriptures and doctrinal emphasis, while greatly emphasizing, psychology, counseling, family therapy and self-improvement. While all of the latter things are useful and have a place in our teaching, it is over emphasis of them to the neglect of the gospel that is dangerous. We can have happy, well-adjusted individual and families who will be destroyed for lack of divine knowledge (Hos. 4:6).
7. Virtual silence in the face of the never ending attacks by the promoters of humanism, evolution, and hedonism through our public schools and media. While our people are being corrupted and led away into these errors, their church leaders stand mute watching them go!
8 Many Christians accept and live by the world's code of dress, conduct and moral behavior while elders and preachers say nothing to call them back to God's standards. Some even seek to defend the way of the world as harmless.

Satan could not destroy the early church by the sword of persecution (Rev. 12:2-11). He was able to swallow up the church by absorbing it into the pagan culture or Rome. This was done in the name of liberty and freedom from persecution, via Constantine's edicts. It occurred in a climate of unprecedented growth in numbers, prestige, recognition, and power for the church. So thrilling were the triumphs of the fourth century that the Christians never realized that the cause they loved and for which their fathers had died was being reshaped into an apostate, counterfeit church, eventually known as the Holy Roman Catholic Church.

Awareness of the problem is not enough. There must be a workable knowledge of the Scripture and unswerving faith and loyalty thereto if we are to survive this modern onslaught against the faith once delivered (Jude 3). May God grant us wisdom to correctly read the signs of the times and to apply the divine remedy to every problem. Let us never forget our charge, "Be not conformed to this world" (Rom. 12:2). One of the major objections to the program of the change movement is that secularizes the Lord's church.

11. APOSTASY: IS IT A POSSIBILITY?

Our preachers use to frequently preach on the possibility of apostasy. In so doing they were addressing the popular false doctrine of Calvinism which says that once a person is saved, he cannot so sin as to lose his salvation. The question was easily answered, for Paul said to Christians who sought justification by the law, "Ye are severed from Christ . . . ye are fallen away from grace" (Gal. 5:4). Sadly, our generation does not hear many lessons on this important topic although such teaching is still needed.

We who preach and teach still need to address the possibility of apostasy. We must consider the question, not just of individual Christians, but the possibility of congregations, Christian schools or even our brotherhood departing from our commitment to Christ. That commitment is to restore and practice the faith revealed in the New Testament. That commitment many among us seem to have forgotten, or even have rejected, and some have embraced a new and different approach to serving God. That such can happen is affirmed by Paul in his warning to the elders of the church at Ephesus. "I know that after my departing grievous wolves shall enter in among you, not sparing the flock; and from among your own selves shall men arise, speaking perverse things, to draw away the disciples after them" (Acts 20:29-30).

When the question of apostasy is raised, the liberals among us laugh. They brand those that pose such questions as dinosaurs. They accuse them of disrupting our brotherhood. They paint them as unscholarly bumpkins. They suggest that they really don't understand the restoration plea. But it is precisely those liberal minded brethren who are the promoters of change; changes that are departures from the old paths of the Bible. They would be disappointed if their plans were unmasked and thwarted by the discussion of the possibility of a widespread apostasy.

Those who are familiar with our history know without doubt that the potential for a general apostasy involving a majority of our preachers, congregations and schools is real. It happened to our brotherhood here in America at the end of the 19th century. The first manifestation of that apostasy was a movement to create a governing body to manage our mission efforts. They called it the American Christian Missionary Society. Next was an agitation to incorporate instrumental music with our song worship. Those who were the vocal agents of change in those efforts were generally the more sophisticated and erudite preachers from the large city churches. They persisted in their determination to have these extra Biblical things until division occurred. So effective had they been that upwards of 85 percent of our churches were lost. A struggling handful was left, primarily in the South. David Lipscomb and a small band of fellow preachers waged a valiant battle to salvage and rebuild the shattered brotherhood. Today the heirs of those who abandoned the Biblical pattern are known as the Christian Church-Disciples of Christ. For the Disciples the apostasy is complete. They bear little or no resemblance to the church of the Bible. Many of their leaders have publicly declared the attempt to restore the primitive faith as an unworkable failure.

We have many simple-minded brethren among us. They believe the Bible and respect its authority. They are happy to walk in the old paths, but they are naive. They open their pulpits to unsound men who are promoting and introducing strange ideas and practices among us. They support and promote schools that are seed beds of apostasy. They support and circulate publications of those who would preach a different gospel. They appoint such men to be elders and deacons. They remain silent when such are given classes to teach. They speak not when such men are considered for the pulpit. They can't bear to take a stand; to be found in opposition to error or to stand with a minority, or, god-forbid, to stand alone. One of the great needs of our people is for good, level-headed men who know God's Will and have the fortitude to stand foursquare for it. Often one person can make the difference in the direction a congregation will travel. God sought for such an individual in Ezekiel's day. "I sought for a man among them, that should build up the wall, and stand in the gap before me for the land, that I should not destroy it; but I found none" (Ezek 22:30).

Like our brethren of a century past, we see standing before us the possibility of apostasy. May God help each of us respond with courage and conviction to defeat that possibility before it can do its evil work. We must be prepared to "fight the good fight of the faith" if we would lay hold on eternal life (I Tim. 6:12).

12. CHANGE YES: APOSTASY NO!

An army of younger church members is clamoring for change in the worship, faith and practices of our churches. They have naught but criticism for the efforts of the past and are certain they have discovered a far superior way of "doing church" as they are fond of saying. They leave the impression on immature and gullible disciples that those of us over 50 are stubborn, close-minded and impervious to change, no matter how beneficial it might be. In this they are less than honest. Some ultraconservative types might well be that intractable, but for the majority of us it is not change that we reject, it is unlawful departure from God's authorized Word and way.

* We are willing to change such things as the hour, the length or the order of our services, but we are not willing to change the nature and substance of them. God has specified singing, praying, communing, offering and instruction as acceptable aspects of his worship.
* We are willing to try new songs or new hymnals, but not a new kind of music. Only singing did the Spirit authorize (Eph. 5:19). Instruments, other than the voice and heart, we will not, we cannot accept.
* We are willing to consider different methods of observing a communion service, but we cannot mix the sacred meal with a common meal (I Cor. 11:20-22). Nor can we observe the feast on a day not ordained by God (Acts 20:7).
* We are willing to accept any or all Biblical names for the church, but we will not brook those who seek to dismiss or discredit the Biblical name "church of Christ" used by Paul (Rom. 16:16). It is never wrong to give due glory and honor to Christ the founder and head of the church.
* We are willing to change our methods of evangelism but not the gospel message given by Christ. Methods flourish and grow obsolete but the message is divine, perfect and eternal (Rom. 1:16).
* We can tolerate those who prefer other reputable translations than the King James Version but not those who reject the authority of the Bible.
* We can adapt to modern improvements in our meeting houses but we cannot be party to those who would "modernize" the church which Christ built, which is revealed in Scripture.
* We can admit our failures to measure up to the divine pattern for faith and practice, but we can never admit the church which Christ built is any less than perfect.
* We can preach salvation by grace through faith (Eph. 2:8-9), but we will never be able to preach salvation by grace alone or faith alone (Jas. 2:24).

Change in nonessentials, in matters of judgment and expediency our people have been making for the last 200 years. Changes in the God-given faith and practice of Christianity apostates have been engaging in for the same period of time. Sydney Rigdon's changes took him into Mormonism. Dr. John Thomas' changes led him into the Christadelphians. The changes of instrumental music and missionary societies took their promoters into Disciples of Christ/ Christian Church denomination Changes regarding the doctrine of the kingdom of Christ and His return lead Robert H. Boll into Premillennialism. Changes in the teaching of the role of miraculous gifts of the Spirit led Don Finto and the Belmont Church of Christ into Pentecostalism. Changes in the government of the church and the doctrine of Christian liberty led Chuck Lucas and Kip McKeen of the Boston church into the International Church of Christ cult. The changes proposed by the "change agents" centered in Abilene, Texas are leading toward a new denominational body with which we want no part.

13. THERE ARE SCHISMS AND THERE ARE SCHISMS

Many who read these lines may think, yes, we have a problem with this "change movement," but we have had other problems in the past and they soon played out and the church has moved on. They surmise, that the church is strong and will survive it. Those who think thusly are not well informed as to the nature and extent of the danger before us.

We have had numerous problems that were centered around one or a handful of preachers and involved but a scattered group of congregations. We have had a few legalistic brethren break fellowship and form their own brotherhoods. Most of these have withered and declined over the years. Yes, there were a few premillennialists and charismatics that flourished for a brief season and then moved on to the more accommodating fields of denominationalism. Today's challenge is different. Not since the end of the 19th century have we faced a threat so dangerous.

What we call the change movement is an uncommon danger. Consider the following aspects of it:
* It is already spread throughout the nation and is affecting our churches in most major cities.
* Already its proponents have control of our two largest universities (Abilene and Pepperdine) and have a significant foothold in some others.
* They have captured several of our largest, most influential congregations.
* The leaders of this movement are not poorly educated country preachers. They are talented men with advanced degrees. They fill important pulpits and university chairs.
* They have at their disposal wealth, influence, position and power.
* They are influencing large numbers of young future preachers in their schools.
* They are making their appeal to the under 50 segment of our brethren, many of whom are so deficient in Bible knowledge and have so absorbed the culture of our age that they readily embrace their human concepts and schemes.
* The promoters of change are aggressively promoting their agenda. They understand the value of working together to attain their goals. They know the value of disseminating their doctrines in print form.
* Their scholars are busy rewriting our brotherhood history so that future generations will not know their roots and true heritage and thus be susceptible to their deceptive message.
* These false brethren have no intention of leaving our fellowship. They are determined to stay and change us into their own image.
* They have been able to operate with only scattered and minimal opposition thus far. No major opposition has been mounted against their program.

We will survive this onslaught only if:
* A sufficient number of brethren awaken to the threat facing us.

* If they are willing to take up the sword and shield in defense of the faith (Phil. 1:16).
* If they are willing to invest the necessary time, energy and money into providing the supplies and materials needed for this spiritual conflict.
* Only if they are willing and able to band together with others of like faith and fight for the common good.
* Only if they can bear with the infirmities of each other and abstain from fratricidal infighting that leaves us divided and helpless in the face of a determined enemy.
* Only if they will stay the course and not grow weary in well doing until the victory is won (I Cor. 15:58).
* Only if they will act quickly, before the enemy has gained such strength and numbers that they will be like a tidal wave, sweeping every thing before them.

Brethren, this is no ordinary, run of the mill, schism. This is like a 100 year flood. Only when the danger is understood can we hope to successfully confront and contain it. "Quit ye like men." "Fight the good fight of the faith" (I Tim. 6:12).

III.
WHAT IT IS THEY WISH TO CHANGE

14. WHEN IS A CHURCH OF CHRIST NOT A CHURCH OF CHRIST?

There is a Church of Christ of the Philippines, a denomination that bears no resemblance or relation the church of Christ of which we are part. There is a Protestant denomination called the United Church of Christ. In the South one encounters the Immanuel Church of Christ, a radical Pentecostal body. The International Church of Christ is a denomination with its headquarters at Boston, governed by a body of men who fancy themselves apostles of Christ. Many have had the experience of entering a meeting house with the name Church of Christ over the door, only to find an organ, a choir and a reverend pastor within. In reality it was a Christian Church, in spite of the name. The name on a church building or on the deed of trust is not sufficient to make a worshiping group a bonafide church of Christ. Nor does the fact that the people choose to call themselves by that Biblical name necessarily make them truly a church that Christ will own and accept.

To be a church of Christ, certain basic essentials must be met. The disciples must be born again by the birth of water and Spirit or they cannot enter the kingdom of God (John 3:3-5). They must have been buried with Christ in their baptism (Rom. 6:3-4) for the forgiveness of their sins (Acts 22:16). It is that one baptism (Eph. 4:4) that puts people into the one body or church of Christ (I Cor. 12:13). They must recognize Jesus to be head over all things to the church (Eph. 1:22) and submissive to his authority (Heb. 5:8-9). They must be willing to worship and serve the Lord according to his revealed will (Luke 6:46).

The question posed in our title is pertinent because of problems that have surfaced among us in the past twelve years. There are people who still wear the name church of Christ who have long since abandoned the very truths that identify them as a church of Christ. Regardless of the name a body of people might wear, a church is not truly a church of Christ if any or all of the following factors are evident among them:

* If they no longer accept the New Testament of Christ as the ultimate and absolute authority in determining matters of faith and practice. The words of Christ will judge us in the last day (John 12:48).
* If a congregation no longer worships according to the New Testament pattern. This is true whether it is in their communion, their song worship, their day for sacred assembly or any other aspect of worship.
* When a congregation is no longer content to be governed as Christ ordained. There is no acceptable alternative to elders and deacons to lead His church. (Tit. 1:5).
* When a congregation places women in positions of leadership which God has forbidden (I Cor. 14:33-34; I Tim. 2:8-11-12).
* When a body of people no longer teaches sinners to be saved in Christ's appointed way. Grace and faith can never eliminate the need for obedience and specifically for baptism in salvation (Acts 22:16).
* When a body of people despise and ridicule Christ's church, his doctrine, his worship and his faithful servants they make it clear that they are not a congregation of Christ's people, regardless of the name they may wear.

When any or all of these conditions are found in the life and teaching of a church that identifies itself as a church of Christ, it is a case of false identity or at the very least, mistaken identity. Remember the congregation at Ephesus? Without genuine repentance they would have ceased to be a church of Christ (Rev. 2:1-5). The church in Sardis had a name . . . but they were dead in the eyes of the Lord (Rev. 3:1).

15. COMMUNITY CHURCHES AND CHURCHES OF CHRIST

We all understand that God did not assign a specific name to his church. Rather, several different names are used to designate his people: church of God, church of the Lord, churches of Christ and the church. When there was but one body of people in the world that honored Christ as their founder, head and Lord there was no need for any further identification. We, however, live in a society were there are upwards of fifteen hundred different kinds of churches. This situation creates a state of confusion as to which body of people one is referring to when he speaks of or asks about "the church." This situation necessitates that we have some way of identifying ourselves so we can communicate, find each other and point others to a body of brethren in a given place.

In the early days of the Restoration Movement three different streams of people came together to unite on the Bible and restore the faith and practice of the original church. Those led by Alexander Campbell most often referred to themselves as Disciples of Christ. Those led by Barton Stone most often used the name Church of Christ. Those coming from the James O'Kelly, Elias Smith and Abner Jones movement preferred the name Christian Church. There was not a strict adherence to any particular one of these names and all the brethren recognized each other as fellow-Christians serving God in one body. When schism occurred at the end of the 19th and the beginning of the 20th century, those preferring to have instrumental music, missionary societies, women in positions of church leadership, etc., generally identified themselves as Christian Churches/Disciples of Christ. Our brethren distinguished themselves by the biblical name Churches of Christ, found in Rom. 16:16. Over a period of 25 years this distinction of names became virtually complete. Our brethren continued to hold and use the name Churches of Christ, not because it was the exclusive Bible cognomen for the church but because it was biblical and was helpful in identifying our people, wherever they might be.

Over the last 40 years, liberalism has slowly eroded the Biblical foundations of many of our younger preachers. They in turn have failed to properly instruct and indoctrinate our people. A new generation of leaders arose who seemed to be ashamed of their association with the brotherhood of people known as Churches of Christ. They craved acceptance with their neighbors of the Evangelical churches. They did not want to bear the stigma of being exclusive and different from the worldly churches around them. Since they no longer believed the exclusive message of salvation and the one church of Scripture, they did not want to be publicly identified with those who still held to such exclusive beliefs. Hence they began to cast around for a name that would do two things:

* It would mask from the people of their community that they were affiliated with other Churches of Christ.
* It would make them appear like other "Community Churches" that were experiencing phenomenal growth. We know that many of those who have taken this route have chosen as their models, "Nondenominational Community Churches" such as the Saddleback Community Church of Orange County California and Willow Creek Church in Barrington, Illinois and Robert Shuller's Crystal Cathedral. Of course those churches are thoroughly denominational in their faith and practice since they prefer the doctrines and commandments of men rather than the authority of the New Testament of Christ as their standard. Numerous Baptist, Methodist, Reformed and other denominational congregations have also taken this same moniker of "Community Church." It seems that some of our brethren prefer to be identified with such groups rather than with their brethren of Churches of Christ.
* Another probable motive is that under the name of Community Church, the typical congregation places little or no emphasis on doctrinal loyalty. Thus a typical Community Church might employ a Methodist minister this year and a Disciples of Christ man the next, and a female Presbyterian the following. Indicators are that some of our brethren who have chosen this route have a similar laxness about doctrinal standards. Church for them is all about fellowship, fun, doing good and feeling good. Such things as abiding in the doctrine

of Christ (II John 9-11) are given little emphasis.

Those of our people who have chosen to identify themselves as Community churches seem to have a commonality about them. They all have embraced the agenda of the change movement which seeks to transform our people into the likeness of our denominational neighbors. Such things as salvation by grace through faith before immersion, a failure to emphasize the importance of baptism, a willingness to tolerate the use of instrumental music in worship, a willingness to allow women to assume leadership roles in the life of the church, acceptance of denominational churches as in good standing with God and other related issues seem to be part and parcel of those wishing to be known as "Community Churches." Several of our Universities and Colleges have given encouragement to the Community Church movement: among them Abilene Christian University, Pepperdine University and Harding Graduate School of Religion.

It would be as scriptural to identify ones congregation as the Community Church of Christ as the State Street Church of Christ. But for most of these folks, they want the "Community Church" without the "of Christ" designation. As Jesus said, we can only judge them by their fruits (Matt. 7:16-21). The direction of this movement is away from New Testament Christianity and from obedience to the message of Christ. It is away from the brotherhood of Churches of Christ of which they once were a part. In my judgment it would be a mistake for a congregation to take such a name as it creates confusion as to whom they are. It also identifies them with those who are abandoning the Bible as their standard of faith and practice. It reflects on their part a sense of shame to be identified with the gospel and the body of Christ. Paul was not ashamed of the message he preached (Rom. 1:16) With Jesus, he gladly endured the shame of the cross (Heb. 12:2; Gal. 5:11) and so should we. If the world despises us for what we believe and stand for, so be it; they hated Jesus for his faith and convictions (John 15:17-20).

16. THOSE WHO CRITICIZE THE CHURCH

As the church of sails the stormy waters of the 21ˢᵗ century, she is subjected to criticism from many quarters.

Skeptics and unbelievers hate God, Christ, the Bible and the church. They never miss an opportunity to hurl their insults and criticisms at the Lord's people. The church stands for all that they oppose. She is an obstacle to their ambitions to impose their secular views and values on our society and bring all into their tow.

More criticisms come from the spokesmen of the many churches founded by men. Imposters hate the true bride of Christ because she teaches and practices pure and undefiled religion. They are offended and embarrassed by her faithfulness to her Master and his revealed will.

There are times when the church is criticized by her friends. Being composed of fallible souls, the church never measures up one hundred percent to her Lord's expectations. Like the church in Ephesus, some forget their first love (Rev. 2:4). Like the church in Pergamum some tolerate false teaches in their midst (Rev. 2:14). Like the church in Laodicea, some grow lukewarm in their love and zeal for Christ (Rev. 3:15-16). When such failures are evident, faithful servants of God will "reprove, rebuke and exhort" the church to mend her ways (II Tim. 4:2). Solomon wrote, "faithful are the wounds of a friend" (Prov. 27:6). Friends of Christ do not relish the job of criticizing the church. They do so "even weeping" (Phil.3:18). They do so gently as a nurse would correct her ward; as loving parents would their beloved child (I Thess. 2:7,11). Their criticisms are tempered and measured. They are spoken in love (Eph. 4:15). They are constructive and given with the intention of helping the church, building her up (I Cor. 14:26), saving those who have gone astray (Jude 21-22) Because their criticisms are presented in this constructive way and spoken in love, the church will prosper and be better for it.

There is yet another kind of critic in our midst. These are disillusioned brethren who have made shipwreck of the faith (I Tim. 1:19-20). They have disdain for all who do not share their denominational view of religion. They are embarrassed by those brethren who went before them and built the schools and congregations wherein they now earn their living. They have no sense of pride of membership in the church. In fact they find nothing about her to be proud of save themselves and the few disciples that follow their lead. Like hostile enemies, they stand aloof and cast their stones of criticism against the church they claim to be members of. Many are the blows they have inflicted upon her. Other enemies of the church rejoice to see the fratricidal attacks they make under the guise of "reforming, renewing or changing" the church. They would destroy her by making her into yet another ignoble human denomination.

The church can expect the criticisms of those without. She can be benefitted by the constructive criticisms of her friends. But she suffers most from the treasonous blows of those who appear as sheep in her midst but inwardly are ravening wolves (Matt. 7:15).

17. TWO KINDS OF CRITICS

There is a difference between those who see a problem and with good will, desire to help fix it and those who look for flaws and failures to justify attaching the person, institution or church they hold in low esteem. The former group help us grow. Their criticisms are to be cherished (Prov. 25:12). The latter crowd discourages and destroys those that they propose to help. Edmund Burke asked, "Is it in destroying and pulling down that skill is displayed? The shallowest understanding, the rudest hand, is more than equal to that task." Beaconsville wrote, "It is much easier to be critical than to be correct." David was the victim of men who "sharpened their tongue like a serpent; adders' poison is under their lips" (Ps. 140:3).

A certain class of political liberals sees no good in America and thus they magnify every fault and problem. They seem to hate the nation of their nativity and wish her ill in her undertakings. So do religious liberals treat the church. They see no good in her. They exaggerate every flaw and failure. They hold up her shortcomings for public ridicule. They treat their spiritual predecessors with contempt. They are spiritually arrogant and reflect an air of superiority toward the common folk of the church. They hold in admiration, the religious bodies around us who embrace doctrines and practices patently foreign to Scripture. They dare to lay their profane hands on the sacred things of the Lord's church, his bride; her worship, her doctrines, her practices. They destroy the church they inherited from their fathers in the faith. They do so, while assuring us that they are doing so for beneficial purposes and our own good. Such is a fair description of the change agents at work among our churches.

Such destructive criticism is not new. Through the years, wise men have observed it at work and passed harsh judgments against it.
* J. C. Sharpe understood that "Criticism is not religion, and by no process can it be substituted for it"
* H. C. Trumbull believed that "An over-readiness to criticize or to depreciate a minister of Christ is proof of a lack of devotion to Christ.
* Washington Irvin opined, "There is a certain meddlesome spirit which, in the garb of learned research, goes prying about the traces of history, casting down its monuments, and marring and mutilating its fairest trophies. Care should be taken to vindicate great names from such pernicious erudition."
* Addison rightly observed, "I never knew a critic who made it his business to lash the faults of other writers that was not guilty of greater himself . . . as the hangman is generally a worse malefactor than the criminal that suffers by his hand"
* Henry Longfellow wrote, "Some critics are like chimney-sweepers; they put out the fire below, and frighten the swallows from their nest above; they scrape a long time in the chimney,

cover themselves with soot, and bring nothing away but a bag of cinders, and then sing out from the top of the house, as if they had built it."

Let this be our daily prayer: "Lord, save me from critical faultfinding habits into which so many people fall. Keep my heart tender, sympathetic and hopeful. Help me to be firm and steadfast in my loyalty to truth and always clear as to what truth is." (Unknown).

18. FAULTY ASSUMPTIONS OF CHANGE AGENTS

On every hand we are bombarded with the message from those among us who are agitating for changes in churches of Christ. As I read through the stream of books being issued by the proponents of this movement, I am struck by the many false suppositions under which they labor.

They falsely assume that churches of Christ (other than themselves), do not believe or accept the Old Testament as a part of God's divine cannon of scripture. This is one of the principal theses of the book, **"God's Holy Fire"** by Bros. Cukrowski, Hamilton and Thompson of ACU, Abilene Christian University Press. We have long heard uninformed people of the world make similar unfounded charges, now these men who teach in one of our Christian schools are repeating the falsehood. They should know better. In the same vein, they falsely assume that gospel preachers do not teach and preach the stories of the Old Testament. While some may have neglected the Old Testament and others may have failed to incorporate all of its rich treasure in their preaching, none reject it and none refuse to preach from it. Perhaps they could find just one specimen of their mis-shapened and misinformed preacher and put him on display for all the rest of us to see. He would indeed be a rare and exotic find for in 46 years of preaching and circulating among our people I have yet to meet one who held such views of the Old Testament.

Another faulty assumption is that preachers in "traditional" churches of Christ do not understand or preach the great truths about God's grace. If they should say that none our preachers teach salvation by grace alone, we could agree with their charge. But again I challenge them to find even one man who does not believe in salvation by grace through faith (Eph. 2:8-9). Such is preached today in every pulpit in even the most conservative congregations. Of course some emphasize the topic more than others, just as some might emphasize faith, baptism or prayer more than others. But such is a matter of degree, not of rejection.

They falsely assume that our preachers don't understand or preach about the role of the Holy Spirit in the life of Christians. While there are some who don't give enough attention to this glorious theme and there are some who have a limited understanding of the benefits the indwelling Spirit provides God's people, the vast majority are not so. All believe in the separate existence of the Holy Spirit; all believe he works on behalf of God's people. But none, save perhaps among the disciples of change, believe that the Spirit of God yet works in miraculous ways, or that he reveals any additional truth to God's people since apostolic times.

It is mistakenly held that the average preacher, outside of their change fellowship, does not know how to correctly interpret God's Word. The arrogance of this claim is seen when we observed that from the beginning of our American Restoration movement, till some 20 years ago, all the conversions, growth, programs and accomplishments of our brotherhood were made by men who never heard of the "new hermeneutic." Be they college professors, college-trained or self-made preachers, they all believed that God's Word should be read just as we would read any other serious book containing history, instruction, regulations and promises. They all understood that God revealed his will to man through generic and specific commands, approved examples and necessary inferences. All understood that while the entire 66 books were inspired of God and inerrant, the will of Christ, found in the New Testament, regulates the faith, worship and practice of Christians. They understood that the Old Testament was profitable for our study; that it revealed important and essential truths; but that the ordinances of the Mosaic system were not binding on us today. Those enlightened by the "new Hermeneutics" have planted few, if any churches, no schools, nor have they opened any new mission fields. They, like parasites, prefer to invade healthy bodies and draw the life and energy from them. The end result, if they prevail, is decline and eventual death to their victims.

Positing these faulty assumptions regarding these and other points, the promoters of change proceed to beat their straw man as they present themselves as the deliverers of the church. Those who are informed know that their assertions are just as faulty as their assumptions.

19. SEEING THE END FROM THE BEGINNING

Sometimes it helps a person in deciding whether to take a certain road if he can know ahead of time what he will confront as he travels that route. Of course only God can see and know the future with absolute certainty but we can make some reasonable projections based on facts and past experience.

If you choose the path set forth by the "change agents" at work among us, you can reasonably expect some if not all of the following situations to await you.

* If you prefer the charismatic approach to worship you may well end up like the Belmont church of Nashville. Once a strong, faithful church of Christ, under the leadership of Don Finto, a 1960 forerunner of the "change agents," they first nibbled at the bait of Pentecostalism and then swallowed it whole. Today they are the Belmont Church, no longer affiliated with Churches of Christ. They are fully Pentecostal with instrumental music and

their own apostles. That's where changes led them.
* If you accept the assertions of the "change agents" that we have misread Paul's restrictions on the role of women in the church, you may well find yourself in fellowship with the West Islip Church of Christ of Long Island, New York. Katie Hays is their associate minister who shares all ministerial functions including pulpit duties. This is no urban legend. The West Islip elders related this on the Christian Chronicle website: www.christianchronicle.org (Sept. 2002).
* If you choose the agenda of the "change agents," in time you will almost certainly find yourself worshiping with instruments of music. Such is high on their agenda. The Community Church of Christ in Hendersonville, TN reached that point a few years back as has the Northwest church in Seattle, Washington state to name only a few (See Milton Jones in **The Transforming of a Tradition**, edited by Allen & Anderson, pp. 75-84).
* If you choose the road of change you will find your church accepting as members those claiming to be saved by grace and faith alone before baptism. Such is being taught by notable change agents such as Rubel Shelly and Max Lucado.
* By choosing change, you will cease to be a members of the church purchased by the blood of Christ (Acts 20:28); established by him (Matt. 16:18); which will be saved by him (Eph. 5:23). That sacred church is exclusive. It is unique with no competitors or equals. The churches that embrace the "change doctrine" see themselves as a denomination established by Alexander Campbell and Baron Stone. Christ did not die for a church established by those men nor has he promised to save it. It is a disservice to them to attribute that to them which they repudiated. Campbell's enemies loved to call him the founder of a sect called the Campbellites. Now some who claim to be his friends do so! Shame!

We recently read of a tragedy where a bridge collapsed in the night and unsuspecting drivers plunged into the dark waters below. The "agents of change" are trying to lead our people down a dark, dark road of error. The bridge is out and those who follow them face a fearful end in the murky waters below.

IV.
HOW WE GOT TO THIS POINT

20. HOW WE GOT INTO THIS SITUATION

Many brethren have recently awakened to discover that serious problems are erupting in congregations all across the nation. They are especially evident in many of our large city churches. Several of our colleges and universities are actively promoting a program of innovations that change the faith, worship and practice of churches of Christ. These changes are not merely cosmetic or surface matters, they are profound and if implemented will transform a church of Christ into a humanly created denomination of no eternal worth or value. Having spent the last forty-seven years working among our churches, it seems the following things have paved the way bringing us to this critical situation.

I. For some 40 years many of our preachers have neglected doctrinal instruction in their preaching and classes. They preferred to deliver "self-help" lessons, lessons on marriage, family and child-rearing. These along with pleasant, inspirational talks in time left their hearers spiritually illiterate and anemic. They were thus vulnerable to new-winds of doctrine that Satan's agents introduced into the life of the church.

II. During that same 40 years our churches depended heavily on Christian Colleges and universities to educate and train their preachers. With few exceptions these schools have failed in the stewardship entrusted to them. Trying to imitate their peers in the denominational world, they placed minimal emphasis on the text of Scripture and even less on the doctrinal distinctives of Christianity. They preferred to train young men for pastoral roles, with heavy emphasis on counseling, public relations and "church growth" strategies based on denominational patterns. Many of the graduates of these schools have gone forth with a weak view of the authority of the Scripture and a distorted view of the church and our history here in America.

III. A third factor that brought us here is the use of denominational Bible school literature to educate the children in our churches. For some 30 years most of the elementary level literature offered by our Christian publishers and book stores has been prepared by denominational teachers and publishing houses. While lightly edited by our distributors, it has two serious flaws: the errors that are woven into it and the basic truths that are neglected and left out. While many bodies know the value of early indoctrination, we have not and now we reap what we have sown.

IV. A loss of faith in the power of the gospel to save the lost has occurred. Even though God clearly states that the gospel is his power to save the lost (Rom. 1:16), a generation of young preachers now fill our pulpits who obviously do not believe this. No matter what they say, their conduct betrays them. They have chosen instead to depend on storytelling, entertainment and gimmicks to attract people and persuade them to make a commitment to their churches. Rejecting the pattern given by the Holy Spirit they have preferred a new pattern; that of the Saddleback Church or the Willow Creek Church's pattern, We see the result of thus following these man-made patterns.

V. We have raised a generation of preachers who are ashamed of the Lord's church. They are pained that it is different, exclusive, old fashioned, not concerned with pleasing men or popularity. The books and lectures of the change agents demonstrate this embarrassment. They blush at our acappella singing, our childlike dependance on Scripture, our insistence that Christ has only one church; that we will not yield on the necessity of immersion for remission of sins.

VI. Some of our sisters have abandoned the standard of Christ for the philosophy and program of the Feminist movement. They rationalize and discount Paul's authority to forbid women a public leadership role in the church (I Cor. 14:33-34; I Tim. 2:11-12). They use the logic and arguments of humanistic feminists to justify their violation of God's law. Already we have a few churches with women preachers. Unless the righteous arise and man the walls, more will follow.

VII. Weak leadership, elders and preachers have yielded to the clamor of young, worldly-minded members who demanded changes that would satisfy them God ordained that older, seasoned men be appointed to lead his people (Acts 14:23). They are expected to hold fast the faithful words (Tit. 1:9). Elders themselves are under the authority of the written Word of Christ. The only discretion they have is in nonessential or optional matters where Christ has not legislated.

Thus it has been in hundreds of congregations. We have sown to the wind and reaped the whirlwind!

21. FINDING THE SOURCE

When the Anthrax attacks occurred, a massive search was begun to find the source of the deadly substance and those responsible for loosing it on an unsuspecting public. Across the country a harmful situation is springing up in numerous congregations of the Lord's church. It enters the life of a church quietly and almost imperceptibly until it has had time to incubate and establish itself. When a foothold is gained, it has the potential to wreak havoc and destruction on the church body and lead a multitude away from the wholesome doctrine of Christ (Tit. 2:1).

The symptoms of this spiritual plague are several. Most notably, those infected are unhappy with the simple singing of hymns, prayers, communion, offerings and lessons from God's Word. They crave entertainment. They have little appetite for the great hymns of the church. They need interactive songs with hand actions and applause. A choir would give them relief. They can tolerate the sound of the piano or guitar with their singing. They choke on Bible lessons that emphasize doctrine, but relish those that savor of feel-good psychology. They have an adverse reaction when the faith and practice of our spiritual forebearers are mentioned. Embarrassment is experienced when great heroes of the past are cited as good examples of faithfulness. They have severe cramps when anyone mentions that Christ's church is exclusively one and that denominationalism is sinful and wrong. Improvement is immediately felt however when a "doctor" tells them that we are just another denomination and that other religious groups are equally pleasing to our Lord. They feel a compulsion to move female members of their groups into positions of public leadership and experience melancholia when they encounter folks who cannot appreciate their point of view.

Observation tells us that this spiritual condition springs from a few primary sources. Published materials advocating these views have sprung from a handful of our Christian Universities. Ministerial Students who have received their training in those schools seem most likely to reflect the symptoms cited above. Lectureships of those schools seem to be show cases for the champions of the new way to worship and serve.

In many cases these symptoms invade congregations by way of a youth minister who first introduced them to the youngsters under his guidance. Most of those youth ministers got their infection while in a Christian school.

Another hot spot for the promotion of these infectious views and practices are the special events that are hosted and directed by those already infected with the noxious virus. University lectureships have already been mentioned. In addition to them are some workshops, retreats, encampments and youth camps that are promoted by those who wish to introduce and impose such changes on the churches. For a number of years many of our campus ministries have been staffed by young men who mistakenly thought entertainment was worship, that recreation was the Lord's work and counseling was teaching God's Word. A few religious journals have aided the spread of these debilitating views.

The activities of all of the above-mentioned groups have for a long time been conditioning young people. They then take these views and practices with them when they return to local congregations. In the absence of strong and watchful elders and preachers, they soon introduce their new approach to worship into the life of the church and the disease begins its deadly work. Conflict ensues as the younger folks push for change. Older members often find it easier to leave than to resist those who are making the changes. Some churches are so weak and malnourished in Scripture knowledge that they easily fall victim to the invading host. In fevered delusion, they even think they are growing and prospering when in reality the apparent growth is but the swelling of a decaying body. Interestingly this same disease has already born its morbid fruit in many of our denominational neighbors. Those who are wise would not want to see such harm come to their church families.

If a congregation is to remain strong and healthy before the Lord Jesus, those who lead will have to be willing to stand firm and say No to those who wish to remake them after the pattern of a denomination body which is unknown to God (Gal. 2:5). They will see that strong doses of Biblical medicine are administered to combat the infection among them.

22. A SELF-CAUSED DISASTER

Russia suffered a great tragedy when her nuclear submarine, the Kursk, sank, taking the lives of 118 good men. Not only was the disaster costly in terms of men and money, it cost the struggling

Russian government prestige and credibility. Her citizens were angry at the loss of their loved ones. Government spokesmen suggested it might have been an old mine left from World War II or a collision with an NATO sub. An official inquiry was made and after a year of waiting the truth became known. The Kursk sank because one of her own torpedoes exploded aboard ship. The faulty weapon leaked propellant and when it detonated, the ship was destroyed.

The moral of this unfortunate story is that it is easy to blame our disasters on someone else, when often they are of our own making. A disaster is now unfolding in the brotherhood of Churches of Christ that likely will result in a division comparable to that of last century when the Disciples of Christ and Christian Churches abandoned the platform of New Testament authority. Tragically much of this disaster is of our own doing.

* Some of our Christian Universities, in their quest for academic recognition, have recruited professors on the basis of their advanced educational credentials and not on the basis of sound faith. Some of these men have brought with them a corrupt, tainted faith which they have successfully passed on to hundreds of our young preachers who studied under them.
* The same schools have displaced emphasis on rooting and grounding Bible majors in sound doctrine with "ministry programs" that sent them forth with lots of people-skills, but no skills in, nor loyalty to God's Word.
* Those preachers, elders and parents who continue to encourage Christian young people to attention schools that are no longer faithful to the Word of God and New Testament Christianity. They are converted to a denominational type of worship and come home to demand it in their home congregations.
* Those who continue to fund such schools, enabling them to do their work of subverting the faith of young students.
* Publishers of our Bible School literature who found it more profitable to purchase denominational literature and put their covers on it than to have Christians write it. The children who spent their formative years being taught from such tainted

material are now the young adults of the church and care not for sound doctrine. To use such literature is similar to loading a submarine with leaking torpedoes.
* Many elders have mistakenly thought that doctrinal preaching would not build up a church and thus have selected and encouraged preachers to feed their congregations a diet of stories and pop-psychology. Now they have a membership who has no understanding of Biblical Christianity.
* Elders, who while sound in their personal faith, have allowed men to stay in their employment who were obviously unsound and adrift in seas of denominational error. Such men can eventually turn the hearts of the congregation away from the principles of Christ.
* Elders who continue to invite men for special services even though it is widely known that they no longer are loyal to "the faith once delivered to the saints" (Jude 3), have made it possible for them to enjoy respect, support and acceptance while they undermine the faith of multitudes.
* Elders, who rather than confront and refuse a noisy element clamoring for change, compromised and agreed to have both "traditional," i.e., Biblical worship and "contemporary," i.e., charismatic worship.
* Elders who help to finance or encouraged their members to participate in lectureships and forums whose purpose is to promote radical, unscriptural changes in the Lord's church. Many preachers have done the same.
* Good men, who would never preach or approve of error, have spent years preaching nice Biblical sermons that failed to indoctrinate their hearers in the essential fundamentals of Christianity, especially those distinctive points that distinguish Christ's church from denominations. Now that a militant wave of heresy has appeared such members are in no position to resist it.
* Preachers who have seen this problem evolving over the last 20 years, but have stood with muted tongues unwilling to speak out against it. What could have been extinguished in a month is now

threatening to overwhelm us.
* Many youth programs have been essentially recreational and the devotional activities were allowed to be shallow, subjective and entertainment oriented. Now those young people are the young adults of the congregation and expect the same from the pulpit.
* Congregations whose campus outreach programs have been allowed to become seed beds for a new kind of worship and faith that is based on the teachings of men rather than the Book of God. Rather than being strengthened and kept loyal to Christ, it is often the case that students in these programs go on to create problems in the churches where they clamor for changes like they learned while in school.

It is bad when the church is attacked from without by those who hate her, it is worse when she is damaged by those who should be her friends and guardians. Brethren take heed to what is happening where you serve.

23. SOUND MEN WHO HELP MAKE APOSTASY POSSIBLE

As efforts to corrupt the faith and turn churches of Christ into a denominational body expand, we face special challenges in recruiting a viable army of soldiers to resist the incursions of those who are enemies of New Testament Christianity. There are numbers of brethren who are sound in their faith, who would never knowingly engage in any practices contrary to the will of Christ, who are inadvertently helping the promoters of apostasy in their mission. Consider the following types who fall into this category:

* Preachers who behave as if we have no problems facing the church. Thus their members are totally unprepared when they move to a new location where false teachers have been influential or when they show up in their home congregation.
* Preachers who refuse to inform themselves about our problems.

Yes, it is time consuming to read and learn what unfaithful teachers are promoting. Yes, such is not a pleasant pastime, but it must be done if we are to be the watchmen God expects us to be (Ezek. 3:17).

* Preachers who never get around to alerting and warning their people of the problems we now face. Thus they leave them ignorant and vulnerable to false teachers who will one day come knocking (Hos. 4:6) .
* Preachers who refuse to address the false doctrines being promoted by the change agents. It is our job to teach all things that Christ commanded (Matt. 28:20), to declare to them all things profitable (Acts 20:20) and thus to fortify the faith of our hearers. Sound preaching necessarily involves some lessons exposing and refuting error (II Tim. 4:2; Tit. 3:10).
* Preachers who fail to point their brethren to available, useful and sound materials that would inform and fortify them against the destructive errors being promoted. There are good books, tracts and gospel papers that would inoculate any dedicated saint against the doctrines of the change agents. To fail in this respect is much like the doctor who fails to advise his patient of medicine that would heal his disorder.
* Elders who employ men without asking, probing questions about their faith and relative to today's problems. They thus run the risk of inadvertently bringing in a man who will sow the seeds of discord among their flock.
* Elders who invited guest speakers with no concern about their views on the change issues. This gives change agents credibility and opportunity to do their destructive work.
* Elders who encourage Christian Schools, Camps, Seminars, Workshops, Encampments and Magazines with no thought to who will be teaching and what will be taught. To encourage brethren to attend and participate in programs that are indoctrination sessions for the change movement is irresponsible.
* Elders who allow folks to serve as teachers, deacons, etc. who hold weak, compromising views of the faith, and are

sympathetic to the change movement. To place such brethren in positions of trust and leadership is like inviting a person infected with the plague into your home.
* Elders who fail to provide specific teaching to educate, inform and forewarn their members of the dangers abroad. The teaching of the church is first of all the duty of elders (Acts 20:28). They must give account for the souls entrusted to their care (Heb. 13:17).
* Editors who are so determined to be positive and avoid controversy that they completely ignore the dangers abroad. Each month they have opportunity to strengthen their readers against heresy that if left to flourish, will destroy the church. Even while sticking to their positive approach, they could help their readers by systematically addressing the fundamentals of the faith that are being challenged.
* Editors who are personally not about to embrace the change doctrine, willingly provide space to erroneous authors, enabling them to promote their destructive views.
* College administrators, who though sound themselves, employ or maintain on their staff teachers of unsound faith. Even one such man can plant his poison in the hearts and minds of hundreds of naive students.
* Conservative preachers and elders who exhibit such a caustic and hateful spirit that they drive folks into the waiting arms of the liberal change agents.

The threat to our existence as a faithful church is real and present. Every man who loves the Lord is desperately needed to ensure that Christ's church will survive. Brethren, don't be part of the problem!

24. ENABLERS: GOOD PEOPLE WHO HELP OTHERS DO BAD THINGS

Once again the Lord's people are facing the problem of liberal false teachers working to change the faith and practice of the church.

From many quarters we hear of preachers and others set on bringing about unscriptural changes they wish to see implemented. They would change the way we worship in song, the role of our women in public worship, the way people receive salvation, our relationship with the denominational world, the way we interpret and apply Scripture, even the way we view God's Word. If they are successful, they will bring chaos and division to the church as their predecessors have done in the past.

There are determined false teaches who have a mission and goal of subverting and gaining control over congregations and eventually the whole church. There are others who **enable** the church-wreckers to succeed. These brethren love the church; they would not intentionally harm her. In their naivete they operate very much as the family member who enables the alcoholic to continue his destructive behavior. The writer of Hebrew speaks of some who entertained angels unawares (Heb. 13:2), so also some entertain liberals unaware.

* Some enablers have had such faulty Bible training that they truly feel it would be rude and unchristian on their part to speak up against a teacher of error.
* Some are novices in the faith or in leadership. Thus they allow unsound teachers to enter in and influenced the congregation they lead. They are hesitant to challenge the false teacher, even though they are uncomfortable with his message or proposals.
* Some are clearly deceived. They would not knowingly be party to harming the Cause of Christ. False teachers always depend on smooth and fair speech to deceive the hearts of the innocent (Rom. 16:18). They use cunningly devised fables (II Pet. 1:16) when spinning their web.
* Some lack adequate knowledge to discern the error being propagated. Now as always people and churches are destroyed by lack of knowledge (Hos. 4:6).
* Some mistakenly think that unity at any price is preferable to maintaining a pure Biblical faith and church. Unity is precious.

We must work to maintain it (Eph. 4:3) but Christ never intended that we sacrifice truth and faithful obedience to have unity with those who promote a false way.

Innocent of evil intent these brethren may be, but they nevertheless enable the enemies of the church to gain an entrance and commence their destructive work. Some folks by their failure to protect the flock of God are unconscious enemies of the cause of Christ.

25. THE LURE OF THE NEW

"The whims of fashion govern not only what we eat and how we dress but also what we venerate and how we worship. But as trends come and go will the church survive the fickle tastes of her worldly members?"

Our parents and grandparents grew up in a day when truth, institutions and values from the past were appreciated, respected, venerated, and cherished. By the 1960s that appreciation for the past began to fade. Today there are many people who are so addicted to that which is new and different that they despise anything that is old . . . no matter how sacred it may have been to their predecessors. This unpleasant change is evident in patriotic, political, social and cultural fields, but most noticeably in the area of religion.

Those obsessed with changing things operate under the mistaken notion that the new is always better than the old. The patriotism of the average young America is not equal to, much less superior to that of his grandparents. Contemporary political behavior is certainly no better than that of 50 years ago. Modern schools pale beside the schools our parents attended. The social virtues and values of modern America do not compare favorably with those of generations past. Contemporary art and entertainment are but a shadow of that which was produced in days past.

The "lure of the new" is especially dangerous and destructive in the area of Christianity. The God of Christianity is timeless. He is also perfect. A thousand or even ten thousand years of human progress does not mean that God must change. He changes not (Mal. 3:6). Christ lived and died two thousand years ago. But he is the same yesterday, today and forever (Heb. 13:8). Like his Father, he changes not. He does not need to be updated. The New Testament is upwards of two thousand years old. It is the word of Christ and will never pass away (Matt. 24:35). It is truth (John 17:17). It is timeless, as meaningful and applicable today as when first written. We are forbidden to try to change it (Rev. 22:18-19). We can only obey or disobey its precepts.

The church, purchased by the blood of Christ and established on the grand truth that He is the Christ, the son of the Living God, is likewise two thousand years old. But being the creation of God the Son, its eternal aspects cannot be changed. Those who lay profane hands on the bride of Christ will answer to him for their brazen effort. We can change our time of worship, our place for meeting, the decor of our meeting houses, but we cannot touch the way we worship, the way God organized his church, the way converts are added to the church or the doctrines of the faith. Those things were ordained by the founder and must be held in sacred respect and unalterable.

Enjoy your new car or home. Accept new hair styles and dress. Benefit from new drugs and medical, procedures but don't presume to change that which God has established for his kingdom. To do so will place one in jeopardy of the same consequences that befell Nadab and Abihu, Korah, Dathan and Abiram, and Uzzah and Ahio. In religion the lure of the new may prove to be as dangerous as the new lure is to the trout in the lake. The new ways promoted by our change agents may be pretty, flashy, intriguing and exciting but hidden within is the deadly hook that leads to destruction.

V.
OUR HISTORY IS BEING REPEATED

26. *DEJA VU* ALL OVER AGAIN

To folks who are unfamiliar with our brotherhood's history, the current clamor for change emanating from the halls of our Christian Colleges and Universities may seem new, strange and different. But those who have studied the history of our movement from 1850-1925 know that today's events are a virtual replay of brotherhood events in that distant generation. As Yoggie Bera, that famed philosopher of New York use to say, "It's deja vu all over again."

* In 1849 D. S. Burnett of Cincinnati, Ohio led a drive to persuade our brethren to create a Missionary Society to do the mission work of the church.
* In 1859 Dr. L. L. Pinkerton of Midway, Kentucky introduced the first musical instrument into a church of the Restoration Movement.
* In ca. 1885 Bro. Isaac Errett of Michigan was being addressed as reverend.
* By 1880 Sis. Emma Babcock was preaching among the "progressive" churches.
* Bro. J. H. Garrison and others progressives began to speak of our denomination and work for our inclusion in ecumenical religious organizations.
* The Disciples' Divinity House at the University of Chicago was a generating plant for liberal thought. They indoctrinated a multitude of young preachers and educators who moved into our churches and schools with their message of skepticism. Religious papers, such as the **Christian Standard, The Christian, The Christian Quarterly** and **The Disciple** kept up a continual drumbeat for progressive change in our faith, worship and practice.

* Congregations were convinced that to grow and prosper, to compete with their denominational neighbors, they had to embrace the changes and the vast majority joined the progression away from the simple faith of the New Testament Christianity.

A few lonely voices were raised against that tidal wave of apostasy. Noble sons of God such as Jacob Creath, Jr., Tolbert Fanning Benjamin Franklin protested but to no avail.

It was Fanning's pupil and protege David Lipscomb, a humble farmer from rural Tennessee who dug in his heels, rallied a small but determined band of courageous men and drew a line in the sand. The progressives swept away some 85 percent of our people, all of our schools, and most of our mission work. Our forefathers in the faith had to start over again, virtually from scratch to rebuild the body of disciples known as Churches of Christ.

What is being promoted among our universities and churches today is "***deja vu*** all over again." Pray that God will raise up a courageous band of Creaths, Fanning, Franklins and Lipscomb to lead his church in this mortal struggle against the progressives of our day. They identify themselves as **agents of change**. In reality they are apostates, kin to those Paul warned would depart from the faith in later times (I Tim. 4:1).

27. VALUABLE LESSONS FROM THE PAST

A century and a quarter ago our brotherhood was being decimated by a powerful change movement that eventuated in the separation of the Disciples of Christ/Christian Churches from our fellowship. The parallels between that apostasy and our current change movement are remarkable.

David Lipscomb, a country preacher from Middle Tennessee,

emerged as the most effective leader of the opposition. Although he was neither a profound Bible scholar nor a polished orator, Bro. Lipscomb was a man of much wisdom, determination and great patience.

While doggedly opposing the digressives, who were determined to change the worship of the brethren by introducing instrumental music, and the polity of the church by organizing missionary societies, Bro. Lipscomb patiently sought to lead good men out of their error and into useful positions of service in the church.

When Theophilus B. Larimore was trying to maintain fellowship with the digressives and the conservatives was well, Bro. Lipscomb and others worked patiently to convince him that he must break his ties with error and take his stand with those who were loyal to the Bible way. They eventually succeeded and Bro. Larimore went on to be one of the most effective and successful preachers among us. When Lipscomb was criticized for befriending Bro. Larimore, he wrote, " . . . I have no sympathy with the idea that we must jump on and denounce every brother that does not do things our way. This is selfish bigotry" (Robert Hooper, **Crying in the Wilderness**, p. 219).

Hall. L. Calhoun served under the inimitable John W. McGarvey at the College of the Bible in Lexington, KY. He was then encouraged to enroll at Yale University's Divinity School where he earned his Bachelor of Divinity degree. His doctorate was earned at Harvard. He returned to teach at the school in Lexington. He was McGarvey's choice to succeed him as head of that school (A. Doran & J. E. Choate, **The Christian Scholar**, p. 93). When the theological liberals were able to grab control of the College of the Bible, N. B. Hardeman, F. W. Smith and H. Leo Boles were able to persuade Bro. Calhoun to leave the camp of the digressives and cast his lot with our brethren. The rest of his days were spent effectively preaching the word among our people.

The lessons for us are these:
* Lipscomb's doctrinal soundness and loyalty were tempered by his love for his brethren and his desire to salvage every good man he possibly could.
* Men who are champions in opposing error can still afford to extend a helping hand to a brother who needs some help and encouragement.
* Men like Bros. Larimore and Calhoun remind us that not everyone in the camp of the change agents is a hopeless case. Some of them can be salvaged, and we must make every effort to do so.
* One man salvaged from error is worth all the labor and patience it took to win him.
* We must do more than oppose error. We must labor to build up the kingdom in positive ways as well.
* The most effective leaders in the kingdom are not always the great scholars or preachers. Few have equaled Lipscomb's greatness, influence or success yet he was no great preacher or scholar.

28. OUR PAST IS THE KEY TO OUR PRESENT PROBLEMS

Across the nation Churches of Christ are faced with a host of preachers and teachers who have undertaken a campaign to mold and changed them according to a new pattern. These "agents of change" think they have found something new and better for the Lord's church, but in reality what they are promoting is almost identical to the changes proposed by the progressives among our churches in the 60 years from the end of the Civil War to World War I.

The changes they insisted upon ravaged our brotherhood with strife and division. When the dust was settled there were two separate bodies; Churches of Christ and Disciples of Christ/Christian Churches. Those who departed from us had begun a journey which continues to this day, farther and farther from the Biblical ground their fathers occupied.

* Those brethren were unhappy with our acappella singing. They desired choirs, soloists, pianos and organs.
* They felt that a brotherhood of independent congregations could never do the Lord's work in an adequate way. They proposed all sorts of brotherhood organizations to manage that work. They created missionary, Bible, tract, publishing, benevolent and other societies, believing they could do it better.
* They were convinced that our preachers were not reaching their full potential as simple ministers or evangelists, and so they reshaped theirs to be pastors and reverends.
* They felt lonely and alienated from their ministerial peers in other religious bodies, so they joined their ministerial alliances and eventually the Federal Council of Churches (Now, The National Council of Churches).
* They were embarrassed at their fathers' resolve to be Christians only and the church which Christ built and blessed. Such an approach seemed narrow and ungenerous to others, so they began to seek acceptance as fellow denominationalists.
* They felt shackled and restricted when obliged to abide by the authority of the New Testament in their faith and practice. They needed the Old Covenant to broaden their range of options for worship. Eventually, even that did not provide adequate latitude for their innovations.
* They concluded that we were mistaken in not placing women in our pulpits and leadership offices. So they remedied that by doing so.
* Eventually they concluded that the whole idea of restoring the original faith and practice of the church was an obsolete and unworkable idea and abandoned it.

Within 40 years (by 1906), the differences between the progressives and our fathers were so great that it was clear they were two different bodies of people. Today you can examine the mature fruit of their progressive ideas by visiting a Disciples of Christ church. They still talk about our common past, but in faith and practice there is little that we hold in common.

Today the seeds, if not the plant, of all of these departures from the faith are found among us. Many of the great grandchildren of those courageous men who stood in the forefront of the battle and salvaged a small remnant of faithful disciples are prepared to embrace the apostasy that was rejected by their forefathers. Like Hymenaeus and Alexander, they are making shipwreck concerning the faith (I Tim. 2:19-20). Let all who love the Lord reject their overtures.

29. WHAT IF "CHANGE AGENTS" HAD BEEN OUR LEADERS

As I wade through the plethora of books being issued by those who are seeking to impose changes on Churches of Christ, I am led to ponder, "What if the 'change oriented' preachers, university professors and editors had lived in earlier generations and been the ones providing leadership for the church when crises appeared?"

If they had been among us in the years following the Civil War, they most surely would have sided with those promoting instrumental music in worship, human organizations to do the mission work of the church (i.e., missionary societies), women in leadership roles and fellowship with denominational churches. All of these items and more are on the agenda our "change agents." Had they been our leaders back then there would be few if any Churches of Christ today. We would all be in the Disciples of Christ or some other denominational communion. Thank God for Tolbert Fanning, David Lipscomb, Austin McGary, J. D. Tant and that noble band of faithful men who stood against those "change agents" of yesteryear and saved the church from apostasy.

If they had been our representative leaders in the generation between the two World Wars (1920-1940), it is very possible that we would all be caught up in the speculations of premillennialism just like most of our Protestant neighbors. Our change agents think our fathers made a mistake to oppose those who sought to introduce that popular error among us. We can be thankful that we had H. Leo Boles, R. L. Whiteside, Foy Wallace, Jr., John T. Hinds and other good men who would not abide those who promoted that change in the thinking of our people.

Had they represented us in the 1960s, when Charismatics began to surface among us, we very well could be a Pentecostal body today. In fact, if our contemporary promoters of change succeed, they will most certainly lead us in that direction. They cannot find it in their code to oppose error that appears in the garb of "spirituality," excitement and miraculous workings of the Holy Spirit. Thank God for Guy N. Woods, James Bales and others who quickly extinguished the Pentecostal flame.

If they had been our leaders in the 1970s and 80s, we might all be a part of the Discipling Movement of the International Churches of Christ (i.e., Crossroads/Boston) denomination. A few good men stepped forward, wielded the sword of the Spirit effectively and exposed the promoters of that movement for the heretics they were. Our change advocates have no stomach for such negative, confrontational teaching and action. A favorite saying of the promoters of change is, they prefer "function over form." Since the Boston folks won lots of converts, how could anyone object to their methodology?

If today, we as a body of people allow the advocates of change to be our teachers and leaders we are like the man with a "death wish." They will change us from the Church of Christ purchased and founded by the Lord Jesus into a denomination founded by Barton Stone and Alexander Campbell. They will change our worship from that ordained by Christ in his Word to that designed and demanded by men who do not revere God's Word. They will change our faith from that derived from the New Covenant of Christ to that borrowed from Luther and Calvin and modern Pentecostal leaders. Rather than salvation by grace through obedient faith (Eph. 2:8-9), they will have us teaching salvation by grace and faith alone. If our children and preacher students are sent to their universities, they will likely emerge as denominational disciples rather than as strong faithful Christians. Rather than come home to strengthen and build up our congregations, they will come as missionaries of a new faith and practice inspired to impose changes on a church they no longer believe in.

Reader, as you listen to the sweet, inviting sirens of change, ponder these "What If" questions. They will help you to say "No!" to them.

30. STANDING AT THE CROSSROADS

Churches of Christ are standing at a critical crossroads. It is the same one our ancestors faced and it is one most of our religious neighbors have had to deal with.

At the turn of the last century our fathers arrived at this same crossroads. The road to the right led to ultraconservatism and extremism. Led by Daniel Sommer of Indianapolis, a handful of disciples chose that path. As they traveled, their road grew ever more constricted. They continually tightened their circle of fellowship. Again and again they quarreled and broke fellowship with each other. Today, a half dozen or more small bodies still trudge this dreary path.

The vast majority of our fathers paused and pondered the future and chose the path to the left. They had grown weary of the straitened and narrow road which they and their predecessors had traveled for a hundred long years. The road to the left was broad and smooth. It was throughly modern. Vast multitudes of other religious folks were choosing it. It was not a lonely road. That road abounded in things exciting, entertaining and popular. All who chose it were applauded and welcomed by the crowd along the way. Bold leaders like W. K. Pendleton, Isaac Errett, J. H. Garrison and Herbert

Willett challenged the masses to reject the old narrow road and follow them down the new broad road of spiritual adventure. Fully 85 percent rushed after them. Today they are known as the Disciples of Christ/Christian Churches denomination.

The remnant that was left cast their eyes about. They consulted again their road map to eternity and studied it carefully. They besought God's will and guidance in prayer. Convinced that the way straight before them was the Savior's Way, their leaders challenged them to go forward. They were bound for New Jerusalem and were not going to be diverted. There was only one way to go. God-fearing men like David Lipscomb, F. D. Srygley, Austin McGary and J. D. Tant exhorted and encouraged their fellow pilgrims. They shepherded the stragglers and urged them to keep their eyes upon the goal. As the journey proceeded, others took note and joined their caravan. Individuals and families, even congregations realized that theirs was the glory land way and fell in beside them. Their numbers swelled until well more than a million joyful souls streamed along the upward path. Men and women of every tribe and nation were invited to join them and multitudes did. They were trudging the old paths that led to the Father's home.

Now a century has past. We have come to yet another crossroads. Three options are before us. A noisy throng is trying to convince us to take the road to the right. Ultra-conservatism always leads to radicalism and faction. A larger crowd is already streaming down the road on the left. They are following their Protestant neighbors on that broad road. Again the emotion, excitement and popularity of the left are drawing them onward. Learned professors keep telling them it is the way to go. They ridicule the old paths as obsolete and boring. The majority have yet to decide. Shall we follow the old paths our fathers trod or shall we turn aside to the right or the left? If the pilgrims are to be encouraged to stay on the highway of holiness, strong and faithful preachers and elders will have to step forth and lead the way. Congregations tend to follow their leaders. May God raise up such leaders, for the future of His

Son's church hangs in the balance.

31. POOR BENJAMIN'S ALMANAC

The great statesman philosopher, Benjamin Franklin (1706-1790) gave us "**Poor Richard's Almanac**" filled with choice proverbs and accumulated bits of wisdom for Colonial Americans. The great gospel preacher, Benjamin Franklin (1812-1878), gave us the **American Christian Review**, the most widely read gospel paper of his day. Because of his lack of wealth and formal education, he was scorned by the sophisticated progressives of his day. As he watched the liberal wing of the brotherhood rapidly abandoning the original plea for New Testament Christianity, he expressed the elitist air of the progressives in his pungent way, saying,

> "We are a long way ahead of these old books, read and admired by old fogies. These were good books in their time, and plain, old-fashioned men did their work in their day; but we are philosophers, geologists, astronomers, historians and reasoners, not going by the *Word*, but *general principles*; not confined to the *letter of Scripture*, but the *spirit*" (As quoted in **The Churches of Christ** by Richard Hughes, p. 51).

If we did not know better, we might conclude that Bro. Benjamin was a prophet led to describe an attitude that would surface among Churches of Christ a hundred years later (1960-2002). Such an attitude is now common stock in many of our Christian Schools where worldly "scholars" are training tomorrow's young preachers. It is vividly displayed by Bro. Hughes, in his book, **The Churches of Christ**. It is an established part of the sales pitch of the agents of change. In Bro. Franklin's day, the progressives evolved into the Disciples of Christ/Christian Church denomination. Ours are clamoring to be received into fellowship by those same people and no doubt will be. They long to be accepted by their peers in the evangelical world.

Although he was poor and humble, Benjamin Franklin taught more truth, saved more souls, planted more churches, strengthened and helped more people than any progressive of his day! We look back to him as a true hero of the faith, the others will forever bear the stigma of men who divided the body of Christ. The grandchildren of the progressives of Franklin's day are asserting themselves in our day. They are our agents of change. Their end will be that of their ancestors. May we be faithful and unmoveable as was Bro. Benjamin Franklin.

32. A MYSTERY AND A MARVEL

It is a mystery to me why those universities among us, who have already, or are in process of rejecting the very concept of "restoring New Testament Christianity," solicit funds for preserving and housing Restoration literature, journals, books and memorabilia. Why do their professors publish books on a subject and cause they no longer believe to be a legitimate and viable approach to serving God in the 21st century?

Could it be that they are trying to convince those who provide money and students, necessary to the survival of their enterprises, that they are still faithful and loyal to the Restoration Cause? Or are they trying to persuade themselves that they really haven't abandoned the faith?

No one demonstrates more interest in the early history of our movement than the Disciples of Christ, yet they have long ago abandoned every aspect of the Restoration Plea. Strange how history repeats itself in so short a time.

33. THE SLIPPERY SLOPE

A popular analogy is that of the novice on the ski slope who stands nervously at the top of the run. Not quite sure of himself or what lives ahead of him, he takes a little step, then another, testing the pack. Suddenly gravity takes control and down he goes to an uncertain fate. While there is a remote chance he might make it safely to the bottom, it is far more likely that disaster awaits him.

So it is in Christianity. Apostasy is a slippery slope with spiritual ruin as its final destination. To see this in bold relief, one needs only look at the history of the great Protestant churches that surround us. Once bastions of conservatism, Methodist, Presbyterian, Lutheran, Episcopalian and Congregational churches now bear only faint resemblance to their past or to the Christianity of the Bible.

The **Disciples of Christ** are an even more pertinent example for us. Their complete and total drift into apostasy and the extremes of liberalism took them little more than 100 years. In 1849 the first of our spiritual forebearers stepped upon the slippery slope of departure. It all seemed so harmless, just an organization to coordinate mission work of the churches. They called it the **American Christian Missionary Society**. The second step was easier. As they relaxed their grip on the necessity of following the Bible in all things, they introduced **instrumental music** into their worship. Then in quick succession came women preachers and elders, open membership, participation in the Federal Council of Churches and the full agenda of theological liberalism. Today it is gay rights, a rejection of Biblical authority and the concept of restoration

We now see many congregations of Churches of Christ standing at the slippery slope of apostasy. Large numbers of preachers and elders, unaware or uncaring, are testing the icy pack of change. Some are testing new forms of expressing worship. The traditional ways of worship seem drab and boring compared to those of Neo-Pentecostalism. It is exhilarating for them to lift up the hands, or have an unseen choir. Some are testing the ice on the matter of salvation. Having fed on the sweet tasting doctrine of salvation by grace and faith alone, they are gingerly testing these teachings on their listeners. They aren't quite ready to boldly repudiate the need for baptism, but they have downgraded it to a "maybe" status.

Others on the slope are toying with the role of women in the leadership of the church. They are not strongly wedded to the Biblical limitation that forbids women to teach or have authority over men (I Tim. 2:12).

Some are slipping on the uniqueness of Christ's church in a world of denominationalism. Although Scripture knows nothing of denominations, these men are heard speaking of our brotherhood as a denomination or sect. If that we are, we stand in competition with the church that Christ built and in shame should close our doors and disband. This certainly is not what our fathers believed. Once you start down the slippery slope, just where does it end?

These are but a few of the examples before us. Some are already plunging headlong down the slope to certain destruction. For them there is little hope. Others are yet flirting with the ice at the crest of the slope. Perhaps by God's mercy they can be snatched back before they are lost beyond recovery (Jude 21-22). Those elders and preachers who are wise will avoid the slippery slope by planting their feet firmly on the plainly revealed truths of the gospel.

34. THE WAY ERROR GAINS ENTRANCE INTO A CONGREGATION

A false teacher will never walk up to a congregation and announce, "I am a heretic, I have come to capture or destroy your church." Paul says that such men use, "Smooth and fair speech" to "beguile the hearts of the innocent" (Rom. 16:18). He speaks of their "cunning craftiness" (Eph.4:14) and their "cunningly devised fables" (II Pet. 1:16). When false teachers are unable to take a congregation in one fell swoop, they settle for an incremental approach . . . a little here, a little there until one day that are in full control.

A hundred years ago those brethren who wished to introduce instrumental music into our churches were determined to take all with them. Their strategy, used over and over again, was as follows. At first they pretended to accept our acappella practice. They would occasionally drop snide remarks about the poor quality of our singing. They would lavishly compliment the worship of those who used instruments and praise the beauty of their worship. To build a constituency and gain a following, they carefully, promoted their agenda privately to gullible souls who could be easily swayed. They eventually suggested using the instruments for young people's meetings and classes, always reassuring the congregation that such would never affect their worship assembles. When that goal was reached, they would bide their time and continue their quite promotion in private settings. When they were confident that they had a majority in their camp, they would raise the question, "Would the congregation prefer to use an instrument in worship?" By that time the elders and other brethren, content to abide in the apostles' doctrine, were totally outnumbered and out maneuvered. They were faced with the option of accepting the change; objecting and being labeled as trouble makers; or to leave in search of a sound congregation where they could worship "as it is written."

By the time our brethren figured out their strategy and were able to alert fellow-Christians, the loss was devastating. Those determined to add to the worship prescribed in Scripture swept upwards of 85% of our churches into their camp. Today when you see a Disciples of Christ or Christian Church, remember the strategy their ancestors used to win their victory. That will help you understand why elders generally said, no to bringing an organ or piano into their church building, for any purpose. That is why property deeds for meeting houses had restrictive deeds that forever forbade the use of a musical instrument in worship conducted there. That is why preachers who thought the question of instrumental music in worship was "not a salvation or faith issue" were not invited to preach for them, even in a revival meeting. That is why preachers routinely delivered lessons explaining the Biblical basis for our acappella worship.

We are now some 70 years removed from the apostasy described above. A third generation has now reached the level of leadership. Most of them are unfamiliar with our past, and many of them not well-grounded in Scripture. Consequently we see churches dangerously drifting toward a maelstrom of error. Many of our people have never heard a Biblical lesson teaching why we worship as we do. Others openly state that they see nothing very serious about the use of instruments in worship. We frequently hear of preachers who now boldly say, that to them "instrumental music is not a salvation issue." Some congregations are allowing instruments to be used in youth programs and in "concerts in their meeting places." One by one, the incremental steps are being taken that will eventuate in them having instruments in their worship. It is only a matter of time. I plead with all brethren to consider the past and take heed lest ye fall (I Cor. 10:12).

35. FULL CIRCLE

In 1849 progressive members of the Restoration movement meeting in Cincinnati, organized the American Christian Missionary Society. In 1859, Dr. L. L. Pinkerton and the church at Midway, Kentucky introduced the first instrument of music into our worship. By 1857, Tolbert Fanning, Jacob Creath, Jr. and others had seen the errors in the Missionary Society and launched their opposition. In the 1880s some of the progressives had moved women into leadership. By 1906 the apostasy was full grown, our circle of fellowship was broken. Those who preferred human organizations to do the Lord's work and humanly devised methods and styles of worship went on to evolve into the modern denominations known as the Disciples of Christ and Independent Christian Churches. By 2,000 an element of preachers and educators among our brethren had evolved away from their historic Biblical roots and embraced human organizations to do the work of Christ's church, instrumental music in worship, women in church leadership and the same approach to Bible authority as the digressives of yesteryear. These modern expressions of apostasy are openly expressed in such books as **The**

Crux of the Matter and The Transforming of a Tradition.

This leads us to the following necessary conclusions:
A. Either our fathers were wrong in objecting to missionary societies, instrumental music, choirs, soloists, and female church leaders or our liberals are wrong today. If the fathers were wrong, then they were guilty of the grave sin of dividing the body of Christ and forming a schism that has no right to exist.
B. If the fathers were wrong, the Disciples of Christ are the legitimate extension of the church and we all should repent of our erroneous and divisive practices, ask their forgiveness and seek a place in their fellowship.
C. If our acappella worship is only our tradition, then in shame, we should renounce that human tradition that we have allowed to divide the body of Christ. We should no longer object to the piano, organ or rock band.
D. On the other hand if our fathers were correct in their objections and the digressives were acting contrary to the doctrine of Christ (II John 9), then our contemporary preachers and professors who have embraced the errors of the Disciples are as guilty of false teaching and causing division in the Body of Christ as were those a century ago. They should repent and turn away from their destructive program or be rejected and marked as enemies of the Cause of Christ (Rom. 16:17-18).

In a century we have come full-circle. Because the lessons of our past history were not learned, some among us have repeated the mistakes of the past. Our fathers were right in their stand against digression last century because they stood on solid Biblical grounds. May God raise up a band of loyal and courageous leaders in the mold of David Lipscomb who will lead us in this hour of trial.

VI.
A PROFILE OF THOSE WHO ARE PROMOTING THESE CHANGES

36. CHANGE AGENTS: A BIBLICAL PROFILE

From the beginning there have been those among Christ's disciples who were not satisfied to abide in the simple system that the Lord inaugurated for this church. Paul mentioned several he had encountered: namely Hymaneaus and Alexander, Phygelus and Hermogenes (I Tim. 1:20; II Tim.15). Jesus cited the Nicolaitans, those who held the teaching of Balaam and that evil woman Jezebel (Rev. 2:6, 15, 20). Today the church is being troubled by a band of men who have embraced a new and different approach to Christianity. Their faith and practice they borrow from the denominational world. They reject the old standards of the Scripture for new standards that are designed to please 21st century man. They have boldly announced their desire and intent to change the church. The church image they greatly admire is that of independent, Protestant community churches like the Willow Creek Community Church in Illinois or the Saddleback Valley Community Church in California.

The Holy Spirit chose several striking metaphors to describe first century disciples who were not content to abide in the doctrine of Christ (II John 9). Paul called them "enemies of the cross of Christ" (Phil. 3:18). Those who wished to add ordinances of Moses's Law to the message of Christ, he called, "evil workers" (Phil. 3:2). He foresaw disciples who would "fall away from the faith, giving heed to seducing spirits and doctrines of demons" (I Tim. 4:1). They were teachers with seared consciences (I Tim. 4:2). Those who taught a different doctrine than Christ had given, he described as "puffed up, knowing nothing . . . men corrupted in mind and bereft of truth" (I Tim. 6:4-5). In his letter to Titus, those who disrupted the peace of the church by their teaching and agitations he called "factious" men (Tit. 3:10). Peter called them false prophets and false teachers. They were promoters of "destructive heresies" (II Pet. 2:1). Jude depicts them as hidden rocks in a harbor, lurking beneath the surface, waiting to rip the bottom out of the ship whose steersman thought he had found a safe haven. They are like shepherds, who without fear feed themselves while the flock is torn and scattered. They are like "clouds without water" promising a blessing but delivering nothing (Jude 12). How do you suppose the Spirit views those today who are busy sowing discord throughout the brotherhood and leading disciples away from the simplicity of the gospel?

The Holy Spirit also instructs us how we should deal with those who trouble the family of Christ. We must not allow ourselves to be deceived by them (II Thess. 2:3). We should mark them and turn away from them (Rom. 16:17-18). We should reject them (Tit. 3:10) and refuse their message. We should in no way lend them support or encouragement (II John 9-11). Those who think they can have detente with the agents of change are deceiving themselves. Jesus warned, "Beware of the leaven of the Pharisees and Sadducees" (Matt. 16:6) We must also beware the leaven of the change agents. Like leaven their doctrine will work silently and unnoticed until they have permeated a sufficient portion of the entire congregation and then they will be in control of the whole. He that hath an ear . . . let him hear!

37. VARIETIES OF CHANGE AGENTS

From every sector of the nation we hear of churches being troubled by promoters of the change agenda. Although those engaging in this promotion have a common goal, not all are of the same stripe.

There are skeptical Bible professors at work in some of our schools. They have been educated in a worldly, skeptical environment where simple Bible Christianity was considered obsolete and foolish. Some of them were subjected to and succumbed to a rationalistic view of Christianity others were indoctrinated in a denomination approach to Christianity. Now they have secured a place in our Christian Schools. Filled with arrogant pride, they feel it is their mission to debunk and destroy the foundations of faith of their students. They send them forth as missionaries of change. They crave recognition from their intellectual peers in academia rather than the glory and approval that comes from God (John 12:42-43). They write the books promoting change and poison the minds of young Christians in our schools.

There are ambitious young preachers who want to be recognized as successful. They are determined to have large flourishing congregations, no matter the price. With limited Bible knowledge, they have no strong convictions about the faith, worship or practice of the church. Anything can and will be sacrificed to the idol of success. They love to test the limits. They seek to justify themselves by pointing to the number of their disciples, and by discrediting those who were their fathers in the faith. Such men are unworthy of the post they occupy.

There is the worldly crowd that has found a place in some of our congregations. They have taken the name of Christ, but not his cross (Matt. 16:24). They want the respectability and social benefits of Christianity without the limitations of the king and his law (Matt. 28:20). They crave entertainment, fun and excitement. They want a religion that does not demand separateness from the world (I Pet. 1:16). They don't want to be different. They insist on a religion that is subservient to the spirit of the age.

There are hapless elders who either know not the Scriptures or care not that God's will be done. Increasing or maintaining attendance figures and keeping the restless young crowd pacified takes preeminence over all other considerations. Some are willing to hire a preacher and let him do whatever he wishes so long as the attendance and contributions stay up. Some are willing to allow the clamoring crowd set the agenda for their congregation. They are willing to listen with uncritical ears to the alluring advice of the "church growth specialists" who would throw the restraints of Scripture overboard to attract a crowd.

Theses four groups, if left unchecked and unchallenged, will wreck and destroy that which our predecessors in Christ have worked 200 years to build up. God forbid that we allow it to happen! "Please holy Father open the eyes of our brethren and stir up their hearts to reject those who lay sordid hands to the sacred things of your church and fill them with righteous zeal to seek the old paths and walk therein. In Jesus' name."

38. GETTING ACQUAINTED WITH A LIBERAL

We live in a world of competing ideologies. In social matters, politics, morality and religion we see those who are conservative and those who are liberal in their convictions and policies. Only those who know and understand the beliefs that underlie the two approaches are able to make an informed and wise decision as to which ideology they will accept. Uninformed of the doctrines, methods and goals one is vulnerable to deception and manipulation. Paul urges us to "know them that labor among" us (I Thess. 5:12). In upwards of half a century of preaching, I have observed the following characteristic of those preachers and leaders who have embraced a liberal approach to Christianity.

* The liberal preacher will always **present himself as a scholar** who knows more than those poor, ignorant conservatives who prefer to hold to those traditional Biblical ways of doing things.
* The liberal brother **wants to be known as a man of compassion**. He says or implies that conservatives are harsh, unloving and uncaring for others.

* He **wants to gain control of a congregation and its meeting place that others have built and paid for.** It is not often that he will announce his new views, go to a new community and start a church from scratch. That is much too hard; so he works his way into an established church and gradually subverts the faith of its members.
* A liberal **is evangelistic;** not necessarily for the lost, but to make converts for his cause. Like the Pharisees they compass land and sea to make proselytes . . . but their converts end up further from, rather than closer to God (Matt. 23:15).
* A liberal **is like a chameleon**. Around strong conservatives he can talk and sound like one of them, around fellow-liberals or those who are unaware, he speaks a different language.
* A liberal **is usually a patient worker**. He can wait for months or even years as he quietly undermines the faith of the disciples and manipulates into leadership roles those who sympathize with his theology.
* A liberal **will not boldly announce his intended agenda** to those he hopes to change. While doing his destructive work, he will continue to use traditional vocabulary and expressions and identify himself with the great heroes of the past until he has gained the confidence of the targeted audience.
* Once he has set his hook in a congregation, a liberal **will not give up or walk away if a protest is raised**. He feels he is on a mission for God and will see a congregation wrecked rather than admit his wrong or abandon his effort.

The best way for a congregation to deal with liberalism is to never allow a man of such persuasion into their pulpit; not for a meeting, a seminar, a class, or for employment. If such a false teacher is already in your midst, the best method of saving your congregation is to immediately dismiss him and send him on his way . . . without recommendation. Otherwise, left undisturbed, a church will experience grief untold.

39. DELUDED DISCIPLES WHO LOATH THE LORD'S CHURCH

Since the Youth Rebellion of the 1960s we have witnessed the bizarre phenomena of Americans who are so disenchanted that they loath their nation, their race, their culture, their parents, ancestors and their religious heritage. They even hate themselves and seem ashamed of the life they enjoy.

This self-loathing is nurtured by many academics, media types and politicians of the left. The amazing aspect of this self-loathing is that America offers more equality, freedom, opportunity and advantage to its citizens than any other nation on earth. We have rescued more people from aggression, protected more weak nations, fed and financially supported more people then any nation in history. In the climate of freedom which America offers, tremendous advances have been made in medicine, science and technology; progress that we have shared with all the world. Here freedom of religion, thought and speech has flourished as nowhere else, yet these poor deluded souls, spend their days loathing America. "President Reagan set about to change their self-loathing. He openly proclaimed that America was great and that the traditional values of faith, family, community, enterprise—remained the building blocks of a decent and good civic society."

It is doubly strange that a similar self-loathing has arisen among some members of the church of Christ. Howard Norton in the Preface to **"Directions for the Road Ahead: Stability in Change Among Churches of Christ**, offers interesting insight into this strange behavior. He cites Dr. Gordon W. Allport of Harvard (The Nature of Prejudice), who notes that people have an **"in-group,"** i.e., those folks whom they can comfortably refer to as "we." They also have a **"reference group"** i.e., a group by which they measure themselves and with which they prefer to be recognized. When a person identifies with a "reference group" different from his "in-group" he finds himself in conflict. He may "repudiate his own "in-group" and develop a hatred for them.

This analysis well describes those among us who are so unhappy with the church of their fathers and who are determined to restyle her in a new mold. A number of our intellectual preachers and professors look to the Evangelical churches and scholars as their reference group. They long for the acceptance and approval of those men and institutions where they have gained their advanced education. They wish to be respected on the same level as men like Billy Graham, Robert Shuller and other notable and successful Evangelicals. The problem is, the leaders of the Evangelical world, as a rule, hold Churches of Christ in contempt because of our unyielding commitment to the commands of Christ and our refusal to compromise our faith for their approval. Thus, "unable to receive approval from the Evangelicals because of the 'in-group' to which they belong, (i.e. fellow-members of Churches of Christ), a kind of self-loathing develops, and churches of Christ, (their fellow-disciples jhw) become to them the enemy; the cause of their discomfort."

This helps us understand the bitter, hateful criticism the change agents are hurling against the Lord's Church. They despise us, yet for some reason they are not yet willing to leave us. They find a hundred grounds for complaint and virtually none for commendation. Like Israel of old, they long to be like the world around them (I Sam. 8:5). Jesus said, "Whosoever shall be ashamed of me and of my words in this adulterous and sinful generation, the Son of man also shall be ashamed of him, when he cometh . . . " (Mk. 8:38).

Precisely because we love the church of Christ and seek approval only from Christ, we will reject the criticism of these self-loathers and the changes they want to force on us. With saints of old, with true conviction we will sing, "I love thy kingdom Lord . . . the church our blest Redeemer saved with his own precious blood."

40. UNWORTHY CHILDREN

One of life's saddest sights is that of children whose behavior is unworthy of their noble parents. God's word often speaks of children who bring shame to their parents (Prov. 19:26). Some become entangled in drugs or alcohol, others in crime or immorality. Interestingly while the child in such cases is the one who has failed to live up to the standard of his progenitors, he may be so absorbed in self, or so calloused by his sin, that he feels no sense of shame. The shame and embarrassment falls upon his parents.

In God's family we also see unworthy children. By their faith in and baptism into Christ, they are children of God (Gal. 3:26-27). They are privileged to wear the name of the Savior (Acts 11:26), and to have a place at his table (Luke 22:29-30). They enjoy the honor of working in his cause, sharing his message and of being heirs of all of heaven's treasures (Rom. 8:16-17). But in spite of all these blessings and honors, some live unworthy lives. Some live worldly lives that bring dishonor on their heavenly Father. Others are disloyal to the will of the Father in spiritual matters. Only those who do his will can expect to enter the kingdom of heaven (Matt. 7:21). Some dishonor their Father by conduct that casts shame on his church; some by trying to dominate their brothers and sisters. Some rend the unity of the body in pursuit of their own agenda. Some have a hateful, spiteful attitude that is shameful to themselves and grievous to the Lord in whose kingdom they wish to serve.

Today, there are unworthy members of the Church of Christ here in America. Two hundred years ago, devout men, realizing the inadequacies of denominationalism, shook off those shackles and set their sights on restoring the faith and practice of the primitive church. From small and humble beginnings, God blest the cause they launched and it took hold of the public mind. Soon thousands stormed the gates of the kingdom of heaven, seeking entrance (Matt. 11:12). By the end of the first century upwards of a million souls had embraced the plea for restoration. But unworthy children grew weary of the simplicity of the ancient faith. They grated under New Testament authority. Consequently they began to agitate for change. They preferred to sing with instruments of music. They craved a national organization to lead the churches. They wished to place women in leadership roles. They wanted acceptance by their denominational neighbors. Disregarding the pleas and protests of their brethren, they forged ahead, rending the body. Their actions result in the emergence of the Disciples of Christ and later the Independent Christian Churches.

Today, a century later, we see scattered among our people another generation of unworthy children. They too are weary of the old paths. To be limited to things authorized by the New Testament is burdensome. They see us as only another denomination of human origin. They would accept the use of instrumental music. They yearn to have fellowship with their denominational neighbors. They would move women into roles of public leadership. They would change us into their image or destroy us. Their actions are shameful. They are unworthy children who have betrayed the cause of their ancestors in the faith. The cause they plead is not the restoration of New Testament Christianity, rather it is the destruction thereof. May God help them see their mistake and grant them time to repent.

41. SOME THINGS AN AGENT OF CHANGE CANNOT DO

Churches of Christ here in America are presently confronted with a sizeable number of preachers and educators who are determined to bring about major changes in the body of Christ. These are not anti-Christian unbelievers, nor are they members of other church bodies. They are men who claim membership among us and fill pulpits of our congregations and classrooms in our Christian Colleges. Among the things they are busily at work to change are the following:
* The way we worship God in our public assemblies.
* The role of women in the leadership of the church.

* The way we approach the Bible in our efforts to determine right and wrong.
* The way we do our work as a congregation of Christ's people.
* The way we perceive ourselves. They reject the idea that we are the church which Christ established. They see us as just another denominational body. They have a very poor opinion of the brotherhood of churches of Christ as evidenced by the scathing criticism they continually heap upon us.
* The manner and way in which we teach lost sinners that they must be saved.
* The way we deal with those who embrace and promote false doctrine.
* The name by which we identify our congregations.

Most of these agents of change are well-educated men. Many of them preach for large, well-known churches. Not a few of them hold teaching positions in our Christian Colleges. They have already gained a significant foothold among our people and have succeeded in influencing many of our younger members and a number of congregations. However successful these teachers may be in their quest to rework and reshape our people, there are some things they can never do.

*They cannot claim to be a part of the great Restoration Movement of the 19th century. They do not believe restoration is a valid way to approach Christianity.
* They cannot identify themselves with the great men of the past who preached God's Word among our people. Any time they invoke the names of David Lipscomb, Austin McGary, G. H. P. Showalter, N. B. Hardeman, G. C. Brewer, C. R. Nicol, Gus Nichols, R. L. Whiteside, Otis Gatewood or any of the great men of the last 200 years, they are speaking a lie. This is true because those men all loved the church as we have known her for the last two centuries. They taught people to be saved upon confession of their faith, repentance and baptism. They worshiped each Lord's Day with acappella singing, prayers,

contributions and the Lord's Supper. They all repudiated denominationalism. They all loved and honored the name Christian. They believed the Bible to be an inspired, authoritative book that determines all things spiritual for Christians.

* They can take no credit for the congregations they serve, or the schools in which they teach, for the folks who founded those churches and schools were committed heart and soul to the Church of Christ of their generation for which the promoters of change have only contempt.
* They cannot identify themselves with and take joy in the great host of missionaries who took the gospel of Christ to the nations of the world in the last century. The reason being, all of those who went out carried the same message, faith and practices held by churches of Christ in America to the lost of humanity.
* They cannot boldly preach their message with the conviction that it is right because it is biblical. Their motive is to sow doubt, not faith. They reject the approach that looks to the Bible for "book, chapter and verse" proof of what one believes and does in Christ.
* They cannot stand in the face of the competing claims of denominationalism and present a way that is right and cannot be wrong because they do not think that such exists. Nor are they sure denominationalism is wrong.
* They cannot with confidence say "I have fought a good fight . . . I have kept the faith" (II Tim. 4:7). The fact is, they have betrayed the faith that was passed down to them by those who went before them. Like Esau, they have given up their birthright for a mess of pottage (Heb. 12:16).

42. ARE THEY TRULY CHRIST'S DISCIPLES?

Jesus said to those Jews that had believed in him, "If ye abide in my word, then are ye truly my disciples" (John 8:31). This reminds us that there are two types of followers of Christ. There are some who are truly, and some who are not truly His disciples. The differential is whether or not they "abide in his word." Later John enlarged on this thought saying, "Whosoever goeth onward and abideth not in the teaching of Christ, hath not God: he that abideth in the teaching hath both the Father and the Son" (II John 9). With this in mind, consider the following.

* We have disciples among us who read Acts 22:16, which says, "be baptized and wash away thy sins" and then teach folks that we are saved by grace alone, before, thus without baptism. "My salvation is on grace alone, not by anything I've added to it." "The one step of salvation is faith . . . " "It (baptism) is not the fifth step (in the plan of salvation)." (Quotes from Rubel Shelly's recorded sermons, cited in **Change Agents and Churches of Christ** by William Woodson, p. 236).
* Some brethren read Paul's prohibition, "I permit not a woman to teach, nor to have dominion over a man, but to be in quietness" (I Tim. 2:12), then say, but such does not apply to us. They encourage women to seek leadership roles in the church. Bro. Paul Casner wants to see "men and women serving alongside one another in all aspects of church life" (Allen and Anderson, **The Transforming of a Tradition** p. 100).
* Some read Paul's charge to Timothy to "Hold the pattern of sound words which thou hast heard from me" (II Tim. 1:13), then deny that there is a divine pattern and ridicule those who strive to follow the pattern God has provided. "...the Bible does not provide a constitution or pattern for church organization" (Cukrowski, Hamilton & Thompson, **God's Holy Fire**, ACU Press, p. 48).
* Some read about the "law of the Spirit of life in Christ" (Rom. 8:2) and the "perfect law of liberty" (Jas. 1:25) and then insist that we must not view the New Covenant of Christ as God's law for us. They obviously think they know more and better than the apostolic writers.
* Some read that divisions among Christ's disciples and the practice of identifying oneself by the names of men are contrary to his will

(I Cor. 1:10-13; 3:1-6) yet they work diligently to fashion the church of Christ into just such a denomination founded by Barton Stone and Alexander Campbell. Also they teach our people one can be saved and serve God acceptably in such human organizations (Holloway & Foster, **Renewing God's People**, ACU Press, p. 138).

These scenarios are not illusions or theoretical cases. They describe the scores of "change agents" that are circulating among our churches and teaching in our schools. They call themselves Christian and members of the church of Christ, but given their attitude toward the Savior's Word, the question must be raised, "Are they truly His disciples?" What say ye?

43. THEY MUST BE DIFFERENT KINDS OF CHURCHES

Churches of Christ are faced with a revolution in their camp. A band of skilled, articulate men has launched a movement to reform (i.e., change) the faith, worship and practice of the brotherhood. If they are successful, we will no longer be a church modeled after the Biblical pattern; the church our fathers and mothers knew. The seriousness of the challenge is illustrated by the contrasting views of the church held by those who are promoting change and those who are determined to cling to the old paths of the Biblical standard.

Our view of the church is that it is stable and unchanging in its essence. We want to believe and worship just as the first disciples did and as faithful saints have since the beginning. The church was established by Christ (Matt. 16:18) and given a standard of faith and practice conceived in heaven, suitable for all men of all nations and forever binding on those who wish to please him (Matt. 28:20). **Their view**, in contrast, is of a church that theoretically can be different in every age, culture and community. Their churches are the products of their culture and are shaped by those who are significant leaders. They reject the idea of the Bible as our divine pattern and ridicule the idea as "patternism."

Our view is that the Church of Christ is the spiritual body of Jesus in this world (Eph. 1:22); purchased by his blood (Acts 20:28); established by Christ (Matt. 16:18). It is God's family of saved people (I Tim. 3:15), which will live with him in eternity (I Cor. 15:24; Rev. 21:2). **Their view** is that the church of Christ is a human organization founded by Alexander Campbell and Barton Stone in the early 1800s. At best, it is only a denomination, merely a part of the real church. They see it as seriously flawed and of no lasting value. To them, ones salvation certainly does not depend on being a part of it.

Our view is that the faith, worship and work of the church have been ordained and commissioned by Christ (I Cor. 11:23). The Scriptures provide us all things that pertain to life and godliness (II Pet. 1:3-4). They constitute a "pattern of sound words" to which we are to cling (II Tim. 1:13). We are explicitly taught to "observe all things whatsoever (Christ) commanded" (Matt. 28:20). In his Testament, Christ sets forth the doctrines, we are to believe, the kind of worship we are to offer and the mission his church is to pursue. Our duty is to acknowledge him as Lord (Rom. 10:9) and render submissive obedience to him in every way (Heb. 5:9). **They** see belief and worship as something derived from our history and culture and that human leaders have set the standards for the church. They specifically deny that there is a standard or pattern to which we must conform. They can adapt their message and worship to meet the felt needs and demands of society. They feel comfortable in allowing or doing things Scripture specifically forbids such as placing women in positions of public leadership in the church (I Cor. 14:33-34).

These examples demonstrate that although these two groups of people both call themselves churches of Christ, **they clearly are different in important and significant ways.** In fact they represent two different kinds of churches; one divine, the other human; one guided by Scripture, the other by the will of man. Just as counterfeit money looks remarkably like genuine money, so the churches of the change movement appear to the unsuspecting to be churches of Christ, but their similarity is only surface and their value is no more than that of a counterfeit bill. Christ built but one church (Matt. 16:18); He has "but one body" (I Cor. 12:20). Although counterfeits may exist and even flourish in our midst, they will not stand the inspection of the Great Judge of all (Matt. 7:21-23).

44. CHURCH OF CHRIST NUMBER III

In the 1920s A. T. DeGroot wrote an interesting little book entitled **Church of Christ Number Two**. DeGroot was a liberal scholar and spokesman for the progressive wing of the Disciples of Christ. His book was a sarcastic criticism of the conservative wing of his church which was in the process of breaking ranks with the liberal leadership. They eventually separated themselves and became known as the Independent Christian Churches. Unhappy that anyone would dare reject the progressive leadership of himself and his liberal comrades, DeGroot wrote his book to heap scorn upon them. Since all in the Disciples of Christ/Christian Church body had elected to repudiate the conservative, bible-based stand of our forefathers in the churches of Christ, he sought to embarrass them by suggesting they really were just as old fashioned, narrow and out of date as were they. To those unfamiliar with our past, the issues that separated us from those folks were: human organizations such as missionary societies to do the work of the church, the use of instrumental music in worship, allowing women in leadership positions of the church, fellowship with denomination bodies and theological liberalism. To call his Independent Christian Church brethren a "Church of Christ Number Two" was a pointed insult.

Today we truly do have a new religious body, emerging on the religious scene that wears the name "Church of Christ." These disciples and their preachers have ties to the that body of people known for more than a hundred years as churches of Christ. Most of their leaders grew up in congregations of that brotherhood, and attending schools operated by them. Somewhere along the way their faith was subverted and they turned away from the faith of their fathers. They are known today as "agents of change" who are devoting themselves to imposing significant changes in the faith, worship and practice of the church.

They hold their predecessors in the faith to be old-fashioned traditionalists who are hopelessly out of touch with the Postmodern world. Among the changes they have embraced are a willingness to accept instrumental music in worship, the creation of numerous "extra-church" organizations to do the work of the church, allowing women roles in the public leadership in the church, embracing a Pentecostal type of worship environment with an entertainment format and physical expressions such as hand clapping, etc. They believe that salvation is by grace and thus they no long believe that baptism is essential to salvation. Having concluded that they are a denomination, they are quite ready to embrace other denominational bodies in their fellowship. They have repudiated the idea of restoring the faith and practice of the New first century church and the New Testament as a standard of authority which must be conformed to by all who would be pleasing to God. Other points could be cited but these are sufficient to demonstrate that regardless what these folks call themselves, they are not members of the church of Christ that most of us know and love. They are a new variety or genre of church using the same name as the church they once were part of. It seems to me entirely appropriate that they should take a new name lest they be confused with us. They feel we are hopelessly mired in Biblical tradition. In the spirit of A. T. DeGroot, I would like to suggest that they henceforth be known as **Church of Christ Number Three**. If that does not please them, perhaps they could be part of the **Church of Christ Number Two** that DeGroot had in mind. Since nearly all of these are eager to embrace the Independent Christian Churches in their fellowship, they could share that cognomen with them.

45. SPIRITUAL LSD

Forty years ago a strange phenomenon arose among many young Americans. It was called "the Hippy movement." Searching for meaning, purpose and direction in life, they tried drugs, sensuality, poverty, freeloading, a gypsy life style and mystical cultish religions. Finding no satisfaction in those unproductive fields, many of them decided to try God. But having rejected the traditional way their parents worshiped God, they wanted alternative approaches. They tended to blend elements of mysticism, Buddhism, New-Age Hinduism and other failed systems with their worship to Jehovah through Christ. In their state of mind, they needed and wanted an emotion-based kind of Christianity filled with their own kind of music, and compatible with their hippy lifestyle. The result was religious aberrations such as the "Jesus Freaks" and Moses David's "Children of God" cult. Pentecostalism fit nicely into their mental and spiritual framework. Some of them preached "Let's Get High on Jesus." Others continued to need the help of psychedelic drugs, guitars and tambourines to get the desired high they craved.

Today, although the Hippy movement has largely faded, their spiritual legacy is still to be observed at work in the religious world, and sad to say in some circles within the Lord's Church. A growing number of young Christians cannot find spiritual satisfaction in merely worshiping God as Scripture directs. They need some outside stimuli to stir their passions to acceptable levels. Witness the innovative worship stimulants of the change agents. For some it is new "campfire type songs," for others it is to dim the lights. Others need entertainers to prime them. Still others can only reach the heights by lifting their hands and swaying with the music. Others crave a more "interactive" worship experience.

The demands of the worship market have brought forth a new breed of spiritual entrepreneurs who make a living by selling their latest worship enhancement potions. There is "The Road to Emmaus Program. And the ZOE worship program. Advertisements for the

ZOE program offer their product for fees ranging form $65 to $85 per person. Early registrants get bargain prices. Using concepts borrowed from the world of commerce, the specialists promise spiritual wonders to those who will to step up and buy their product. Shrewd businessmen, they get churches to provide the facilities, promote and advertise their product for them. Some of our Christian Schools are eager to feature such new products on the lectures and seminars.

Back in 1851, when some of our brethren first began to clamor for pianos, organs and choirs to enhance their worship, Alexander Campbell wrote the following insightful lines:

> "That all persons who have no spiritual meditations, consolations and sympathies of renewed hearts, should call for such aid is but natural. Pure water from the flinty rock has no attraction for the mere toper or wine bibber. A little alcohol, or genuine Cognac brandy, or good old Madeira is essential to the beverage to make it truly refreshing. So to those who have no real devotion or spirituality in them, and whose animal nature flags under the oppression of church service, I think that instrumental music would be not only a desideratum, but an essential prerequisite to fire up their souls to even animal devotion. But I presume to all spiritually-minded Christians, such aids would be as a cowbell in a concert." (**Millennial Harbinger**, 1851, p. 581-582)

These words aptly describe the jaded faith and spiritual appetites of those promoters of change who insist they must have soloists, choirs and vocal bands to entertain them, or musical instruments of varied sorts to stir them to acceptable levels of worship. They are eager to pay someone to show them how to get high on Jesus, or in today's climate "high on the Holy Spirit."

Simple worship derived from God's sacred Word cannot satisfy such satiated souls. They must have a stimulant to endure a service. Such reminds us of those citizens of Aldus Huxley's **Brave New**

World who could not deal with even the ordinary things of life without a boost of soma! In fact if one could create a "spiritual LSD" he likely would find a ready market among those who are clamoring for change.

46. CONFESSION IS GOOD FOR THE SOUL

An old Scottish proverb says, "Open confession is good for the soul." Not all confessions are intentional or for the purpose of acknowledging one's faults. Yet, the results can still be beneficial, especially for those who might be endangered by the deeds inadvertently confessed. The knowledge of the deed allows them to protect themselves from the adverse consequences.

In his book, "**The Churches of Christ**" published in 2001, Dr. Richard Hughes, formerly of Abilene Christian, now of Pepperdine University, states some facts that brethren need to know for their own well-being. Dr. Hughes is an eloquent spokesman for the "change movement" which is flourishing among us. While some readers might be hesitant to believe what I say, they cannot accuse Professor Hughes of exaggerated or prejudicial reporting.

He tells us, "In a real sense Carl Ketcherside and Leroy Garrett helped to launch the progressive (i.e., change) movement among Churches of Christ in the 1950s" (p. 139). This quote is significant because most liberals stoutly deny their dependence on Ketcherside and Garrett, even while they are repeating the doctrines and programs those arch-heretics developed and promulgated.

Hughes pinpoints the origins of the change movement. "In that decade (the 1960s) a veritable ideological chasm opened up between progressives and conservatives in this tradition (i.e., Churches of Christ). That chasm resulted in part from the influence of higher education among Churches of Christ" (i.e., Christian Universities; in particular, Abilene Christian and Pepperdine

University, jhw) (p. 139). Abilene Christian professors "subsequently encouraged many students to pursue doctoral work in religion at Harvard and comparable institutions" (p. 140). "Through this process a core of top-flight scholars in biblical and related studies emerged from the very bosom of Churches of Christ" (p. 140). "This development in higher education was critical for the development of a progressive (i.e., liberal) tradition in Churches of Christ that would challenge conventional orthodoxies in a variety of ways" (p. 140). "After all, Harvard-trained scholars were not likely to rest content with traditional in-house debates as they played out in papers like the **Gospel Advocate** and the **Firm Foundation**" (p. 140). These quotes are noteworthy because they identify the sources of the change movement that has emerged among us. Some of the men who pursued higher education in bastions of liberalism such as Harvard lost their faith in simple Bible Christianity. They did not however, abandon the fellowship of churches of Christ, they came back and sought teaching positions in our Christian schools and sowed their seeds of liberal thought in the minds of students who came under their influence. Such men felt themselves superior in knowledge and judgement to lesser types not privileged to study in the Ivy League seminaries. With disdain they set about to reconstitute our people according to their liberal templet.

Dr. Hughes shows us what the change agents hope to accomplish. "The most enduring response, however came in the form of a wide spread attempt (by change agents jhw) to renew and even reinvent this (Church of Christ) tradition" (p. 152). "...the renewal did bring significant change to many of the larger, urban congregations that stood in the mainstream of this tradition" (p. 152). These quotes simply verify what every observant person knows; those of the change movement are not content to be simple Bible Christians. They are laboring to "reinvent" the church of Christ as a modern denominational body whose faith, worship and practice will not be determined by a strict adherence to Christ's Word, but by the will of the people.

Hopefully, these confessional statements will help some who are presently uninformed or undecided, to see the perils that confront us and thus to stir them to make a committed stand for the Cause for which the Lord Jesus died.

47. SOME INCOMPREHENSIBLE THINGS

Solomon confessed to his sons that there were some things that he just could not understand (Prov. 30:18-20). I confess that I cannot understand the people described below.

I cannot understand the Arab Muslim immigrant who hates America. He went to great trouble to escape his homeland and immigrate to America. Yet he hates the land that welcomed him and in which he has made his adopted home and prospered. If he so dislikes the institutions, laws and values of America, why does he not go back to the land of his nativity? There he could be happy.

Nor can I understand the American citizen who is a liberal-minded socialist who dislikes and even hates virtually every aspect of our nation's Democratic institutions, culture, social values, economy and government. Why does he not immigrate to a socialist paradise like Cuba, North Korea or China? He could even go to some of the more liberal European states where he can be happy and a positive, constructive influence rather than an Ishmaelite here at home (Gen. 16:12)?

Neither can I understand those preachers of churches of Christ who hold the church in utter contempt. They draw their income from the church. They enjoy many privileges and benefits because of their position in her ranks, yet they manifest no love or appreciation for her. They see every aspect of her faith, worship and practice as terribly flawed. They spend their time and energy criticizing her past record and former leaders. They stir unrest and dissent in our congregations. The acknowledged nothing good and commendable save in their own narrow circle of comrades. They heap lavish praises on those who are enemies of the church. If we are truly such a flawed and failed body, why do they stay among us? Would it not be far more reasonable for them to make their exit and go to those denominational bodies which they find so worthy and where their hearts dwell?

We can't help but wonder if the unhappy Muslim stays because he would like the opportunity to do us harm. Nor can we help but wonder if that is the motive of our unhappy agents of change? Back during the Cold War era, we used to see bumper stickers that read **"America: Love Her or Leave Her!"** Such a recommendation I pass on to our change agents. It is the church of Christ. Love her or leave her!

48. POWERLESS PREACHING

People were amazed at Jesus' preaching "for he taught them as one having authority, and not as their scribes" (Matt. 7:28-29). Paul's preaching was with "power and love and discipline" (II Tim. 1:7). While his speech and "preaching were not in persuasive words of (human) wisdom," there was a "demonstration of the Spirit and of power" (I Cor. 2:3-4). So powerful was the preaching of the apostles that the foundations of Judaism were shaken (Acts 4:16-18). Gentiles protested that they had "turned the world upside down" (Acts 17:6).

What Was the Source of Their Power?

The power of their preaching did not rest in large numbers, social standing, worldly education, wealth or political clout. They were deficient in all of these. In the eyes of their contemporaries, "they were unlearned and ignorant men" (Acts 4:13). They were viewed as "a sect ... everywhere ... spoken against" (Acts 28:22). The fact is, they were weak in all the areas the worldly mind would see as essential to success. Yet God's power was "made perfect in weakness" (II Cor. 12:9). The source of their great power was in the gospel they preached. "It is the power of God unto salvation" (Rom. 1:16). Paul "determined not to know anything... (in his preaching) save Jesus Christ, and him crucified" (I Cor. 2:2). With the gospel, they had the power of truth to oppose error (John 8:32). They had the sharp two-edged sword of the Holy Spirit (Eph. 6:17). The all-powerful Jesus was with them as they preached his gospel (Matt. 28:18-20). Like a mighty tidal wave, they were invincible; nothing could stop them.

Powerful Preaching of Our Predecessors

Our forefathers in the movement to restore original Christianity, found this power and harnessed it in their preaching. Satan was defeated on every hand. Sinners surrendered to their Lord. False teachers gave way before the assault. Multitudes were saved, churches were planted, the cause grew and prospered. With their famous book, chapter and verse delivery, they were revered by their brethren, feared by their denominational peers. Their gospel message was irresistible to thousands who crowded into the kingdom of Christ.

A New Approach

In our day a generation has arisen that went to a different school. They have imbibed a different spirit. A new way has been found to preach to modern sinners. We hear them presenting a beautifully crafted message with no gospel. They quote little or no scripture, they make no mention of God's will for man. Christ's church, his plan of salvation and his will for his church are downplayed or omitted. They much prefer drama, story telling and relating of personal experiences. They falsely assume:

* That the old Jerusalem gospel will not attract modern man.
* That words from the Bible will not be heard, understood and accepted.

* That sinners would rather hear the speaker's ideas or quotes of some notable theologian or philosopher than God's Word.
* That they can be faithful preachers of God even though they omit most, sometimes all of God's own message.
* That converts they make will automatically learn and accept the Lord's true doctrine and church once they are recruited by their own non-Biblical approach.

Tragically, these "non-gospel" preachers are wrong on all counts. It is tragic for the lost souls who desperately need to hear the gospel (Mark. 16:15-16); tragic for the preachers who have failed to speak his words faithfully (Jer. 23:28); tragic for the church that supports such preaching and gets little or nothing in return. Is it too much to expect gospel preachers to preach the gospel? Is it unreasonable that the church of the New Testament present the message of the New Testament to a lost world?

Observant brethren know that liberal preachers of denominational churches have generally deleted God's word from their message over the last 40 years. Consequently, their faith is dead and their numbers are shrinking. Their missionary forces are drying up. Their seminaries are closing. Why should we follow them down the broad road that leads to destruction?

May all who would speak for Christ, "Preach the word" (II Tim. 4:2). May every eldership insist that those who occupy the pulpit of their congregation be "men of the Book" who are not ashamed of the gospel (Rom. 1:16), and who preach the "whole counsel of God" (Acts 20:27). When God's word is exalted, Christ is glorified, souls are saved, the church is edified and increased. To leave Scripture out of our message is to preach a powerless gospel! Satan is not threatened by such a message.

49. POLITICAL AND RELIGIOUS LIBERALS

Liberals resent being bound by the authority of a written code. In our country, liberals tell us our Constitution was never meant to be a permanent, unchanging code. To them it is fluid and should be reinterpreted by each generation as circumstances and conditions change. Of course they reserve this right of reinterpretation to themselves. Religious liberals are no different. To them the Bible is not a book containing the commandments of God. It is a "love letter" from Him to us. They have invented a "new hermeneutic" to allow themselves to avoid acknowledging his written commands.

Liberals have very little love for their country. They watch for every opportunity to criticize their homeland and to magnify every flaw. They have no respect for the heroes of the past. They prefer heroes of their own ilk. They interpret even noble deeds of patriots in the darkest light. On the other hand they have glowing praise for our enemies and can overlook any wrongs they many commit. In religion, liberals despise the church of which they are members. Every flaw is magnified. They are harsh in their criticism of the great preachers and teachers of the past. Contempt is exhibited toward the writings and accomplishments of the past. But they love denominational teachers. They can see only good in other religious bodies, no matter how far removed they are from the church Jesus built.

Liberals are usually elitists who are bred and fledged in the halls of academia which their progenitors usually control. Their elitism is manifested toward those who do not share their philosophy, especially those with lesser academic credentials. In religion, the situation is identical. From colleges and universities, dominated by liberal administrators and professors, graduates, thoroughly indoctrinated in liberalism, are sent forth to fill the pulpits of our churches. It is safe to say that in the absence of the liberal "Christian" universities, there would be little or no liberalism plaguing God's church.

Liberals rarely identify themselves until they are confident of their hold on power. We have seen judges appointed who were thought to be conservative in their reading of the Constitution. Later they were later discovered to be unabashed liberals. So also politicians often sail under false flags to win their votes of those who would never vote for a liberal. In religion the parallel is evident. A liberal preacher will conceal his views when applying for a lucrative pulpit position or a teaching post in a Christian school. Quietly and carefully he will begin sowing his seeds of doubt and rallying converts for the day when he can assert his influence openly.

Liberals rarely build institutions. They much prefer to move in and capture those built by the sacrificial work and finances of conservatives. A look at the universities of our nation will aptly demonstrate this fact. So in religion, liberals don't establish churches, build buildings or establish schools. Their method is to take over those built by conservative Christians and turn them to their own purposes.

These parallels could be extended but the analogy is obvious to those with eyes to see. Jesus warns us to "beware of false prophets, which come to you in sheep's clothing, but inwardly they are ravening wolves . . . " (Matt. 7:15). May those who lead God's church and the schools among us be wise and watchful and keep the gates secure against men whose approach to Christianity is based on human philosophy rather than the Word of God.

50. SOME OBSERVATIONS REGARDING CHRISTIANS WHO WORK IN THE BILLY GRAHAM CRUSADES

We have reached a new milestone in the history of the Lord's church here in America. Just this last year we have heard of three of our largest congregations and their preachers participating in the Billy Graham Crusades in their cities. There was a time, not many years ago, when involvement in these interdenominational programs would have left a preacher or church scorned by fellow-Christians as unsound and unfaithful. Today, in the wake of the "change movement," such is quite acceptable to the more liberal sort among us.

For Mr. Graham to have our people come and work in his campaigns is quite a victory since for 50 years they had spurned his invitations. For him it poses no problem to accept our preachers and churches into his team. In his view one church is as good as another; churches of Christ are just another denomination and most doctrine really doesn't matter so long as you believe in Christ as God's Son. No doubt he has always viewed us as narrow and misguided and now at least a few of our people have finally come around to his point of view.

For our preachers it is a different story. For if they really believe the Bible to be God's Word, they cannot believe that one is saved by faith alone. Such contradicts the plain teaching of God's Word (Jas. 2:24). They cannot believe that one church is as good as another for that would mean that the creations of men are equal to the body of Christ. They cannot believe that a sinner can be saved by a simple prayer, when Scripture plainly teaches that remission of sins and the gift of the Holy Spirit comes with baptism (Acts 2:38). Thus if our brethren participate in the counseling of respondents to Dr. Graham's lessons, they have to tell them to do something they know is foreign to God's will in hope of salvation and encourage them to choose any kind of church they wish. Such is a betrayal of Christ and the church for which he died (Acts 20:28). To do this one of the following things has to be:
* Either they believe what Dr. Graham teaches and thus they are only pretending to be loyal members of the church of Christ. Or,
* They don't really believe the doctrine of the Graham team but have to pretend to do so in order to be involved in his crusade.

In either case they are being dishonest. If they believe the doctrine and practice of Dr. Graham they should be honest and severe their ties with churches of Christ and seek membership in a denomination that holds such views. If they do not share his views, they should be ashamed of themselves and repent of their involvement in the crusades.

Many of the ancient Hebrews desired to be part of God's holy people and still be acceptable to their heathen neighbors. To win their approval they would participate in the religious activities of the worshipers of Baal. Attempting to mingle two disparate religions is called "syncretism." When confronted with such a problem, Elijah, the mighty man of God, challenged his people saying, "How long go ye limping between the two sides? If Jehovah be God, follow him; but if Baal, then follow him" (I Kings 18:21). To those brethren standing with one foot in the church of Christ and one in the denominational circles of Mr. Graham, Elijah's question is pertinent, "How long go we limping between the two sides?"

51. TWO KINDS OF HERETICS

From the beginning there have always been heretics who taught error and sought to lead God's people astray. (II Pet. 2:1). Those who pursued their wayward course to its conclusion were branded apostates and denied fellowship (Rom. 16:17-18). It should come as no surprise to us that there are heretics among us today . . . and that many of them are well on the road to complete apostasy. Only in heaven will such departures from the Lord cease to occur. Studying the history of our people is an enlightening experience. In doing so, we see a never-ending stream of unfaithful men who lost their faith in the ancient gospel and began teaching a new and different message. Two different types of heretics are also seen: those who are respectable and those who are not.

Respectable heretics will admit their loss of faith. They will acknowledge that they have embraced a new doctrine. They will openly declare that they are no longer in sympathy with the church of Christ. They will resign their posts as preachers or as teachers in Christian schools because they cannot in honesty continue in something they do not believe in. They will leave behind the church they no longer sympathize with and seek fellowship and positions among those who share their new beliefs; whether it is Catholic, Baptist, Pentecostal or Unitarian. While this degree of honesty will not forgive their abandonment of the way of Christ, nor will it give them any advantage in judgment, at least they will not have compounded their sin and guilt by dishonesty.

Unrespectable heretics, on the other hand, will hide and deny their loss of faith. They will cloak their false ideas in the language of the old acceptable doctrine. They will protest and feign great hurt and dismay when they are charged with departures. They will cling to a paying position rather than gracefully leave for a new field. They will try to lead a band of disciples away from the faith, practice and worship of the church they entered upon becoming Christians into something new and different. They will generally do so without being forthright and frank in so doing. To start a new congregation from scratch is too hard for such heretics. They will try to commandeer the meeting house of a church or a school built by those who did not share their new faith. In every departure, without exception, those leaving, always try to get control of the church's property. They don't want to have to raise the money, sacrifice and struggle to build their own meeting places. They want the prestige and respectability that go with the property that has long housed a congregation of God's people. By securing the building, they hope that other Christians will not exclude and shun them as the heretics they are. There is a sense of conquest and victory if they can storm and take the fortress of the owners they would overthrow.

Although I regret to hear of any brother departing from the faith, I confess I do have a degree of respect for the man who forthrightly tells me, "I no longer believe what I used to believe. I am resigning my position and going elsewhere." But I have nothing but contempt for the apostate who lingers among us to rob from Christ all the members, and resources he can before he is driven out. Let us watch to see into which category those who are determined to impose unscriptural changes on us will place themselves.

VII.
THE STRATEGY THE PROMOTERS OF CHANGE ARE USING

52. TO DESTROY A PEOPLE

America's long war with Communism was fought on two fronts. There was the military side and there was the ideological side. Russia and China tried, unsuccessfully, to undermine the democratic nations of the world with their false propaganda and manipulation of mindless people. They used subversive agents to persuade the ignorant and gullible that Communism was good and Democracy was evil. Theirs was a classic attempt to conquer a people without engaging them in open combat. Today churches of Christ are confronted with a band of people who wish to capture the minds and hearts of her members and transform them into a worthless human denomination. Some of their techniques and methods can be clearly identified.

They are working to destroy the history of the Churches of Christ by rewriting it. They cast doubt and aspersions on the heroes of the past and our accomplishments. Such historical revisionism seeks to separate a people from their past so they will more readily follow the new leaders in paths they would otherwise have rejected. In the last 15 years, there has been a steady stream of revisionist books purporting to be historical studies of the American Restoration Movement. These were written by change agents at work among us. Among them are **Discovering Our Roots** by Leonard Allen & Richard Hughes, **The Churches of Christ** by Richard Hughes, **Reclaiming a Heritage** by R. Hughes and **Renewing God's People** by Gary Holloway and Douglas Foster.

They wish to confuse and bewilder members of the church regarding the foundations of their faith. Questions are raised about every point of doctrine and every practice. Doubts are sown in young, immature hearts. The motives and goals of great leaders of the past are questioned. That which we have held to be good, because it was based on Scripture, they call mistaken and that which we believed to be wrong, because it was contrary to God's Word, they say is good (Is. 5:20). Sarcasm and ridicule are used to bolster weak arguments. They tell us that for 200 years we have not even known how to correctly read and understand the Bible. They offer us a new hermeneutics or way or understanding Scripture that allows all of the things we thought to be wrong to be made right.

They have gained control of the schools that we have depended upon to help educate and train our young people and young preachers. Christian schools and universities have ever been the targets for those who wish to subvert the religion of Christ. Already we have lost to these apostates some of our schools and others have been infiltrated. Instead of graduates going forth with strong, robust faith that will strengthen the congregations where they attend, many of them will go forth to promote the agenda of change they learned in school. Preacher students in such schools are indoctrinated in their new approach to Christianity (which is but old denominationalism). They will soon be filling pulpits of churches and seeking to lead them in the paths of change.

They wish to prepare the literature children and adults study in their Bible classes. There they can sow their doubts about the old ways, and replace them with their new ideas about faith and worship. When the children grow to maturity they will be mentally prepared to change the direction of the congregations they are part of.

They desire to revamp the worship of our congregations. Worship is our link not only to God, but to our forebearers in the faith. If younger people can be persuaded to embrace new ways of worship, it effectively separates them from their parents, grandparents and ancestors. Having successfully separated them, they can quickly be molded into something totally different and foreign to the church of their ancestors.

In case you may have missed it, these methods of destruction are precisely those of the change agents at work among us. Let every Christian beware; every elder and preacher alert to defend their flock from those who would wrest it from them. The kingdom of Christ is under attack this very day!

53. DESTROYING OUR HISTORY

When the barbaric Taliban ordered the demolition of Afghanistan's gigiantic statues of Buddha, the world was aghast and outraged. But many members of churches of Christ are standing by in virtual silence as a hostile band of liberal scholars labor to distort and destroy the history of our noble movement to restore New Testament Christianity.

Professors from some of our Christian Universities have issued a number of books that are carefully contrived distortions of the history of our people. Historical revisionism is common in both the secular and the religious world. The Japanese have revised their history books to lessen the guilt and shame of their brutal aggressions in World War II. Marxist academics are promoting a revisionist statement of our nation's history. They eliminate many things honorable and noble and replace them with sordid, ignoble insinuations and innuendoes. Every aspect of the past is interpreted in the darkest light. Every failure is magnified. Every noble deed and accomplishment is discounted or discredited. Special attempts are made to delete the influence of Christianity in the founding and shaping of the nation. It is clear that such revisionist historians hate America, her institutions and heroes.

We have revisionists among us, operating primarily in our Christian Universities.
* They tell the unknowing that Alexander Campbell and Barton

Stone were the founders of churches of Christ.
* They tell us that the goal of the early pioneers was simply a unity movement with denominational churches such as today's ecumenical movement.
* They say that churches of Christ actually began in 1906 as a breakaway splinter group from the Disciples of Christ/Christian Churches.
* They imply that our fathers were in the wrong a century ago for objecting to the use of instrumental music and missionary societies,
* They play down the great growth and victories of our brethren over the last century.
* They cannot see any progress in racial relations in the church, preferring to dwell on the failures of the past; failures typical of most churches of that era.
* They denigrate and dismiss great brotherhood heroes of the past, implying that they were unlearned and ignorant men who distorted the gospel and led us into the morass of legalism.
* They glorify liberal false teachers such as W. Carl Ketcherside and Leroy Garrett. They paint them as having credibility and influence among the mainstream churches which they never had.
* They use selected quotes and experiences from the lives and writings of early restoration preachers, ignoring the larger picture, and use them to rewrite the record of what actually happened.
* All of this is done under the guise of scholarship and a pious pretense of loving the church of Christ and just wanting to tell the story of our past.
* If they are left unchallenged, the church as she once existed, will eventually cease to be. In her place will be another Protestant denomination bearing the image of their revised story of the churches of Christ.

Our revisionist historians bear the same disdain for the church that the Marxist historians bear for our great nation. The message of both should be rejected and they should be ejected from their teaching posts. If the Marxist's professors so dislike America and love Cuba, let them go teach in Cuba's university. If our historians have such a low appreciation for the church and so a glowing view of the Christian Churches/ Disciples of Christ, let them seek employment there.

It is tragic that such revisionists harbor such dislike for the church of their fathers. It is more tragic that so many Christians are watching in shameful silence while the destruction transpires.

Examples of our historical revisionism can be seen in **Reclaiming a Heritage** and **The Churches of Christ** by Dr. Richard Hughes, **Renewing God's People** by Drs. Garry Holloway and Douglass Foster and **The Crux of the Matter** by Jeff Childers, Douglas Foster and Jack Reese. All of these professors are associated with either Abilene Christian or Pepperdine Universities.

54. BEWARE THE REVISIONISTS

In recent years we have witnessed the deceptive work of historical revisionists who have rewritten certain areas of history in order to inject their personal views into the words and deeds of past leaders. By this dishonest method, they seek to exonerate the guilty and condemn the honorable. They make good evil and evil good (Is. 5:20). Revisionists have succeeded in dishonoring and belittling the founders of our nation. They are disguising Japan's brutal aggressions in World War II. Now the aims, purposes and goals of our Restoration Movement are being revised by some of our own preachers and educators.

As I read and listen to our revisionist preachers offer their critiques of the Lord's church my reaction varies from disbelief to disgust. It is clear that many of them see no value or benefit, much less scriptural necessity, for restoring New Testament Christianity. Many of them see nothing sinful or wrong with the denominational variety of Christianity prevalent in our world. It is evident that many of them have little knowledge of the genesis of the Restoration Movement. Certainly they have not done much reading in original sources such as the biographies, sermons and gospel papers of the first 150 years of our history. Most of them share an obvious and pronounced dislike for the preachers and publications of our brotherhood prior to c.a. 1960. Few if any of them have ever done pioneer work, planting churches in difficult mission fields where they had to do battle with error and wrest souls away from malignant error. Virtually all of them live handsomely and comfortably off the labors of those older pioneers whom they despise.

Our revisionists can find serious flaws in the best of our past leaders that discredit them, while finding only admirable virtues in liberal heretics and denominational leaders. When they tell the story of our beginnings on this continent, they use carefully crafted, partial truths that are designed to convince the unknowing that our pioneers were attempting to do something different from what our brethren were trying to do in the 20th century. One such brother's eyes twinkled as he boldly proclaimed that our earliest pioneers were all actually denominational preachers, not bothering explaining that they all chose to leave their denominational connections behind them.

Let every Christian remember that in interpreting the past as in interpreting the Scriptures, only truth can make us free (John 8:24). If these men had a modicum of integrity, they would simply renounce the churches of Christ and their goal of Restoring New Testament Christianity, embrace the denominationalism they love and abandon their attempts to revise our history.

55. GAMES THAT LIBERALS PLAY

Among those who claim membership in churches of Christ are people who abhor conservatives; who do not share their views of Bible authority and the sacredness of the church, her doctrines and ordinances. Since these folks are certainly not legalists nor conservatives, there is only one label that adequately describes them: i.e., liberals. In forty-five years in the church I have observed that liberals love to play games. Some of their games are as follows:

* **Let's pretend** is a favorite game of liberal brethren. They pretend that they are faithful members of the church of Christ when in reality they hold the church in contempt and are determined to change her or destroy her. They pretend to love and honor the pioneers of our brotherhood, all the while poking fun at and ridiculing them as bumbling, uncouthed Bible bangers. They pretend that they are kind, loving, disciples of Jesus, superior in heart and actions to those "old meanspirited" conservatives they would discredit. They pretend that they love and honor the Bible, while questioning its authority and ignoring its precepts. They pretend they haven't really changed in their faith and practice when anyone with eyes to see knows how far they have departed.
* **Snatch and grab** is another of their favorite games. While you close your eyes, they will snatch away your congregation's meeting place, your Christian School, or your mission outpost. This game they are very good at.
* They also like to play "**exaggeration**." They love to exaggerate the problems of the church in order to discredit her. They exaggerate when they describe our past understanding and preaching regarding topics like the Holy Spirit, grace and our attitude toward outsiders.
* They love to play "**king of the mountain**." Those with terminal degrees from prestigious secular and denomination schools pretend to be the ruling authorities who tell the rest of us peons what to believe.
* They play "**imitation**." They love to see who can best imitate the Tele-evangelists or other successful Charismatic-denominational preachers.

Those who are knowledgeable in God's Word and the history of our people recognize the games these liberal brethren are playing. They are neither new nor harmless kid's games. They are machinations of full-grown men who are diligently working to capture the minds and hearts of the brotherhood of people known as churches of Christ. They would remold and reshape them into denominational bodies modeled after the mega Community Churches of our denominational neighbors. Should they prevail, the church we know and love will be swallowed up and destroyed. "Let no man beguile you" (II Thess. 2:3)!

56. LURKING IN THE SHADOWS

I once encountered an atheist who was an apostate Christian, who liked to prowled Christian websites, trying to confuse and overthrow the faith of weak Christians. She actually described herself as a "lurker." Jesus spoke of thieves who lurk in the darkness, waiting for an opportunity to enter the sheepfold and steal the sheep (John 10:8-10). Such does happen in literal sheep folds but he had in mind those evil persons who are looking for opportunities to steal his disciples from his church.

He describes these rustlers of souls as pretenders. They are deceptive as wolves in sheep's clothing (Matt. 7:15). They are thieves and robbers (John 10:8). They are like predatory beasts that attack and destroy his people.

Among those who lurk in the shadows, awaiting an opportunity to capture unwitting disciples are:
Radicals. Radicals come in many varieties but all have the same mind-set and spirit as the Pharisees. They are ultraconservative or legalists. Since the beginning of the church, Christians have had to deal with radical brethren who were determined to bind their personal views about how to practice the religion of Christ (Acts 15:1). Paul warned about brethren who would depart "from the faith . . . forbidding . . . " certain legitimate practices (I Tim. 4:1-3).

Radical groups of the past left the larger body of the church and went their separate ways. Still, we still have a radical element within our rank who wait for opportunity to assert themselves. They often creep into congregations unawares and capture the minds of disciples and if possible an entire congregation with its property.

Liberals also lurk in the shadows seeking for opportunities to draw away disciples after them. They are descended from the Sadducees of Jesus' day. They have little respect for the Word of Christ. They are men-pleasers. They, like their radical counter parts, will also try to grab control of a congregation. They will abscond with the property others paid for and use it for purposes contrary to their intent. Liberals have special talents for gaining control of Christian Schools and turning them into engines of destruction for the gospel and the church. Contrary to the radical, the liberal prefers to stay in our midst and continue his destructive work. He must be driven out.

Our contemporary **change agents** fall within this latter category. They infiltrate congregations, seeking to capture them and their facilities. They wish to change them into a distorted parody of the church which Christ built. Where they are successful, the congregation is stripped of its Biblical attributes and reshaped into a denominational body. They also seek to infiltrate and gain dominance in our schools. Thus far they have met only minimal resistence thus they have been most successful. Daily they grow bolder.

Whether a church is invaded and ravaged by a radical or a liberal, the end result is the same. Division occurs. Disciples are discouraged and scattered. Some lose their faith and go back to the world. Satan gains the victory. Wise disciples will heed Jesus' warning to beware of false prophets who lurk in the shadows. They are deceptive teachers, seemingly harmless as sheep, but behind their sweet facade they are dangerous as ravening wolves (Matt. 7:15).

57. CONGREGATIONAL AUTONOMY: WHAT IT DOES NOT MEAN

A fundamental principle of Christianity is that each congregation of God's people is independent, answering only to Christ. Paul and Barnabas appointed elders in every church (Acts 14:23). Elders are supervisors only of the flock over which the Holy Spirit has made them bishops (Acts 2:28). Christ has all authority in heaven and on earth (Matt. 28:18). No provisions are made for ecclesiastical bodies to govern all the congregations of a community or the world. Leaders of one congregation must respect the autonomy of sister churches and not try to impose their will upon them. Change agents who object to our efforts to expose their schemes to capture unsuspecting churches complain that our outreach violates the autonomy of sister congregations.

* Given the Biblical truths expressed above, we need to remind ourselves that local autonomy does not forbid congregations from cooperating with each other. Thus our brethren have always worked hand in hand to evangelize, care for the needy and in opposing public evils. Several congregations cooperated in sending relief to the needy saints in Judea (II Cor.8:1).
* Autonomy does not forbid us from communicating with each other. Churches routinely exchange their weekly bulletins and other items of information.
* No wrong is done in sending letters to keep each other informed of the progress of the work being done, announcing meetings and activities of common interest.
* Autonomy does not forbid the sharing of important information. For example if professional moochers are going from church to church, begging for assistance, it is proper to advise other congregations lest they be taken advantage of. If a missionary is coming for a visit, it is appropriate to inform other churches who may also wish to have him speak.
* It does not keep us from sharing information about dangers affecting the church. If I knew that a dangerous criminal was

attending a sister church and spoke no word of warning I would be guilty of negligence. If I saw smoke coming from the roof of a church building but failed to issue a warning because it was not my congregation's house I would fail in my duty. If a destructive doctrine is being spread, we owe it to our fellow Christians to speak a word of warning.

Autonomy means that each congregation is free to accept or reject the information we send to them. We can never try to force our views on others, even if we are right and they are wrong. We have no right to penalize a church that does not accept our word of warning. We must never try to subvert or overthrow the leadership of a sister congregation. Scripture forbids us from meddling in other men's matters (I Pet. 4:15). Let us cherish this principal Christ has ordained for his church and never abuse it.

58. EXTREMISTS AND ALARMISTS

No one appreciates an extremist or an alarmist. This is true in the church as in other settings. An alarmist is one who raises unfounded alarms. The word harkens back to when watchmen were posted on the walls of a city to look for danger. The watchman who raised the alarm when there was no danger at hand was called an alarmist. An alarmist may be one with poor judgment. Or he may be a scaremonger who enjoys frightening and disturbing his neighbors by his baseless warnings. An extremist is one who is extreme in his beliefs or conduct. Synonyms of extremist are, excessive, immoderate, exaggerated. He is a person who promotes extreme views.

While all dislike alarmists and extremists, the use and application of these labels are relative from man to man. If the alarmist is expressing warning about things I agree are dangerous, I do not see him as a nuisance or danger. If the extremist believes or practices the same things I do, I see him not as extreme. But if a man warns of something I approve of or see as harmless, it is easy to brand him an alarmist.

One is no alarmist when he sees smoke pouring from the roof of a house and urgently calls the people to evacuate. He is no alarmist who sees a swimmer in trouble in the water and excitedly calls for help. Nor is one an alarmist who sees great dangers enveloping the church and he issues warnings to those threatened by the danger. He is no extremist who tells the truth in a fair and balanced way (Eph. 4:15). The extremist exaggerates his case. He magnifies the danger beyond reality. He is excessive in the remedy he proposes. He is immoderate in the way he deals with the problem.

Paul warned elders of impending apostasy that would threaten their congregation (Acts 20:28-30). He wrote letters warning churches of false teachers who were circulating among the congregations trying to impose changes contrary to the faith and practice instituted by the apostles (Phil. 3:1-2; Col. 2:8). In private correspondence to a preacher he warned of certain men who had made shipwreck of the faith, calling them by name (I Tim. 1:19-20). He also warned of a general apostasy that was approaching (I Tim. 4:1-3). He urged Timothy to "put the brethren in mind of these" warnings (I Tim. 4:6). Peter, Jude and John all issued similar warnings. Yet no sane man would accuse them of being alarmists or extremists. Evidently some of his brethren complained about Paul's warnings because he asked, "So then, am I become your enemy, by telling you the truth?" (Gal. 4:16).

As we raise the alarm and issue warnings concerning the liberal change movement we do not call men to the opposite extreme of ultra conservativism, rather we urge all brethren to stand firmly in the middle road of truth, avoiding the extremes of both the right and left. The alarms we raise are not for sport, nor based on hysterical imagination. The danger is both real and deadly. Those who know our history recognize today's change movement as the grandchild of the digressive (Christian Church) movement that swept through our brotherhood a century ago doing devastating damage. Only some 15 percent of our brethren and congregations survived that ordeal. That is why we write to warn our brothers and sisters of the danger we see.

Those who wish to see the change movement succeed, attempt to discredit those who warn of the danger by calling them alarmists and extremists. So do a few misguided brethren who long for peace at any price and those who do not want their lethargy disturbed. If present trends continue unchecked, a few more years will reveal how wrong they were in so doing. But by then it will be too late to repair the damage done.

59. ISN'T IT STRANGE?

The primary criticism against churches of Christ by change agents is that we have had too many divisions among our people. According to them such makes us unworthy and therefore they are determined to change us into a better kind of church. That there have been divisions we do not deny. That divisions in the body of Christ are detrimental and destructive to the Cause, we freely grant. That those who provoke divisions sin, we totally agree (Rom. 16:17).

We would remind our readers that when two people part company, it is not necessarily the case that all involved are equally guilty. Party A could be totally at fault while party B is totally innocent. Party B could be the one to blame while A is innocent. Both could be at fault. When factious people begin to agitate the body of Christ, trying to impose unscriptural laws on the brethren, we are not obligated to allow them to force their humanly devised rules on the church (Gal. 5:1). When a party chooses to separate from the larger body of Christians, we can only plead for them not to do so. When they leave, the fault is theirs, not ours. As John put it, "They went out from us, but they were not of us: for if they had been of us, they would have continued with us . . . " (I John 2:19).

Just what do the agents of change offer us for our improvement? They want us to acknowledge that we are just another denomination and that we should embrace in fellowship other religious bodies that say they love Jesus. Since we have experienced a half dozen or so schisms in the past, their prescription is that we should embrace the denominational world with its hundreds of schisms. That's like saying that a man with six fractures would be better off with twelve hundred. But then those who embrace postmodernism do not demand logical thinking! Change agents are enamored with the Christian Churches and other religious bodies and are eager to embrace them in fellowship. While scorning us for our schisms, they seem totally oblivious to the divisions those bodies have experienced.

While they blame us for the divisions we have experienced in the past, they are proposing and agitating for changes that will certainly bring about yet another division. In fact, several congregations have already experience turmoil and division because of the promotions of the change agents. They are like the quack doctor who was called to treat a wounded man who had been shot in the right arm. He proceeded to help the poor fellow by shooting him in the left arm so at least he would be balanced in his suffering. After listening to the advice of his three friends, Job called them, "worthless physicians" (Job. 13:4 NKJV). The prescription of the change agents not only does us no good, it is downright harmful and destructive to the Lord's church. Their treatment we surely don't need. Because their proposals are contrary to God's standard and divisive, they themselves should be rejected (Tit. 3:10).

60. A FELT NEEDS MINISTRY

Many of our contemporary ministers, fresh out of "ministry" programs in Graduate Schools, are looking for ways to meet the "felt needs of the people of their community and congregation." This is one of the aspects of the change movement. Bible-based preaching is downplayed and doctrine is considered unfruitful, but needs-based programs are the rage of the day.

Our local denominational neighbors are miles ahead of the "felt-needs programs" of our brethren. For example the Unity Church of Sun City, AZ will offer an overnight trip to Avi Resort and & Casino in Laughlin, NV. The $25 charge covers your bingo fee. Some folks have a felt need to gamble.

The Radiant Church of Surprise provided a Sunday evening festival and concert for the youth of their congregation. It was "Christian Rock" at its best and no doubt met the felt needs of the kids who have been nurtured on Rock music. The only problem was neighbors for blocks around called to complain about the disturbing noise ricocheting through the night and into their homes. Natalie Hearn, **Director of Marketing for the Radiant Church** wrote a letter of apology to the community and submitted it to our local paper. This is a new area of ministry that most of us have overlooked.

The local Disciples of Christ church recently featured "Desert City 4," a Dixieland jazz band, for a Sunday evening program. It met the needs of those who crave Dixieland Jazz.

Besides these classic examples each week we read of services featuring interpretative dancing, travel logs, classical performances, and a large assortment of other entertainment services.

I mention these bizarre examples because they illustrate where the change trail leads. A hundred and twenty-five years ago, the Disciples of Christ took the exit off the straitened and narrow way and went down the broad road they called progressivism. First it was a Missionary Society, then a piano, then fellowship with denominational churches, women preachers, theological liberalism and still they continue to press onward . . . further and further away from Christ and his Word. Denominational bodies such as the Unity and Radiant churches do not honor and respect the written Word of Christ as the final and absolute standard of authority in his religion. They illustrate the extremes to which that failure will lead. It is reasonable to predict that in a few years, at the current rate of drift, some groups formerly associated with churches of Christ will be in the same league with them. A wise traveller will avoid exits that lead him away from the map his Master and forerunner prepared for him. Felt needs won't carry much weight when we stand before the Master and are judged by the words that he spoke (John 12:48).

61. THOSE INFAMOUS 28 DIVISIONS IN THE CHURCH

A few years ago, a singing group traveled the country, making a good living singing **Twenty-six Miles Across the Sea.** Today, change agents travel far and wide singing about 28 divisions among churches of Christ. For them that mantra proves we are an unworthy group and that they with their ecumenical plan for unity are our saviors. A member of their team recently sent me the infamous list. It really shows how desperate change agents are to paint a false picture of their brethren in order to justify themselves in causing yet another division in the body. As we look at their list, note with me the distortions of their accusation

1. The **Firm Foundation faction** (1884). There was disagreement and discussion about whether those immersed without understanding the full purpose of baptism should be rebaptized. There was never an open break in fellowship. Though still discussed, the issue does not constitute a separate brotherhood.
2. **Churches of Christ separation from Digressives** (Sand Creek. IL, 1889). This was a declaration of one congregation declaring they would no longer fellowship digressives who were introducing instrumental music and missionary societies into churches. Had not that congregation and hundreds of others taken a stand against the apostasy of that day there would be no churches of Christ today. All would be in the camp of the

Christian Churches. This would be pleasing to our change agents. The fact is those wishing to have musical instruments and societies went out from us (I John 2:19). We continue to occupy the same ground as did the early leaders of the Restoration movement and the first Christians.

3. **Black Churches of Christ**. Outside of a few Black separatists, no such schism exists. Christians and congregations, be they Black or White, are brethren and fellowship each other.
4. **Those opposed to baptistries** (ca. 1900). While a few folks a century ago questioned the use of baptistries, I challenge the promoters of the list to find us even one congregation holding such a view today.
5. Those who insisted on an **order of worship** (1888). True, a tiny handful of brethren argued that Acts 2:42 provided an order of worship. They have long since died out. No such schism exists today.
6. **Sommerism**. Daniel Sommer was a strong minded, legalistic preacher who had a following that spread into several states. He flourished from 1890-1940. W. Carl Ketcherside led this group after Bro. Sommer's passing but he eventually swung to the opposite extreme of liberalism leaving chaos and confusion among his followers. The survivors, who describe themselves as mutual edification churches, still carry on but are small and few in number. Many of them enjoy fellowship with mainstream congregations.
7. **Anti-Sunday School, anti literature and anti-women teachers** were not three separate schisms but one. Such churches still exist but in many places now have fellowship with the larger brotherhood.
8. **One cup churches**. Some of the anti-Bible class churches also insisted on using only one cup in communion. They divided among themselves over such issues as "fermented or unfermented wine" and "whether the loaf should be broken by the one presiding or by the partakers." Of this group he mentions some who advocated "no plate for communion bread; some who debated whether "to have or not to have a handle on the

communion cup" and some that insisted that "communion must be taken around the table." That a legalistic splinter group should continue to divide among themselves is not the responsibility of the mainstream churches, nor should we bear the blame for their foolishness.

9. **Premillennialism.** In the 1920s a few preachers, led by Robert H. Boll, began to promote the false doctrine of premillennialism and found a following in a handful of churches. The brotherhood rejected their message and they were gradually excluded from fellowship. A few such churches exist today. Most have faded away.
10. In the 1950's a group arose that **opposed cooperation of churches in evangelism, benevolent homes operated by the church and eating in meetinghouses**. These are the only significant schism that has continued to flourish. Today there is some fellowship between members of the two groups and that will likely increase in coming years. Within this group was a schism led by Charles Holt and a more liberal minded minority.
11. In the late 1950s and 60s, W. Carl Ketcherside and Leroy Garrett, formerly of the Sommerite camp, swung to the opposite extreme of liberalism. They called for **unity in diversity** and embraced the Christian Churches and other denominational bodies in their fellowship. They worked unceasingly to influence and seduce young preachers of the mainstream churches. The message of the change movement bears the stamp of these two false teachers.
12. Differing views on **divorce and remarriage** have been warmly discussed by preachers and writers from 1960 to the present. While differences were pronounced and convictions were deeply held, no separate body of people emerged over this issue.
13. Tongue-speaking and supernatural gifts of the Holy Spirit were claimed by a tiny handful in the 1960s. Probably not more than a dozen preachers dabbled in this Pentecostal practice. All of them either left the church ceased to be used by our churches. No schism occurred.
14. Ira Rice's **Contending for the Faith** group. Bro. Rice led an

ongoing war against anything and anyone he perceived as liberal. His harsh and indiscriminate approach alienated him from most mainstream churches. Even many who opposed liberalism as much as he, refused to use or approve of his tactics. These brethren do not constitute a separate body of people.
15. **The International Churches of Christ**. This group, otherwise known as the Crossroads or Boston Movement, consisted of a group of young zealots who embraced a cultish, controlling kind of program. They flourished for some 20 years but now appear to be disintegrating.

To this list we must add **The Change Movement**. This is the merging and flowering of several past groups under a new banner. In its ranks one finds Ketcherside's Unity in Diversity disciples; those who yearn for a Pentecostal experience; those who have lost their faith in the inspiration and authority of the Word of God; those who desire an ecumenical fellowship with denominational bodies, especially with the Disciples of Christ and Christian Churches; those who have embraced the agenda of feminism and those who have been caught up in the philosophy of Postmodernism. The issues of this movement are virtual identical to those that led to the separation of churches of Christ and Christian Churches a century ago.

The authors of the infamous list of schisms badly want to paint the Lord's Church as a flawed and failed movement that must be changed by their more enlighten teachers. The exaggerations of such a list are telling. While there have been issues and trends, actual brotherhood schisms amount to some eight rather than 28. While eight schisms are too many and those responsible for them will have to answer to God for their actions, it is unfair and unreasonable to blame the church for the failure of some of her disgruntled members. To do so is like blaming godly parents who have raised six faithful children, for the failure of one child who has chosen to abandon the faith.

Let us all give diligence to maintain the unity of the Spirit in the bonds of peace (Eph. 4:3). We must not allow the enemies of the church to discourage or dishearten us by the false charges and accusations they make. May every faithful Christian reject the proposals of the promoters of change.

62. INCREMENTALISM: ONE OF SATAN'S DEVICES

Bill and Hillary Clinton accomplished much of their political agenda by a method described as incrementalism. That which was unacceptable and could not be passed in one large package was accomplished in several small incremental steps. This method of reaching unpopular goals has been effectively used by the feminists and the homosexual rights movement. Observing the success of this approach in the volatile world of politics, the change agents at work among us have adopted this incremental approach to reach their goal of imposing major changes on the church.

In his book **Women in the Church**, Carroll Osburn quotes Mary Tolbert who writes, "Feminist hermeneutics stands over against patriarchal hermeneutics (its goal achieved, CO) by small unnoticed acts of subversion. Numerous such incremental changes, like erosion, will eventually bring down the fortress" (p. 32). Those conversant with what is occurring in our churches and schools will immediately recognize some of those small acts of subversion that are transpiring today: a woman chaplain at one of our Christian Universities; a woman associate preacher here; a female co-teacher of an adult class there; schools offering women courses in ministry and featuring women preachers on their lectureship; books advocating expanded roles for women in church leadership. At the end of the day one is not surprise to read that a church here and another there has a woman preacher in their pulpit.

Similarly, change agents are attacking the foundations of the church by a series of incremental changes that "like erosion will bring down the fortress." Many of the proposed changes are small and at first seem of little consequence. But added together and with time, a congregation one day awakens to find that they are no longer a church of Christ. Few change agents are so confident or stupid as to try to grab control of a church in one bold move. It is a step by step process which they patiently pursue. They might ridicule the efforts of past brethren, or seek to shame their hearers for their old-fashioned faith and views. They propose more contemporary services, perhaps a praise team to improve the worship. Guest speakers are brought in to promote the proposed agenda. Young people are gently led to use instruments in their devotionals. Younger ladies who have absorbed feminist views are encouraged to reach for leadership roles in the church. Collegiates and young adults are used as a leverage tool for accepting changes. If we want them to stay or to bring their friends, some changes must be made. Fun is poked at the old faith and practices long held by the church. The great success of certain denominational churches is held up as a worthy example. Young people are taken to programs that offer new and unconventional activities for worship. New elders and deacons are proposed that will be sympathetic to the change agenda. Step by step the process advances until the foundations are totally undermined and finally the resistance crumbles. The few holdouts are encouraged to get with the program or leave. The results: another church has been subverted and changed into a denominational body.

Tragically many elders are totally oblivious to the incremental changes their preachers, youth ministers or campus ministers are initiating in their churches. The majority of their members sit in silence while a small handful who are committed to change, step by step, work their project. Brethren, we are under attack in every quarter. If we continue with the current level of indifference and unconcern, we will surely be overwhelmed. Remember the losses we suffered a century ago. That generation of change agents swept away eighty-five percent of our brethren and congregations; most of our mission work, all of our schools. Shall we suffer the same fate all over again? Remember their goal; "one step at a time until the fortress falls."

63. "LET ME FIX YOUR PROBLEMS"

Scam artists abound in our land. Many are their victims. We read of termite extermination companies whose inspectors release vials of termites under houses and then for a handsome price, offer their services to rid them. We hear of auto repair shops whose repairmen damage customers' cars and then offer to repair them for a hefty charge. Today we have false teachers among us who are like those scam artists. They introduce erroneous teaching and disruptive practices into congregations and then volunteer their advice and service to reconcile the contending parties and restore peace. Frequently the "conflict resolvers" are based in those universities from when the change agents have emerged. The price they extort is compromise; tolerance of the unscriptural views and practices. A frequent scam is the proposal that the church should have two services, one for the old traditionalists and one for those who want change. That makes a good temporary arrangement until they are in position to take control of the leadership and property of the victim church. They write books like the **Crux of the Matter and The Second Reincarnation** to rationalize and justify the problems they have created.

The Better Remedy

God did not leave us helpfulness in the face of our enemies.
* First we are to beware of false teachers who operate as wolves in sheep's clothing (Matt. 7:15).
* We are not to receive into our houses or the pulpits of our churches those who abide not in the doctrine of Christ (II John 9-10).
* We are to reject the factious people who trouble the body of Christ (Tit. 3:10).
* We are to mark (identify) those who cause divisions and occasions

of stumbling contrary to the teachings which we have received and turn away from them (Rom. 16:17-18).

We need to be reminded that there have always been folks, nominally within the church, whose faith and convictions are antagonistic to the principles given us by Christ. Paul pictures them as folks who made shipwreck concerning the faith (I Tim. 1:19). Peter's imagery is that of a dog returning to his vomit or a pig that had been washed, wallowing in the mire (II Pet. 2:20-22). Jude's illustration is that of a "wandering star" trekking endlessly through the blackness of space . . . hopelessly lost. He also paints them as jagged, dangerous rocks lurking just beneath the surface of an otherwise safe harbor (Jude 12-13). Jesus describes them to thieves that seek to secretly enter another's sheepfold and steal his sheep (John 10:8-13).

Should I learn that a local business man deceives and defrauds his customers, I wisely take heed to that information and refuse to patronize him. I tell others of the risk he poses. If we learn that certain preachers and teachers are troubling our churches, teaching new and different doctrines that are contrary to God's word and harmful to the church, wisdom suggests that we should reject them, refuse them a place in our midst and warn others about them. We don't need their "proposed changes" for the faith and practice of the church and we certainly don't need the remedies they offer when our churches have been troubled by their ideas.

64. STRANGE LOGIC OF CHANGE AGENTS

The champions of the change movement lodge many criticisms against their brethren of the churches of Christ. The most notable is that we are a divided people. They delight in numbering and pointing out the varius factions, (be they large or small), that have arisen and then blaming all for the divisiveness of the mainstream church. We are blamed for every kook and crank who draws any disciples and starts his own congregation. We are blamed for refusing to allow assertive folks to bind on us rules of their own making. We are faulted for refusing to abandon the prescribed principles of New Testament Christianity found in the Testament of Christ. To the promoters of change, such is proof that we are not the church we claim to be.

At the same time, change agents are aggressively pursuing a policy that will inevitably cause yet another division among our people. That will occur because they are determined to introduce unscriptural changes into the faith worship and practice of our churches. These items of change are not old truths from the Bible which have been overlooked or forgotten. They are not new Biblical ideas discovered by brilliant minds. They are old items borrowed from the various schools of denominationalism. Notice the following:

* In the realm of salvation, they have introduced salvation by grace through faith, before and even without baptism. This they borrowed from Luther, Calvin and their heirs. They also promote grace and faith as the "all in all" of Christian commitment. Their bashing of the necessity of obedience (works of faith) (Jas. 2:24) is a page out of the latest book of Baptist theology.
* In the realm of Scripture some of them openly question the inerrancy of the Bible. This implies a low view of inspiration of the Scripture writers. This comes straight from the halls of liberal theological seminaries. They question the authority of God's Word, and deny that it is His law for the church. They ridicule the idea that we should feel duty bound to look to the New Testament as a pattern for our faith and practice. This has been the standard approach of Protestantism for hundreds of years.
* In the realm of worship, they would supplant our simple, Bible-based worship for the emotionalism of the Charismatics. In the area of our music they would open the gate to those who want

instruments with their worship, just as the Disciples of Christ and Christian Churches did in the past.

* In the realm of preaching, they would replace gospel proclamation that teaches the doctrine of Christ and tells auditors where they can see it in their own Bibles. They prefer storytelling, entertainment and emotional appeals, with little or no appeal to Scripture. Instead of "teaching them to observe all things whatsoever (Christ) commanded" (Matt. 28:20), they offer lessons that meet the "felt needs" of their hearers. Not accepting the New Covenant of Christ as binding law, they have little inclination to emphasize its doctrinal and legislative content.

Ignoring the heaven-ordained role of male spiritual leadership in the church, they would place women in those roles, with no regard for scriptural prohibition (I Cor. 14:33-34; I Tim. 2:8-12). Liberal Protestant bodies and Pentecostals have done this for generations.

The items cited above are the same package of errors that drove a wedge of division between our brethren a century ago. Now the process is in motion yet again. When the change agents gain the ascendency in a congregation, they don't hesitate to assert their dominance and tell those who cannot in good conscience accept their innovations to leave and go else where! What is that but another case of division in the family of God? Thus those who sow the discord and divide the brethren, blame them for resisting their assault. It reminds us of the robber who blames his victims for resisting his criminal act. Is it not strange that for us to tell them to be gone is blameworthy, while for them to do the same is necessary for building up the church.

VIII.
THE FUNDAMENTALS THEY ARE ATTACKING

65. CHANGES DO MAKE A DIFFERENCE

In a suburb of Nashville, there once was a flourishing congregation of the Lord's people. They had a lovely meeting house and prospered for a season. Because of internal conflicts and poor leadership, the congregation disintegrated and ceased to exist. The building still stands but changes have taken place. The sign identifying it as a church of Christ was taken down. The pews, pulpit and communion table were carted away. The former doors were removed and large garage doors installed. At last report, an auto repair shop occupied it.

No longer do saints assemble there for worship; the gospel is not proclaimed therein. The sacred memorial meal is not observed, nor do sinners have their sins washed away in its baptistry. No children fill its classroom for Bible study. Satan won the victory! The changes have been overwhelming and permanent. It is no longer the home of a church of Christ. It houses a car repair shop.

Across the nation scores of churches of Christ are engaged in a similar process of change. Led by skilled, intelligent promoters of change, they have embarked on a project that will impose significant alterations in every aspect of their being. Consider what their mentors propose:
* Many have already changed their name. They prefer to be known as a "Community Church" or some other cognomen than church of Christ.
* They have rejected the Bible as the divine pattern for the church (II Tim. 1:13), preferring consensus and the example of various successful denominational bodies for their pattern.

* They are changing their doctrine. They have repudiated much of what their fathers taught about grace, baptism, worship, church government, the role of women, the nature of the church.
* They are changing their worship. The plain, simple worship of the apostolic church is not pleasing to them. To be bound and limited by Scripture is too restrictive. They view our acappella singing, our simple memorial feast, our Biblical preaching to be old-fashioned, boring and ineffective. They long for excitement and the freshness of change. They wish to be like their religious neighbors who acknowledge no such limitations (I Sam. 8:5).
* They have changed their message of salvation. Salvation by grace (Eph. 2:8-9) has been replaced by salvation by "grace alone." Baptism to wash away sins (Acts 22:16) has been replaced by baptism to declare one's previous salvation by grace. The one church, which is God's family of saved souls (Acts 2:47; Col. 1:13), has been replaced with a choice of denominational churches, none of which are really important.
* They have replaced the Biblical teaching and practice of exclusive male leadership for the church (I Tim. 2:8-12; 3:1) with a new model, fashioned after the Feminist cult, that allows women to participate in "all aspects of church life," i.e., as preachers teachers, deacons, etc.
* Preaching the gospel has been replaced by storytelling, dramatic skits and other new means of sharing.

More examples could be given, but these suffice to make the point. Congregations that have embraced the above-mentioned changes may once have been faithful churches of Christ. But given these major changes in every essential aspect of their nature and being, are we not correct in concluding that somewhere along the way they ceased to be what they once were? Yes, they may still be a church, but they are no longer the church one reads of in Scripture, or the church they were 25 years ago! They may talk of their spiritual roots in the Restoration Movement, but they have abandoned those roots. Just as that building housing the auto shop in Nashville is no longer the home of a church of Christ, such changed congregations are no longer the church they once were! Actually it would be a blessing, if all of those who are determined to take this course would take a new name and dissociate themselves from us, lest those seeking salvation and the church of the Bible be misled.

66. THINGS MOST COMMONLY BELIEVED AND NOW DISBELIEVED AMONG US

Luke tells the readers of his gospel that there were things "most surely believed among us." He then proceeds to restate those great, foundational truths (Lk. 1:1). Allow me to remind you of things most surely believed among members of churches of Christ; things believed because they are derived from the clear message of the New Testament. These fundamental truths have been held by Christians here in America since the beginning of the movement to restore the faith and practice of the early church that began at the opening of the 19th century. In the last 15 or so years, a band of dissident preachers and teachers have arisen among us who no longer hold these truths and are diligently working to undermine them in the hearts of our people. We all believed:

* That the Bible is verbally inspired of God; that it is from his all-wise and infallible mind (II Tim. 3:16-17).
* Hence the autographs of the various books of the Bible were without error or flaw as they were issued from the inspired writers (John 10:35; Ps. 19:7).
* That the New Testament of Christ claims to be and is in fact a divinely given pattern by which we must model all aspects of our congregational life (II Tim. 1:13; Heb. 8:5).
* That to be acceptable to God, we must accept the Scripture as the sole, absolute and binding authority for our faith and practice (John 12:48; Rev. 20:12).
* That the essential message of the Bible can be read and understood by the common man without the intervention of professional scholars (Eph. 3:4).

* That salvation by grace is conditioned on obedient faith (Eph. 2:8-9; Heb. 5:9).
* That salvation requires both faith and obedience on the part of man (Gal. 5:6; Jas. 2:22-26).
* That baptism by immersion, for remission of sins is essential to salvation (Mk. 16:16; Acts 2:38; Rom. 6:3-4).
* That Christ established, purchased and saved only one church (Matt. 16:18; Acts 20:28; Eph. 5:23; Eph. 4:4).
* Hence denominationalism is sinful and unacceptable (I Cor. 1:10-13; 3:1-4).
* That Christ expects his people to be united and that unity is to be found only in Christ and upon his word (John 17:17-21; II John 9).
* That Christ's church is his kingdom here on the earth (Matt. 16:18-19; Col. 1:13; Heb. 12:28).
* That churches of Christ are in fact his true church or else they have no worth or value and no right to exist.
* That early Christians sang praises to God without instrumental accompaniment. They did so because they had authority to sing and make melody in their hearts but none to use instruments (Eph. 5:19).
* That the early church partook of the Lord's Supper on the first day of every week, as a memorial to the death and suffering of the Savior (Acts 20:7; I Cor. 11:23-26).
* That they gave their gifts to God as an act of worship authorized by the Holy Spirit (I Cor. 16:1-2; II Cor. 8:5).
* That God placed the leadership of the church and all public teaching of mixed audiences in the hands of faithful men and that women are not allowed to teach nor have authority over men in the church (I Tim. 2:12; I Tim. 3:1-2; I Cor. 14:33-34).
* That miraculous gifts of the Holy Spirit were given in the first century to certify the apostles and prophets as true representatives of Christ and to confirm their message as from God (II Cor. 12:12; Mk. 16:20). That those miracles ceased with the completion of the New Testament of Christ (I Cor. 13:8-10).
* That our preaching should indeed be *gospel preaching;* that all

who stand up to preach should speak as the oracles of God (I Pet. 4:11).

It is a shameful fact that every man promoting the change movement among us has rejected part or all of these things most surely believed by our American brethren for over 200 years. Paul predicted that some would fall away from the faith (I Tim. 4:1). Today it is our misfortune to be witnesses to such apostasy. May God have mercy on his people and save his church from those who would corrupt and destroy her. If those who no longer believe are unwilling to repent, may they follow their hearts to some denominational body that shares their unbelief.

67. THE FUNDAMENTAL ISSUE

Agents of change are boldly calling for significant changes in the beliefs, worship and practice of churches of Christ. These changes, if implemented, will alter the fundamental nature of the church as a body of believers. Those who accept the proposed changes will no longer be congregations ordered after the New Testament of Christ. Rather, they will be denominational bodies like those our fathers left in generations past.

Among the beliefs and practices being challenged are:
* The nature of grace and saving faith. Is salvation experienced before baptism?
* The boundaries of Christian fellowship. Should we embrace in fellowship all who believe in Jesus regardless of their faith and practice?
* The nature of worship. Shall it be of a charismatic, emotion-based type or that which we have traditionally held?
* The nature and purpose of the Lord's Supper. Is it an act of worship, a sacred memorial, or is it a dinner meal?
* The nature of Christian praise. Can we add instrumental music and use special singing programs in worship, such as choirs, solos,

quartets, etc.?
* The role of women in the leadership, teaching ministry and worship of the church. Should they fill these roles?
* The authority of the Bible in the life and work of the church. Is it complete, final and absolute, or is it relative, negotiable and changeable?

While all of these are significant issues, the latter point, the authority of the Bible, is greater. It is the fundamental, bedrock issue that determines our response to all the rest.

The message of the New Testament is that the church must be subject to Christ in all things (Eph. 5:23-24). The second half of the Great Commission orders us to teach converts to obey all things that Christ commanded (Matt. 28:20). The only possible way to know his wishes and commands is through the pages of the New Treatment. Christ is founder, head of and savior of the church (Matt. 16:18; Eph. 1:22; 5:23). All authority has been vested in him (Matt. 28:18). The Scripture contains and provides us with "all things that pertain to life and godliness: (II Pet. 1:3). We are strongly warned against going "beyond what is written" (I Cor. 4:6 ASV); failing to abide "in the doctrine of Christ" (II John 9); or adding to or taking from the revelation God has given (Rev. 22:18-19). If the university professors of the change movement can succeed in undermining our faith in the Scripture, their battle is won!

It should go without saying that any preacher, any editor, any author or any Christian school that will not commit to this fundamental principle of truth should be rejected forthwith. They are unworthy of our attention, respect or fellowship and should be counted as outside the household of faith.

This is not a theoretic or hypothetical possibility. This is the fundamental issue of the current change movement. Doubters have only to read the recent books, **"The Crux of the Matter and God's**

Holy Fire" to see this. We who love the Lord and honor his Word must by all means stand fast in the faith and not allow ourselves to be blown about by every wind of doctrine (Eph. 4:14). If we fail this test, and those who do not hold this high view of the absolute and final authority of God's Word prevail, the cause we love will be swept into the junk yard of oblivion.

68. THE BIBLE MUST BE RIGHTLY DIVIDED

"Study to show thyself approved unto God, a workman that needeth not to be ashamed, rightly dividing the word of truth" (II Tim. 2:15 KJV). Bible study can be the richest experience of one's life, or it can prove to be extremely frustrating. One reason some have difficulty understanding God's message is that they fail to make the proper distinctions in the Scripture. The following thoughts will help the sincere Bible student attain the knowledge he desires.

I. **The Bible is a library of 66 books,** written by some 40 men over a period of sixteen hundred years. While each book must be read and studied for its own unique message, we must never neglect to note the interrelations of the books with each other. Moses wrote the first five books of our Old Testament. **Genesis** tells the origin of the Hebrew nation and how they got into Egypt. **Exodus** tells how they became enslaved and then were delivered. **Leviticus** tells how their national religion came to exist. **Numbers** relates how they spent 40 years wandering toward Canaan, their new homeland. **Deuteronomy** rehearses the exodus from Egypt and the 40 years of wilderness wandering. The historical background for the various psalms can be found in the books of **Samuel, Kings and Chronicles**. Paul's epistles must be studied in light of the history of the **Acts of the Apostles**.

II. **Within the Scripture are words of both inspired and uninspired men.** Care must be taken to ascertain who is speaking and if he is directed by the Holy Spirit or not. For example, in Genesis

3:4-5 we read the words of Satan as he tempted Eve. Surely we should not treat them as we would the words of God or an inspired prophet. Inspiration guarantees that we have a true record of what was said, but not that every person quoted was telling the whole truth.

III. **The Bible is written in various literary styles.** Books like **Genesis** and **Joshua** are history. Their message is expressed in simple prose. **Psalms** and **Proverbs** are poetic in nature and abound in figurative language. For example, David writes:"My heart is like wax; it is melted within me" (Ps. 22:14). Surely no one could view these words as literal. So it is with thousands of other expressions. A good rule to remember is, "All words of Scripture are to be understood in the normal, literal sense unless the context (the setting in which they are found) forbids such." Then we look for a figurative meaning. This lesson is extremely valuable when you study the prophets such as **Ezekiel** or **Revelation**.

Another case in point is history and prophecy. Is the writer relating events past or present (i.e., history), or is he predicting things yet to come? **Jeremiah** relates the historical facts of Jerusalem's capture by Babylon (Jer. 52:1-30). But he also predicted the overthrow and destruction of Babylon in 50:21-28, which occurred 50 years later.

IV. **The Bible consists of an Old and a New Covenant.** In Hebrews 8:7, the author speaks of "the first covenant." The first covenant was the Old Testament law that God made with the Hebrew nation when he brought them out of Egypt (Heb. 8:9). The New Covenant was made by Jesus (Heb. 8:13). All men today are subject to the New Covenant of Jesus (Matt. 28:18-19; John 12:48). Thus you do not need to build an ark, even though Noah was commanded to do so (Gen. 6:14). You need not offer a lamb for a sacrifice even though the ancient Hebrew were so obligated (Lev. 1:10). You must, however, obey Jesus in all that his New Covenant teaches if you would please God. Christ asked, "Why call ye me, Lord, Lord, and do not the things which I say?" (Lk. 6:46). Do you ask of what value then is the Old Testament? Much in every way. It is the history of God's scheme of redemption. It tells us our origin and how things came to be as they are. It is of immeasurable value as a background for our New Testament study. Paul writes that things "written afore time were written for our learning . . . " (Rom. 15:4). What great lessons we learn from its study. But if we wish to learn what to do to be saved, we must look to Jesus and his New Testament (Matt. 17:3-5). The same is true for instructions about the church or worship today.

What is the practical application of all this? This concept of the two covenants, properly understood, will keep us from serious religious error. We do not observe the seventh day Sabbath (Ex. 20:8) because it is an Old Testament ordinance given to the Israelites (Deut. 5:12-15). We worship on the first day (Sunday) because it is the day of Christ's resurrection (John 20:1-9); the day the Holy Spirit came to begin his ministry (Acts 2:1-4; compare Lev. 23:15-21); the day the church began (Acts 2:1-47); and the day early Christians worshipped (Acts 20:7; I Cor. 16:1-2). The thief on the cross could be saved by Christ without baptism because he was yet under the old covenant which lasted until Christ died (Heb. 9:16-17; Col. 2:14-16). Under Christ's covenant we must believe and be baptized in order to be saved (Mk. 16:15-16; Acts 10:48).

May each of us study to show ourselves approved unto God, rightly dividing the word of truth (II Tim. 2:15).

69. IS TRUTH RELATIVE OR ABSOLUTE?

Postmodernism says, "What is right depends on the situation." It adherents believe there is no body of eternal unchanging truth. They say truth is relative and may vary from group to group or from time to time since there is no objective standard." Are these views right or wrong?

There are two standards of morality; man's and God's. History demonstrates that man's morality is governed by a changing code of relative values. This is because every code of human law has fallen short of absolute justice and equity. Whatever human intelligence designs and regulates must fall into the class of relative values. There is no human authority to tell us how to act so that the greatest good will come to the race.

God's laws are absolutely perfect. As Creator of all, he knows what is best for the whole of mankind. Being all wise, he knows without experimentation what will work for the best. He sees the end from the beginning. His laws are not relative. They need no revising. God has two kinds of laws: natural laws and spiritual/ moral laws. The laws of nature are absolute, and unchanging. The law of gravity is as true now as in the beginning, in America as in China.

God's spiritual laws are as absolute and unchanging as the laws of nature. Jesus said, "Heaven and earth shall pass away but my words shall not pass away" (Matt. 24:35). "The word of the Lord abideth forever" (I Pet. 1:24-25). "Every scripture inspired of God is profitable for teaching for reproof, for correction, for instruction in righteousness that the man of God may be complete, furnished completely unto every good work" (II Tim. 3:16-17). "The faith . . . was once for all (times) delivered unto the saints" (Jude 3). God's "word is truth" (John 17:17). His word is final and complete. We are warned, "Add thou not unto his words, lest he reprove thee and thou be found a liar" (Prov. 30:6).

Today, conduct once considered wrong is excused. Everyone and everything are blamed except the offender. This is Postmodern morality. Solomon said, "There is a way that seemeth right unto a man but the ends thereof are the ways of death" (Prov. 14:12). God's absolute standard of right and wrong must be accepted if our nation survives. All lying is wrong (Rev. 21:8). Stealing is wrong (Eph. 4:28) Sexual relations out of marriage are wrong (Heb. 13:4). Taking God's name in vain is sin (Ex. 20:7). Postmodern morality is really the old system of immorality.

You ask, "How can I know right and wrong?" God's voice is the absolute authority. Jesus is the example of perfection. The Bible is the absolute code of Truth. Read it. Believe it. Obey it. Be Saved!

70. THE LAW OF CHRIST

Inspired writers refer to the New Testament as "the law of the Spirit of life in Christ Jesus" (Rom. 8:2); "the perfect law, the law of liberty" (Jas. 1:23) and a "law of faith" (Rom. 3:27). This being the case, how say the change agents among us that we are not under a law of God? They love to say that we should not view the Bible as divine law. Are they so ignorant of the book they claim to teach? Do they not believe what the Scripture says of itself? Do they think they know more about God's Book than the Holy Spirit who gave it? Could it be that in order to sell their agenda to a Bible-believing, Bible oriented people, they must first convince them that the Scripture is not law, therefore it will be no great thing if its words are ignored?

If the Bible is not divine law, then no man is a sinner. For "where there is no law, neither is there transgression" (Rom. 4:15). If we have no divine law, how can some be called "lawless" in their conduct? (II Thess. 2:7; I Tim. 1:9). If the Scripture is not law, how could some men in the church be desirous of teaching "the law?" (I Tim. 1:7). If there is no law in Christ, we would have no knowledge of sin, or of right and wrong, "for through the law cometh the knowledge of sin" (Rom. 3:20). If the New Covenant is not God's law, then no man need worry about being judged by it in the last day (John 12:48). If it is not law, then we can do anything we desire in the name of religion and not worry about having to give account unto God (II Cor. 5:10; Rev. 20:12). If the Scripture is not law, then James and Paul were mistaken in calling it that. If that is so, how can we have confidence in other things they said? That would mean the

New Covenant is not reliable and free from error, would it not? If God had wanted to tell us that his written word is His law to guide and govern us in maters of faith, practice and worship, what do our champions of change feel He should have said, beyond what he has said, to make it clear?

It is true that we are not under the Law of Moses (Heb. 8:6-13; Rom. 7:4). It is true that we are saved by God's grace rather than by law-keeping (Eph. 2:8-9). It is a fact that our response to God must be one of faith rather than an attempt to earn salvation by works of law (Rom. 3:21-22). But it is a flagrant error to teach men that God's Word should not be viewed as law. This lesson our change agents need to take heed to.

71. THE PATTERN OF CHRISTIANITY

Those promoting the agenda of change for Christ's church deny that God has given us a divine pattern which we are expected to follow. They ridicule those who believe otherwise. In derision they call them "*patternists*" and their approach to serving Christ "*patternism.*" Of course this is the way members of the church of Christ have been serving Christ since the beginning of our back to the Bible movement. It is also the procedure God in his word teaches us to follow.

To reject the idea that God has given us a divine pattern to follow is the reject what is clearly taught in the following Scriptures:
* Paul exhorted Timothy to "**Hold the pattern of sound words** which thou hast heard from me . . . "(II Tim. 1:13). The Greek term translated "pattern" is *tupos,* which Strong defines as "a model (for imitation)."
* The author of Hebrews quotes God who said to Moses, "**See . . . that thou makest all thing according to the pattern** that was showed thee in the mount" (Heb. 8:5). His lesson to Christians was that they too must observe God's New Covenant pattern.

* Paul reminded the Christians in Rome that in their conversion, they had obeyed "from the heart . . . **that form of teaching** whereunto (they) were delivered" (Rom. 6:17). Thus, there is a pattern for being saved!
* The brethren in Thessalonica were commanded to withdraw their fellowship from every brother that walked disorderly and "not after **the traditions which they received of us**" (II Thess. 3:6).
* Paul believed that Christ used him (Paul) as "**an ensample** of them that should thereafter believe on him . . . " (I Tim. 1:16). He often exhorted disciples to "imitate" his example (II Thess. 3:7; I Cor. 11:1).
* Peter tells us that Christ left us "**an example** that (we) should follow his steps" (I Pet. 2:21). Such examples are intended to be followed!

Students of the Old Testament know that when God ordered Moses to build him a tabernacle, i.e., a portable house of worship, he said, "According to all that I show thee, the pattern of the tabernacle, and the pattern of all the furniture thereof, even so shall ye make it" (Ex. 25:9). If God gave Israel a pattern and expected them to follow it, is it unreasonable that he would do the same for us who serve him under Christ? The reason we need a pattern is that "it is not in man that walketh to direct his own steps" (Jer. 10:23).

All of these verses teach us that God has given us a pattern or example of what he expects of us and that it is our duty to conform to that pattern. That divine pattern is the message of Christ expressed in written words, in a permanent record for all men of all nations in all ages (Matt. 24:35). We know it as our New Testament. Furthermore we are strictly warned to neither add to nor take away from that which he has given us (Rev. 22:18-19; Prov. 30:6). His words will be the standard by which we will be judged in eternity (John 12:48).

We can't help but wonder why anyone professing Christ would deny that which is so clearly taught in his Word. The agenda proposed by the agents of change cannot be implemented where the Divine pattern is respected and complied with. Hence to accomplish their goals, they must deny the concept of a heavenly pattern and persuade brethren to accept things which have no basis in Scripture and might even be contrary to portions of it. If no Divine pattern exists no one could object to their changes!

Everyone desirous of spending eternity in heavenly bliss should focus his mind on that day when he will stand before Christ, the Supreme Judge of humanity. For the dead will stand before the throne and the books will be opened and the dead will be judged by the things written in the books, according to their works (Rev. 22:11-12). God has a pattern for his church. Do you respect it? Are you complying with it?

72. LEADERSHIP BY CONSENSUS

Those who are promoting changes for the church want a new and (in their opinion) improved way of making decisions for the church. We hear them saying, "elders are not to rule over the congregation but govern only by consensus." Strange that the Holy Spirit did not have the advantage of their input when he wrote the Hebrew Christians to "obey them that have the rule over you, and submit to them . . . " (Heb. 13:17). Granted, elders are not to be dictators or tyrants. Granted, they do not lord it over the flock (I Pet. 5:2-3). God describes them as shepherds and the church as a flock of sheep in their charge(Acts 20:28-29). Most shepherds do not guide their flock by seeking consensus of the sheep. They do not drive them, but they do lead them in safe and proper paths. They make the decisions necessary for the welfare of the flock.

The idea of consensus has gained popularity, with change agents promoting it as a vital part of their agenda for changing the church. They find it difficult to penetrate and gain control of a congregation whose elders are not easily deceived. Elders can refuse to hire a smooth talking, impressive preacher even if the congregation is taken with him. If they are uncertain of his soundness they can pass him by. Elders can dismiss a preacher who has embraced the errors of the change movement, even if the majority of the members are fooled by him. Elders can decide who will or will not teach a class; which brotherhood activities will or will not be promoted; which guest speakers will be invited to come. They can determine the direction the congregation will travel. Such is not good for the change agents who wish to commandeer a congregation for their new movement. To change agents, the solution for this problem is governance by consensus. We need only point out that such is a non-Biblical approach to directing God's people. This should be sufficient for all who truly love and honor Christ as Lord and head of the church (Eph. 1:22).

The following quote is most insightful and should be well-considered by all who want to see God's church survive and prosper.

> "Ah consensus-the process of abandoning all beliefs, principles, values and policies in search of something in which no one believes, but to which no one objects; the process of avoiding the very issues that have to be solved, merely because you cannot get agreement on the way ahead. What great cause would have been fought and won under the banner of 'I stand for consensus?'" (Margaret Thatcher).

May the God of heaven bless every congregation with elders who are truly capable of leading His people in paths of righteousness and who will protect them from those who would do them harm.

73. THE SILENCE OF THE SCRIPTURES

In his excellent history of the American Restoration Movement, James DeForest Murch made the following insightful statement concerning us of the Churches of Christ:

> "Within the last generation the Church of Christ has made a phenomenal growth. This is due to two things: (1) Its people have stood like a Rock of Gibralter for 'the faith which was once delivered unto the saints,' amid the doubt and confusion superinduced by liberalism. They have challenged the spirit of compromise and worldliness and dared to be a 'peculiar people' teaching and practicing what they believe is the Bible way of life. (2) They have come to realize that the silence of the Scriptures must be respected as well as the commandments of Scripture, but that obedience to its silences permits freedom of judgment and action" (**Christians Only**, p. 313).

There are two remarkable things about this quote. First, Murch was a national leader in the Independent Christian Churches whose predecessors rejected the law of silence 125 years ago and who almost to a man, still refuse to recognize this aspect of Christ's authority over his church. Second, is that we now have a sizeable number of professors, preachers and elders among us who are preaching and behaving as though there is no such a thing as "the law of silence."

This principle of divine authority is revealed in a half dozen examples of Biblical history. When Jewish brethren journeyed to Antioch and told the Gentile converts, "except ye be circumcised after the custom of Moses, ye cannot be saved (Acts 15:1), Paul and Barnabas took the matter to the apostles at Jerusalem. After an inquiry, the apostle and elders wrote "For as much as . . . certain (men) who went out from us have troubled you with words, subverting your souls; to whom we gave no commandment" (Acts 15:24). Thus a teaching not commanded by apostolic authority is not to be allowed or accepted. Although there was no command forbidding circumcision, in the absence of some positive instruction the practice could not be introduced into the life of the church.

The writer of Hebrews observes that Christ could not serve as a high priest on earth since he was of the tribe of Judah, "as to which tribe Moses spake nothing concerning priests" (Heb. 7:14). No specific statement forbade a man from Judah serving in that exalted station, but it did not have to since God had said that the sons of Aaron the Levite would bear that office (Ex. 28:1).

Two other familiar events of Old Testament history vividly illustrate this point. The tragic case of the priests, Nadab and Abihu, sons of Aaron, who perished while using strange fire in offering incense in Jehovah's sanctuary (Lev. 10:1-3). The fire they used was strange in that it was not taken from the sacred fire on the great brazen altar, as God had instructed them to do (Lev. 16:12; 6:12)

When David ordered the ark of God to be carried up to Jerusalem another tragedy occurred. It was placed on an ox cart and care was taken to insure that proper respect was shown. But when the oxen stumbled and the ark was about to fall, Uzzah reached out to steady it and God instantly struck him down (I Chron. 13:6-10). Shocked and saddened, David ordered the procession halted until they could research the matter and determine why God had so dealt with them. Consulting the Scriptures, they discovered that God had ordered the ark to be carried on the shoulders of priests. Although he had not specifically said, "Don't carry it on an ox cart," such was excluded by the positive directive given (I Chron. 15:2,13).

Today, to our shame and sorrow, many of our young preachers have never heard this lesson explained or else have been convinced it is of no significance for modern disciples. The most notable example of this failure is in the current discussion about our worship. These poor scholars who wish to introduced changes are asking, "Where does the Bible forbid us to do so?" Shame, shame, shame. The above lesson, which you should have learned in freshman Bible, answers you with a thunderous voice.

74. BELIEVING THE PREMILLENNIAL LIE

Thinking folks are amazed at the wild speculation of the various teachers of premillennialism that seems to dominate the religious book market, the journals of most conservative denominations and the religious broadcast media. Almost weekly some new discovery is announced: the man of sin has been identified, Armageddon is just around the corner, the mark of the beast has been spotted, the State of Israel is ready to fulfill Bible prophecy. The date of Christ's return has been repeatedly set and then abandoned. The absurdity of this religious game-playing would be humorous were it not for the precious souls being led astray by its false teachers.

A few clearly stated Biblical facts forever refute this ancient heresy. God is omnipotent. Therefore, the Jewish nation could not thwart his plan to establish his kingdom in the days of the Roman kings (Dan. 2:44). Christ established his kingdom and first century saints were citizens of it (Col. 1:13, Rev. 1:6). Christ now reigns on David's throne in heaven (Rev. 3:7; Acts 2:29-33). No one knows the date of Christ's return (Matt. 24:36). When he does return there will be one general resurrection of the good and the evil (John 5:28-29). These and many other plainly stated Scriptural truths destroy once and for all the foundations of this false system.

Why is Premillennialism So Popular?

The burden of this lesson is to try to understand why this anti-Scriptural teaching is so widely received. It is startling to observe that it is the **cause celebre** of most of the evangelical churches. Generally speaking only the Lutherans, conservative Presbyterians, Mennonites and Churches of Christ are free from its taint. Most other bodies are infected to some degree.

The following reasons help to explain why this strange, contradictory teaching has such an attraction and hold on people's minds.

A. Paul writes of people who believe a lie, "because they receive not the love of the truth ... but had pleasure in unrighteousness" (II

Thess. 2:10-12). Those who have had much experience in trying to teach people who hold this view have observed this amazing lack of interest in those plain, simple truths of God that nullify the millennial heresy. Jesus spoke of a kind of person who "seeing, saw not and hearing, understood not." "For this people's heart is waxed gross, and their ears are dull of hearing, and their eyes they have closed; lest haply they should perceive with their eyes, and hear with their ears, and understand with their heart . . . " (Matt. 13:14-15).

B. Some folks are attracted to the bizarre and incredible. The more unbelievable the proposition the more eagerly they rush to embrace and then cling to it. We see this spirit demonstrated in the huge crowds lined up to view the freak shows at the fair and the masses that pay their money to see movies based upon the occult, the ghoulish and the impossible. Perhaps the human race is not so far removed from the primitive superstitions of yesterday with witches, ghosts and apparitions of demons. Premillennialism abounds with spicy fruits for the superstitious souls.

C. Premillennialism appears to answer question of the unknown future. Men have always had an insatiable desire to know what lies beyond the curtain of tomorrow. With its predictions of the date of Christ's return and the end of the world, it attracts these date seekers even as does astrology its disciples.

D. There are people who relish the thought that they have discovered a mystery that others have not found. This, in their proud minds, elevates them and makes them superior. The infamous Gnostics of the early Christian centuries suffered from a similar illusion. Thus false pride and superior attitude is at least one of the many causes. It will not take many encounters with such teachers to see this elitist attitude demonstrated. Paul warns against being lifted up with pride lest we "fall into the condemnation of the devil" (I Tim. 3:6).

E. Some folks are prone to be naive and gullible in matters religious. They do not like to expend the mental energy required to think for themselves. They reason, "Let the preacher do the studying and then explain it to me." Thus they are like baby birds, they trustingly open wide their mouths to whatever the preacher brings them. Such people need to take heed to all those verses that stress individual responsibility for faith. Study to show yourself approved unto God, "rightly dividing the word of truth" (II Tim. 2:15). The Beroeans were commended because they searched the Scriptures daily to see if the teaching was true (Acts 17:11). In judgment each one of us will give account of himself before God (Rom. 14:12).

F. Some people believe this lie because they have been told that they are supposed to believe it in order to be faithful. They have the sheep complex; they blindly follow their leaders. They should remember that the Judas goat leads the flock into the slaughter pens. God never intended for his people to be blind followers of blind teachers. He warned us that both will fall into the pit (Matt. 15:14). John admonishes us, "Beloved, believe not every spirit, but prove the spirits, whether they are of God: because many false prophets are gone out into the world" (I John 4:1).

G. Some blindly hold to premillennialism because they have heard it proclaimed in a bold, matter of fact way all their lives and they have never thought to question it. Long ago the propagandists learned that a lie oft repeated is soon held to be truth by the thoughtless masses. The early church had men miraculously endowed by the Holy Spirit to be discerners of spirits (I Cor. 12:10). Though inspiration has past, each of us needs to measure what we hear by the infallible Word of God. Jesus warned "Take heed what ye hear" (Mark 4:24).

H. There are some Bible students who have fallen into the trap of premillennialism because they have failed to rightly divide the word of truth (II Timothy 2:15). By that we mean that they co-mingle Old and New Covenant promises. They have not compared Scripture with Scripture to learn of God's fulfillment of his promises to Israel. They fail to distinguish between figurative and literal language. It has well been said that a correct hermeneutic will destroy the premillennial doctrine.

I. Most believers in Premillennialism have not taken the time to review the spotted history of the many millennial movements and thus to discover their numerous false predictions and contradictions. Most glaring are the predictions of Christ's return by William Miller of the Adventists and Judge Rutherford of the Jehovah's Witnesses. One of the recent mistaken premillennial prophets is Hal Lindsey who has repeatedly set dates for the Master's return, only to see them proven false. Moses said "When a prophet speaketh in the name of Jehovah, if the thing follow not nor come to pass, that is the thing which Jehovah hath not spoken; the prophet hath spoken it presumptuously . . ." (Deut. 18:22).

J. Shrewd false teachers have taken advantage of the ignorance and credulity of the believing masses. They feed them their sorry diet of speculation for the notoriety and wealth it brings them. "By their smooth and fair speech they beguile the hearts of the innocent" (Rom. 16:18). They are "false teachers, who . . . bring in destructive heresies . . . bringing upon themselves swift destruction" (II Pet. 2:1). They make merchandise of non-discerning believers.

Brethren, it is not enough that we do not believe these strange doctrines of men. Our task is two fold;

a). To fortify the faith of our brethren lest they be led astray.
b). To liberate those held captive to this false system of premillennialism.

Some of those promoting change have suggested that such millennial speculation is harmless. Others seem inclined to embrace those who advocate it. Most of them are critical of our brethren who stoutly resisted when some sought to introduce it into our churches. They are like the doctor who sees no harm in marijuana. May God give us wisdom to understand the issues and the courage to press the battle in Jesus' name.

75. MAN, THE WORSHIPING CREATURE

Of the several characteristics and traits that distinguish man from the other creatures, worship is one of the most pronounced. In every culture in every age, most men have worshipped something. In their ignorance, the proud Athenians worshipped the unknown God (Acts 17:23). Even the atheistic humanist Auguste Comte proposed a Religion of Humanity complete with his own suggestion for sacraments, saints and rituals . . . "Another unbeliever wrote, "Religion of some sort is probably necessary . . . Instead of worshiping supernatural rulers, it will sanctify the higher manifestations of human nature in art and love . . . " (Julian Huxley ed. **The Humanist Frame**, London, George Allen and Urwin Ltd. 1961, p. 44). A few years ago I read of a government newspaper editorial in Russia exhorting the masses not to adore the statues of Lenin.

Why is man incurably religious? Solomon writes that God "hath set eternity in their hearts" (Eccle. 3:11a). The Creator made man to worship and serve him. Although most men are living in rebellion to Jehovah, they cannot escape their need to adore something or someone greater and more powerful than themselves.

Revealed Worship

The God who made man as he is did not leave his need for worship unfulfilled. He revealed himself to the human family. In Eden, he came down and talked with them (Gen. 3:8-21). The created universe helps man to perceive God's power and divinity (Rom. 1:20). While nature can inspire us to worship, it can never tell us how to worship. God revealed his will for worship through divinely guided prophets who spake as they were moved by the Holy Spirit (II Pet. 1:21). The ancient Hebrews were taught to worship by the Law of Moses (Deut. 6:4, 13). The details of acceptable worship were spelled out for them in the Old Testament. Christians are under the New Testament of Jesus (John 12:47). Their worship is based on the commands of Christ and his apostles (Matt. 28:18-20). The reader should note that Christian worship is not the same as the Hebrews' worship. In both cases worshipers were warned against adding to or taking from God's directions (Deut. 4:2; Rev. 22:18-20).

Our worship is not optional. Jesus commands that we **must** worship God in spirit and in truth (John 4:24). If we would please God and hope to live in eternal bliss, we will worship as he directs.

While most everyone has worshiped at some time, not all have thought out a definition for the term. Our English word "worship" means **worthship** and suggests the worthiness of the person who receives special honor (**Baker's Dictionary of Theology,** p. 560). In the Hebrew and Greek tongues in which the Scriptures were first written, two thoughts are reflected in worship: 1. to serve, to render religious service; 2. to adore, to show reverence to (**Vine's Expository Dictionary of New Testament Words** p. 235-236). Under the Old Law, worship consisted of elaborate rituals, tied to a magnificent temple and professional priesthood. Such a system made its primary appeal to the physical senses.

Under Christ, our worship is "in spirit and truth" (John 4:24). Christian worship is simple and unpretentious and may be offered to God anywhere. It's entire appeal is to the heart. Paul, the apostle, argues that the old system was taken away at the cross and we Christians should not feel bound to follow it (Col. 2:14-18). In our public worship we are to adore the Father and his Holy Son in our songs, prayers, gifts and communion. In our daily life we serve him joyfully.

Different Kinds of Worship

All worship is not acceptable to the great Jehovah. He speaks of vain worship (Matt. 15:9). **Vain** suggests, emptiness, worthlessness. Some worship in ignorance (Acts 17:23). Such are exhorted to know and serve the true God through Jesus. There is an acceptable worship that is offered "in spirit and in truth" (John 3:24). God actively seeks for men to worship in this fashion (John 4:23). Christ put it plainly in Matthew 7:21 "Not everyone that saith unto me, Lord, Lord shall enter in the kingdom of heaven, but he that doeth the will of my Father who is in heaven." Surely this is true of our worship. Good intentions, a heavenly feeling and general approval of one's fellows is not enough. Worship must be **scriptural**, i.e., according to scripture, to be acceptable.

The Church and Worship

The church is God's family of saved people upon the earth. Her primary reason for existence is to worship the Lord. In public assemblies she adores God. In daily activities she serves. We reflect true discipleship and true worship when we "preach the gospel to every creature" (Mark 16:15); when we remember the fatherless and the widows in their affliction (Jas. 1:27); and when we work to strength our fellow Christian (Eph. 4:12).

The God who made man, planted deep within him many powerful urges or drives such as the need for food, shelter, sex, companionship and worship. In all of these cases there is a right and wrong way to fulfill them. May all who love the Lord seek his will for worship in the pages of the New Covenant of Jesus and may we be true worshipers who adore and serve him in spirit and in truth.

76. INFORMATION FOR THOSE DETERMINED TO SPICE-UP OUR WORSHIP

Across the land, we have preachers who are determined to spice up the public worship of our congregations. To the heaven ordained worship of singing, praying, communing, presenting offerings and hearing God's Word, they want to add some or all of the following ingredients: a dash of hand clapping; a few spoonfuls of hugging and an outburst of happy talk; a measure of solos and choir singing; a few sprinkles of testimonials and a large measure of entertainers and entertainment. A few are just about ready to add instrumental music since it is no longer "a salvation issue" with them. Some are toying with letting women exercise their gifts in public worship so they won't feel oppressed or denied. Of course, the New Testament of Christ offers no approval for their additions.

Just today I chanced across the following quote from **The Evolution of Church Music** by Frank Landon Humphreys. "One of the features which distinguishes the Christian religion from almost all others is its quietness; it aims to repress the outward signs of inward feeling. Savage instinct, and the religion of Greece also, had employed the rhythmic dance and all kinds of gesticulatory motions to express the inner feelings . . . The early Christians discouraged all outward signs of excitement, and from the very beginning, in the music they used, reproduced the spirit of their religion–an inward quietude. All the music employed in their early services was vocal" (p. 42).

The illustrious Alexander Campbell understood such brethren better than they do themselves. He wrote; "That all persons who have no spiritual meditation, consolations and sympathies of renewed hearts, should call for such aid is but natural. Pure water from the flinty rock has no attraction for the mere toper or wine bibber. A little alcohol, or genuine Cognac brandy . . . is essential to the beverage to make it truly refreshing. So to those who have no real devotion or spirituality in them, and whose animal nature flags under the oppression of church service, I think that instrumental music would be not only a desideratum, but an essential prerequisite to fire up the souls to even animal devotion. But I presume to all spiritually-minded Christians, such aids would be as a cowbell in a concert" (**Millennial Harbinger**, Series 4, Vol. 1, p. 581).

77. DIMENSIONS OF WORSHIP

The Bible has a great deal to say about worship. We are told to "worship God" (Rev. 22:9). We are warned to have no gods before Jehovah nor graven images (Ex. 20:3-5). We are to be true or genuine worshipers (John 4:23). We are to worship him in spirit and in truth (John 4:24). He expects us to worship him in the beauty of holiness (Ps.96:9). We know that early Christians sang, prayed, communed, presented their offerings to God and received instruction as worship to God (Acts 20:7). They worshiped in their assemblies and they worshiped privately as well.

Worship is something one does intentionally and purposefully. That is one doesn't worship by accident or as a by-product of doing something else. Abraham saddled his ass, clave wood for a burnt-offering and traveled from his home in the land of the Philistines to Mount Moriah. As he and his servants drew near to the mountain, he said, "I and the land will go yonder; and we will worship . . . " (Gen. 22:5). The other things were preparation for worship. The worship was a distinct act he would engage in. In acceptable worship man must be consciously approaching God with the intention of giving him praise and homage according to his will. Private worship can be personal, silent and within the heart of the worshiper. Public worship of a congregation necessarily involves actions of mind, body and spirit of those participating (I Cor. 14:15).

In recent years those who are promoting changes for our churches have come up with the idea that every thing a Christian does is worship. This is usually a precursor to saying, "therefore it should not matter if we take certain liberties with our congregational worship."

While there is both corporate and private worship that does not equal the premise that everything one does is worship. While much of what a Christian does in daily life could be described as serving God; such as being a good husband, wife, parent, employee, etc.

(Col. 3:24), neither does that equal "all things are worship." To see the absurdity of this assertion, image Bro. John Doe's weekly activities. He goes hunting on Saturday and kills a deer, not to feed a hungry family, but as a sporting/recreational activity. Having bagged his game, he guts it. Is this worship? On Monday night he goes to a football game. With the crowd, he cheers his team and roars when a touchdown is scored. Is that Worship? He eats a hotdog and downs a soft drink. Is that an act of worship? He goes home and goes to sleep. Is that worship? On his lunch hour he plays a game of solitaire on his computer, could that be worship? During his vacation he works on restoring his antique car. He sands and paints it. Is that worship? He and his wife have a warm disagreement about how much he has spent on his hobby. Is that worship? That night he sits before the TV, watching Jay Leno, eating popcorn. Is that worship? There are numerous other things, too personal, too private and even too gross to mention that surely are not worship.

We are to present our bodies as living sacrifices, holy and acceptable unto God, (Rom. 12:1-2). This does not mean that every action of life is an act of worship. It means that we should abstain from doing anything we know to be sinful or wrong and we strive to please God in all things we think, say or do. The faithful child of God will strive to live soberly, righteously and godly in his daily life (Tit. 2:12) and he will also be present when the saints assemble to worship and partake of the Lord's Supper (I Cor. 11:20).

78. NEW SONGS AND OLD SONGS

Those campaigning to impose changes on churches of Christ have high on their list, changes in our song worship. They wish to make the use of instrumental music in worship acceptable to our people. They also want to introduce choirs and soloists. They feel driven to replace our traditional hymns with "contemporary Christian music" and "youth songs." To enhance the emotional aspect of song worship, they want to be free to clap their hands, and lift them high in imitation of their Charismatic neighbors and the Tele-evangelists.

In this article we wish to address the choice of hymns we sing in worship assemblies. Some preliminary thoughts are in order: * With the exception of the psalms and a few songs based solely on a scripture text, all hymns are human productions. Their quality and value depend on the poetic and musical skills of the author, his knowledge and understanding of the Bible and the Scriptural sentiments incorporated in them. * All the songs in our hymnals were once new. Thus, being new is not itself a proper objection to using a hymn. * That a song leader selects a song that is not in our hymnals does not make them wrong or suspect. Hymnals for all worshipers are of fairly recent origin. Though they are a wonderful convenience, they are not essential to our salvation or acceptance to God. * That songs are projected on a screen is not a question of right or wrong. It matters not whether we read the words from a printed page in a book or from a printed page projected on a screen.

Some things do matter. If singing is to be congregational, everyone needs to be able to participate in it. If a leader chooses songs, not in the hymnal, that only young people know, then older members have little choice but to sit and listen to the others until they can learn them by memory.

If the use of such songs creates resentment or dissatisfaction within the church family, then we have to think in terms of one person's choice of his favorite songs, causing offense to his brother. This is the same type of issue as the eating of meats which had been sacrificed to idols, which Paul addressed in I Corinthians. The apostle demonstrated the proper Christian response, "If meat causeth my brother to stumble, I will eat no flesh for evermore, that I cause not my brother to stumble" (I Cor. 8:13). If my insistence on changing the type of songs we use in our worship causes division, and it can and will happen, then I will bear the responsibility of having caused division over a matter that at best is a matter of opnion and preference. For such I will surely stand condemned (Rom. 16:17-18).

Without question, many of the contemporary Christian songs have lovely, spiritual lyrics and can be used in our worship without Biblical objection. Some of them will eventually find their way into our hymnals and become a permanent part of our body of hymns. Those that have unscriptural sentiments should be weeded out and cast aside. Those that are trivial should not be introduced as songs of worship.

My concern is that we not cast aside great hymns of the faith that have earned a place in our hymnody and that generations of saints have sung in worship. While popular music is generally on the charts only for a few weeks, or at best for one generation, some Christian hymns have been popular with saints for a hundred years or more. It is arrogant for a new generation to declare such spiritual treasures obsolete or boring and insist on replacing them with their "new" songs.

In one of his great books C. S. Lewis expressed his disdain for those in his Anglican church who were constantly tampering with the worship and especially rewriting or discarding the old hymns. He correctly observed that sacred songs are the ties that link our faith to those gone before. When I sing "The Old Rugged Cross," it evokes precious memories from my youth when with my grandparents I sang it in worship. Goethe wrote, "Music, in the best sense, does not require novelty; nay, the older it is, and the more we are accustomed to it, the greater the effect." Mrs. L. E. Landon observed "Music–we love it for the buried hopes, the garnered memories, the tender feelings it can summon at a touch." By eliminating the great and familiar hymns of the past, we separate today's Christians from their ancestors in the faith

When thoughtless leaders fill their song service with new songs, known only by a select group, it forces those not of that group to listen to the others perform. When one group is relegated to the role of observers, it makes for an easier transition to a choir who sing for the entertainment of spectators. Paul's exhortation to the Corinthians is applicable for today. If your new songs are sung with the most beautiful tongues of men and angels, but you have not love for your older brethren, you are become sounding brass and clanging cymbals. (I Cor. 13:1). If you are truly zealous of spiritual singing, "see that ye . . . abound unto the edifying of the church" (I Cor. 14:12). New hymns should be introduced and used like salt on food; sparingly. Too much will defeat the purpose for using either of them.

79. PRAISE TEAMS FOR WORSHIP: ARE THEY WRONG?

To determine whether or not a practice is wrong it is necessary to carefully analyze the matter in the light of Scripture. Some of our churches have recently begun the practice of having a team of good singers sit together near the front of the auditorium, with individual microphones, to help in leading the song worship. Consider the following observations concerning "praise teams."

* It is no more wrong to have two or more song leaders than to have the one we are use to. Having someone stand before us to lead us in singing cannot be found in Scripture. It is an expedient to help us sing in a coordinated way.
* It is not wrong that good singers sit together. Such has been done in days past in many congregations, although they were not called praise teams.
* It is not wrong that they sit together near the front of the auditorium.
* It is not wrong for them to sing into microphones. The same principle that would allow our solitary song leader to sing before a microphone would allow them to do so.
* It is not wrong to project the words of hymns on a screen so

worshipers can see them. Such has been done in the past but not with the sophisticated technology we now enjoy. The same scripture that authorizes our use of hymnals would authorize the use of projectors and screens.

* It is not wrong for a church to sing new hymns. Every hymn in our book was once a new song.
* It is not wrong to sing hymns that are created in a different style or with a different meter than we are accustomed to. The hymns we are presently use to are quite different in form and style to the hymns sung in the middle ages and in Biblical times. The earliest Christians would have chanted the Psalms or other portions of Scripture. We do little or none of that type of singing. But God did not specify a specific style of music. As long as we are singing "psalms, hymns and spiritual songs" (Eph. 5:19).

There are however, some other important considerations regarding the use of praise teams: If the introduction of praise teams creates conflict and confusion in a congregation, leaders should consider Paul's words, "For God is not the author of confusion, but of peace ... " (I Cor. 14:34). "Let all things be done unto edifying" (vs. 26). To those who insisted on using their gift of speaking in foreign tongues in the assembly, Paul said, "thou verily giveth thanks well, but the other is not edified" (vs. 17). Even if a praise team sings well and with good intentions but their presence causes confusion, the church is certainly not edified. Again Paul said, "Whether therefore ye eat, or drink, or whatsoever ye do, do all to the glory of God" (I Cor. 10:31). To cause confusion among brethren is not to the glory of God.

Those who are obsessed with having praise teams seem to be the preachers and churches that have embraced the broader program of those we know as **agents of change**. **Introducing praise teams is usually part of a package of changes**, some of which are clearly contrary to God's revealed will for his church. Some of these changes are a willingness to tolerate the use of instrumental music in worship, the use of women in leadership roles in the church, essential changes in the celebration of the Lord's Supper, etc. Given this reality we should be very cautious when someone proposes that we have a praise team, lest they also want to change other vital aspects of our faith, worship and practice.

Many of those promoting praise teams are also saying it would be acceptable for us to use soloists, singing groups and choirs in our worship assemblies. Such changes would go contrary to the congregational singing that Christ has authorized, "Teaching and admonishing one another in psalms . . . " (Col. 3:16).

Shrewd deceivers who wish to introduce major changes into the worship of the church know that such cannot be successfully done in one giant step. The people will rebel and throw them out. But they can reach their goal by leading the group in a series of small, seemingly innocuous, incremental steps. Then one day they have them just where they wanted them. The innovation will have been introduced and the people never realized what was happening. Given the prevailing problems facing the church, and given the fact that the promoters of sinful changes are often the promoters of the use of praise teams, we should be skeptical of those doing so. In the current climate, the use of such teams strikes me as unwise and inexpedient. No scriptural criticism can be leveled against the way we have sung God's praise for centuries past. To continue that practice will do a congregation good and no harm at all.

80. THE CHRISTMAS HOLY DAY: A BIBLICAL VIEW

Around the world folks are busily preparing for Christmas. Most churches devote one day per year to celebrate Christ's birth. That is done with an array of human traditions unknown to Scripture. "The day of Christ's birth cannot be ascertained from the New Testament, or indeed from any other source. "The fathers of the first three centuries do not speak of any special observance of the nativity . . ." **(McClintock and Strong, Cyclopedia,** Vol. 3, p.276).

"Chrysostom in 386 states that the celebration of the birth of Christ's according to the flesh 'was not inaugurated in Antioch until ten years before that date'" (**Schaff-Herzog Encyclopedia of Religious Knowledge,** Vol. 3, p.46). December 25th was determined by the decree of Liberious, bishop of the church in Rome, in 354 A.D. The date was widely disputed by others. "The Western Church ordered the feast to be celebrated on the day of the Mithraic rites of the birth of the sun (**Americana**). "The pagan Saturnalia and Brumalia were too deeply entrenched in popular custom to be set aside by Christian influence. The pagan festival with its riot and merrymaking was so popular that Christians were glad for an excuse to continue its celebration with little change in spirit or in manner (**Schaff-Herzog**, Vol. 3, p. 48).

Since Churches of Christ are committed to practicing Christianity as it was in the beginning, we do not observe Christmas as a special holy day. God gave his church only one special day, the first day of the week. This is the day of Christ's resurrection and the day of the church's beginning (Mark 16:1-2; Acts 2). Jesus tells us to "observe all things whatsoever (he) commanded" (Matt. 28:20). But he did not command a Christmas observance. Paul warns us "not to go beyond the things which are written" (I Cor. 4:6 ASV). He was concerned for those who observed "days, and months, and seasons and years" lest his labor with them be in vain (Gal. 4:10-11). While we enjoy the fellowship, and festivities of the season, we believe that we should remember and be grateful for Christ's birth every day and that our charity and generosity should extend through out the year.

There are many great lessons for daily life in the story of Christ's birth.
* We see God's marvelous love. He so loved us that he **gave** his only begotten Son (John 3:16).
* That Christ came into the world as "a child born" demonstrates God's love and respect for the innocence of infancy. Children are not born totally depraved with sin. Rather, we must become as little children if we would enter the kingdom of heaven (Matt.

18:3). This implies their innocence. In a society where one of three children conceived is legally aborted, we are reminded of the sacredness of innocent human life.
* Christ's birth of Mary reminds us of God's concern for woman. Through woman came sin and the fall. God redeemed womanhood by allowing Mary to bring the Savior into the world. In that unique sense, the world is saved through "her childbearing" (I Tim. 2:13-15). Through Christ, woman was saved from the degradation of the pagan world. Before he came, they were little more than the chattel and amusement of men. Now there is no male or female in Christ (Gal. 3:26-28). Now we honor them as "joint heirs of the grace of life" (I Pet. 3:27). We also see God's respect for purity in that he chose a virgin to be the mother of his Son (Lk. 1:34).
* This story teaches us respect for manhood and fatherhood. God gave Joseph the privilege and responsibility of providing for and protecting the infant Savior. We need fathers like him who will nurture their children "in the chastening and admonition of the Lord" (Eph. 6:4).
* The birth of Jesus demonstrates God's respect for and interest in the family. His son was placed in a loving, caring, devout family with a mother, father, and siblings. This sacred concept of family has been seriously eroded in our day, but it is the strength of the church and society and the hope for the future well-being of the race.
* We see in this record, God's respect for the poor of the earth. He could have sent his Son into the home of a rich and noble family, but he chose a poor one in a poor community to receive the blessing. The poor were not neglected in the ministry of Christ (Matt. 11:5).
* God's appreciation for labor and hard work are reflected in his allowing Jesus to grow up as a carpenter with Joseph (Mk. 6:3). There is dignity in labor. Working with one's hands is not shameful (Eph. 4:28), but there is shame in laziness (Prov. 6:6-11).
* The story tells us there is a place for people of all stations in the

kingdom; be they lowly shepherds or wise kings. The gospel is for every social and ethnic group (Matt. 28:19). With God's people there can be no respect of persons (Acts 10:35).

* This timeless story reminds us of our desperate plight as sinners before a just God. If we were to be saved, Christ had to come and "die for the ungodly" (Rom. 5:6).

Our commitment to Christ demands all of our love and service 365 days each year. It also demands that we not go beyond the teaching which Christ left us (II John 9-11).

81. TRADITIONS

A tradition is a belief or practice handed down from generation to generation. All institutions and organizations have their traditional ways of doing things. Traditions can be beneficial, detrimental or inconsequential, depending on how they impact on an institution. Churches are no exception.

There are **holy traditions** passed down to us from Christ through his apostles. We are commanded to "stand fast, and hold the traditions which (ye) were taught, whether by word, or by epistle of ours" (II Thess. 2:15). Holy traditions were given by Christ and must be observed as his divine will (Heb. 5:9). Our faith, worship and practice must be based on these divine traditions. To be a holy tradition, worthy of our observance, it must be as old as the New Testament and found therein. Among those holy traditions are baptism for the remission of sins (Acts 2:38); baptism as the entrance into the church (I Cor. 12:13); communion with both bread and fruit of the vine (Matt. 26:26-29). For disciples to wear the name Christian is a holy tradition (I Pet. 4:16).

There are traditions of men. Jesus told the leaders of the Jews "ye have made void the word of God because of your tradition . . . in vain do they worship me teaching as the doctrines the precepts of men"

(Matt. 15:6-9). Any religious teaching or practice originating this side of Christ and the apostles is a tradition of men, as is any teaching that is contrary to the New Testament of Christ.

Infant baptism: "by a tradition at least as old as the 3rd century . . . children born to Christian parents have been baptized in infancy **(Oxford Dict. of Christ. Church**, p. 689).
* **Sprinkling for baptism**: "In the primitive church, baptism was by immersion . . . the council of Ravenna (1311) was the first to allow a choice between sprinkling and immersion" **(Ency. of Rel. Knowledge**, Vol. 1, p. 201).
* **Frequency of Communion**: "from such passages as Acts 20:7, and various 2nd century writers it seems that the members of local churches all communed at the Sunday Eucharist. But in latter times . . . communion became very infrequent" **(Ox. Dict. Of Christ. Ch. p. 319)**.
* **Instrumental music in worship**: "the general introduction of instrumental music can certainly not be assigned to a date earlier than the 5th and 6th century" **(M'Clintock & Strong's Ency**. Vol. 6, 759).

To prefer these human traditions over the teachings of God's word makes our worship vain (Matt. 15:6). To be pleasing to God, we must be unyielding in our commitment to honor and observe the sacred traditions of Christ and eschew all traditions of men.

82. MORE ABOUT TRADITIONS

Traditions of men that hinder obedience to God stand condemned (Matt. 15:6). Traditions from God and his inspired writers must be honored and obeyed (II Thess. 3:6). Harmless traditions can be followed or rejected according to time, place and circumstances.

* Our choice of **Bible translations** is in part a matter of tradition. For many there is only one Bible to read, the King James

Version. Others prefer more modern versions. Since Scripture was originally written in Hebrew and Greek, the only way most of us can read it at all is by the use of a translation. Some translations are poor and others are better, but by and large it is a matter of personal choice. Use the one you cherish, but allow others the same privilege.

* We have traditions about **Gospel (Revival) Meetings, Vacation Bible Schools, Spiritual Workshops, Bible Camps** and other activities. The longer we observe a particular program, the more sacred and important it becomes to us. God tells us to preach and teach his word (Mk.16:15), but he nowhere prescribes specific programs like those mentioned above. Some churches may decide to do their teaching in a different format. Such is their privilege. We can do it our way and they can do it theirs. Neither sins; neither is more righteous than the other.
* The fact that we have **no female preachers or elders** is a divine tradition handed down from God (I Cor. 14:32-33; I Tim. 2:9-12). We have no choice, we can only obey or disobey God.
* Some denominations **make converts wait for baptism** until an appointed day, or until they have proven themselves. This tradition violates God's example that folks were baptized at the time they came to conviction about their need for salvation (Comp. Acts 8:35-38; 16:33).
* Some folks have a tradition of **baptizing infants**. Such a practice is unknown to the Scripture. There all candidates for baptism were old enough to believe, repent and confess their faith. They made their own choice to be baptized. Thus, this tradition hinders folks from being baptized in God's appointed way.

Part of my job as a teacher is to help folks distinguish between the holy and the common, the unclean and the clean so they may understand and obey the ordinances of God (Lev. 10:10-11). Should you visit a congregation of God's people who do things differently than you are use to, always ask yourself, is it a matter of God's tradition or man's? Is it a sinful or harmless tradition? If it is of the harmless variety, then accept their way as you worship with them.

83. OBSERVATIONS ON TRADITIONS

All churches have traditions. Some traditions are divine in origin and must be honored (II Thess. 3:6). Other traditions originated with men and hinder folks from obeying God's will. Such must be rejected (Matt. 15:6). Still other traditions are harmless. They are established ways of doing things that give continuity and order to our services. With such traditions we know what to expect when we come together to worship.

* We have a tradition of a **one hour worship service**. The Bible nowhere tells us how long to spend in our assemblies. In other countries I have visited, their tradition called for two or more hours in worship. Either is acceptable. Each congregation must decide such matters for itself.
* Our tradition calls for **half hour sermons**. Again God does not prescribe a time frame for a sermon. Such traditions help us plan the use of our time in worship and afterward. Such a tradition is of human origin, but it is not forbidden. We could not however bind it on others.
* Our tradition expects **a preacher to wear a coat and tie** when he stands up to preach. In Bible times they wore no ties or modern style coats. In third world countries, they have different dress styles and a preacher might be perfectly in order to wear casual clothes. We should dress appropriately for the occasion and so as not to cause anyone to take offense at our dress. We must not insist that brethren in all other lands must observe our tradition.
* Our tradition is that we **wear shoes to church**. Most of us would frown on the adult who came barefoot. In many Asian churches, folks are expected to leave their shoes at the door. To wear them in worship would be considered disrespectful. Neither is bound by God. We are free to observe our tradition in the matter.
* Our **meeting houses** are built according to our traditions. We expect them to be suitable for the community in which we live. We heat and air-condition them. We carpet the floors and cover the pews. Christians in other parts of the world have meeting

places that conform to their traditions. Many have no heating or cooling. In some places it is not needed, in others they view such as wasteful use of God's money. Where roads are unpaved, carpeted floors are not suitable. Since God does not address the type of buildings we should have, each congregation is free to make its own choices in the matter. Our choices cannot be bound on others.

Traditions we have. May God help us discern which of them are good, bad and harmless. Let us always be ready to obey those from God; reject those that hinder our obedience to Him and be flexible in those that are harmless and useful our work and worship.

84. FALSE EQUATIONS

"Equate" means to treat, represent, or regard as equal, equivalent or comparable. Experience tells us that many of the equations people try to make are in fact false. Reading the literature of the "change agents" working among us I am struck by the numerous false equations found therein.

* **Old does not equal useless**. They tend to discount, denigrate and toss out anything that brethren did before they (the change agents) came along.
* **New does not equal good**. New methods and approaches may or may not be beneficial. But some are clearly contrary to the revealed will of God and some are detrimental to the body. These folks have a bundle of new ideas and practices for our people. Old timers use to call them innovations.
* **Big does not equal right**. True, the change agents have captured several of our largest congregations. They aspire to build mega churches like their role models of the denominational "Community Church" movement have done. Success and growth are only good and right if they are based upon the Word of Christ (John 12:48).

* **Small does not equal failure or bad.** To read the criticism of the "progressives" the large number of our small congregations suggests that something is missing in our approach. They fail to factor in that the masses of humanity have always and will always reject the gospel call. They don't understand the Biblical truth that "it is the remnant that will be saved" (Rom. 9:27).
* **Faith without obedience does not equal acceptance by God.** God says through James that it is dead and useless (Jas.2:24-26).
* **Grace plus nothing on man's part does not equal salvation** as some of them say. Paul says it is grace plus faith (Eph. 2:8-9) that saves. Jesus said obedience must be factored in (John 12:48).
* **Youth and popularity do not equal being pleasing to God.** The Baby-boomers have now reached the age of leadership. They tend to ignore those who are older as they aspire to lead the younger. That they are wooed by the advertising industry and retailers does not make them special with the Creator. With omniscient eyes He sees the selfish, shallow, presumptuous fickleness many of them demonstrate in their conduct.
* **Applause of the denominational world does not equal approval of God.** That a brother writes books designed to please the denominational world and is praised by them for so doing is an indictment rather than an honor. Its like writing, "In the beginning the world evolved," and being applauded by the advocates of evolution.
* **Advanced educational degrees do not equal Bible knowledge.** Most of the promoters of change proudly display their badges of academic achievement. But those who are steeped in the word of God know that many of them are bloated with human wisdom rather than filled with wisdom from Above.
* **Denial of intent to reshape the church of Christ into a denomination does not equate with reality.** By the fruits ye shall know them, said Christ (Matt. 7:16).
* **Pretense does not equal reality.** Pretending to love the church of Christ, to be faithful members thereof, does not necessarily prove to be true. Again, one must look at the churches where

these men hold forth to see just how they regard the church of our Lord. Results speak louder than pretense.

* **Using a new paradigm for interpreting the Bible does not equal a correct understanding of it.** Read their new book, **God's Holy Fire** (ACU Press), and see just how faulty their "New Hermeneutic," learned from denominational scholars, really is.

Because some dishonest business people use faulty scales to enrich themselves, the government maintains a Bureau of Weights and Measurements. Because of the false equations mentioned above, wise Christians will be extremely cautious of any brother, book or school that promotes "changes" for churches of Christ.

85. I'M NOT ASHAMED

Paul was not ashamed of the gospel. He understood that it was God's power to save men (Rom. 1:16). Our predecessors, who set out some 200 years ago to restore New Testament Christianity, paid a great price for their faith and commitment. They not only loved God and Jesus, they loved the Bible and the Church and were unashamed to stand foursquare on and for them. Today a pathetic situation has emerged among some of our people. We see actions that signal that some among us are ashamed of some of the fundamental aspects of the ancient faith.

Some are evidently ashamed of the Biblical name, "church of Christ" (Rom. 16:16), as they have ceased to identify themselves thereby. They choose rather to be known as "Community Churches" or some other nondescript cognomen.

Clearly there are some who are ashamed of the ancient gospel plan of salvation. They poke fun at the gospel their parents and grandparents believed and obeyed. Their gospel of salvation by grace, varies but little from that of their Protestant neighbors. No longer does one hear the clarion call for believers to repent and be baptized in the name of Jesus (Acts 2:38). They still baptize but almost apologetically and it is very likely many of their converts do not understand why they were immersed.

Some are ashamed of the simple New Testament worship of Christ's church. They thirst for something new and different. Not content with the Biblical worship handed down across the ages, they prefer the expressions of worship they see among their denominational neighbors, especially that of the Pentecostal variety.

There are some who have grown tired of singing the great hymns of the faith without instrumental accompaniment. Sadly, a few have actually opened their doors to the use of man-made instruments. But others are just behind them with their acappella bands. Others groan under the restraints of congregational singing. They long for a choir and soloists. Today their choirs sit in the audience. Ere long they will be in the choir loft and worshipers will watch as the professional singers entertain them for worship.

Without doubt some are ashamed of old time Bible preaching. Book chapter and verse preaching and discussions of doctrinal themes are now passe'. These folks prefer story telling, emotional testifying and entertainment for their sermons.

Some are obviously ashamed of the nondenominational Christianity we have long practiced. They long to be more like their denominational neighbors (I Sam. 8:20). They do not mind being identified as a denomination among the others. It brings respectability. They speak of Alexander Campbell and B. W. Stone as their founders. They speak of our unwritten creed.

Some seem to be ashamed of the concept of one bonafide and genuine Church of Christ. Their fathers believed that there was only one body (church, Eph. 1:22) just as there is one Father and Lord Jesus (Eph. 4:4-5). The sons now believe that many different kinds of churches make up the one body of Christ.

We should pity these brethren. They are not faithful to Christ, his Will and his Church. Nor does their compromise make them fully acceptable with the denominational world. They are lost in a limbo, ashamed of the truth that can set them free. May God grant us courage and conviction so that we will never be ashamed of the Christianity delivered unto us; that we may be faithful unto death (Rev. 2:10).

86. PROFANING THE HOLY

In ancient times things that were sacred and devoted God were described as "holy." Especially were the items associated with the worship of God in his temple considered holy. To misuse or mishandle God's sacred things was the sin of profanation (Lev. 19:8). For profane hands to touch that which was holy was a great offense to God and a shock to the sensibilities of his righteous servants. "They shall not profane the holy things... which they offer unto Jehovah and so cause them to bear the iniquity that bringeth guilt" (Lev. 22:15). God charged unfaithful priests with doing "violence to my law, and have profaned my holy things; they ... made no distinction between the holy and the common ... " (Ezek. 22:26).

When Korah, Dathan and Abiram challenged Moses and Aaron for the leadership of Israel, it was not only rebellion but profanation (Num. 16:1-40). When Uzziah the king of Judah sought to enter the holy place and offer incense it was a profane deed for which God severely punished him (II Chron. 26:16-21).

Some acts of profanation were flagrant and diabolic. Such it was when Antiochus Epiphanes, king of Syria erected an image of Zeus in the temple of God and then ordered a swine to be sacrificed and its blood scattered over God's sacred things. Other profanations were not deliberate or malicious, nevertheless they were harshly dealt with by Jehovah. When David was moving the ark of the covenant from Kiriath-jearim to Jerusalem, he failed to follow the divine procedure that it be carried by staves, on the shoulders of the Levites (Deut. 10:8; I Chron. 15:2). They carefully placed the ark on a new cart draw by oxen. When the oxen stumbled, Uzzah, one of the attendants, fearing the ark was going to fall, reached out to stabalize it. Not being a Levite, he was not authorized to touch the ark. God smote him and he died (I Chron. 13:10). This harsh lesson emphasized for all ages the importance of absolute respect for all things holy to Jehovah.

The church of Christ, purchased by the dying blood of God's Son, is holy (Acts 20:28). His testament is also ratified and sanctified by his precious blood (Matt. 26:28; Heb. 9:17-18). Holy also are the doctrine, ordinances and practices ordained by the founder, head and savior of the church. We are warned against teaching "a different doctrine" (I Tim. 1:3).

No mortal man is authorized to tamper with or change the holy things of Christ's religion. To add to or take from them is to invite disaster (Rev.22:18-19). When preachers and teachers presume to ignore, modify or change the holy practices, principles and doctrines given by Christ they are placing profane hands on that which is holy!

* When God says that we are to "hold the pattern of sound words" (II Tim. 1:13) and promoters of change deny that there is a divine pattern, they profane the Word of God.
* When change agents attempt to change the praise ordained by heaven from "singing and making melody with your heart" (Eph. 5:19) to sing and making melody on an organ, they have profaned that which is holy!
* When they seek to change the Lord's Supper from a sacred memorial (I Cor. 11:25) to a joyous festival and part of a fellowship meal they have profaned the holy.
* When they would replace the proclamation of the gospel (Mk.

16:15; Rom. 1:16) with stories, jokes and promotions of common, ordinary things, they are profaning the holy.
* When they turn the worship of God into a theater for entertainment it is profanation!
* When they would elevate women to position of public leadership in the church even though God has specifically denied that to them (I Cor. 14:33-34; I Tim. 2:11-12), they have profaned God's holy things.
* When they seek to gain possession of houses of worship and schools built and paid for by other Christians for the honor and glory of God and use them for their new doctrines and practices, such is profanation.
* When they discount and poke fun at the sacred name, "churches of Christ" (Rom. 16:16), such is profanation. Such sarcastic expressions as the "Churches of Christ of the yellow pages" smells of profanation.
* When they dare to tell sinners that they can be saved by grace, before they are immersed in the name of Jesus for the remission of their sins (Acts 2:38), they are profaning the holy.
* When they deny that Christians are in any way or sense under the law of Christ, even though the Holy Spirit teaches that we must be submissive to the royal law of Christ (Jas. 2:8), the perfect law of liberty in Christ (Jas. 1:25) they are profaning the Holy will of God.
* When they seek to broaden the fellowship of Christ's family to those not born into it (John 3:3,5), they profane it.
* When the pit their human wisdom against the revealed will of God that too is profanation.

Given the severity with which God dealt with profaners of his sacred things in days past, the prudent man will take care not to take any unauthorized liberties with God's Word, his church, his doctrine and his worship today.

Lest we be found encouragers of these profaners, every man and woman should roundly reject any and every man who proposes to make changes to the holy things of God. We don't want to partake of other men's sins (I Tim. 5:22) lest we share in their punishments.

87. CAN YOU SEE THE WOLF?

Some preachers among us have been **"shouting wolf"** for the last 35 years. Time and again brethren looked but could not find the wolf. After a while, many became inured to the warnings of the wolf-warners. They finally decided those who were constantly sounding the alarm did not merit their attention. Such a response was just what Satan hoped for. Now, with their eyes closed and ears plugged, he could do his work of infiltrating churches with no serious opposition. Muffled and blindfolded, preachers and elders neither saw nor heard as the Adversary's minions did their work. First they captured the administration and Bible departments of some of our schools. The Father of Lies emboldened a few our successful young preachers to launch a program of change. Intoxicated with the taste of their "new wine," they worked evangelistically to recruit others to join their campaign.

When more responsible watchmen saw these **real wolves** savaging many churches and sounded a warning, the majority of our preachers and elders still had their blindfolds and earplugs in place. They could not hear. Many did not wish to hear or see. Such knowledge is disconcerting to the complacent. Warnings were brushed aside as scare-mongering, complaints from preachers jealous of others' success, nitpicking or other ignoble motives.

Last month (Aug. 03) a leading change agent issued a bold announcement that rang a bell even the deaf could hear and caused a flash of light that pierced the thickest blinders. Max Lucado, the most daring of the change agents and the darling of our liberal brothers, preached a sermon announcing a new agenda for his Oak Hills Church of Christ in San Antonio.
* Their name would be changed to "Oak Hills Church." His logic was, "Some people find the name 'church of Christ' to be an insurmountable barrier . . . Let's seek to remove any barrier that would hinder a person from hearing the Gospel." Immersion is also a barrier to many. Jesus as Lord is a barrier to Jews and

Muslims!
* He proposed, "establishing Oak Hills Campuses in other sections of the city. These satellite churches will at least initially, be a part of the Oak Hills family . . . Our multi-site churches could stay linked together by viewing a video of the sermon from the 'mother church.'" In the world of Catholicism, this is called a diocesan form of church government.
* Instrumental music would be used in their Sunday evening services for young adults. Max said, "I will present the . . . message and we will target twenty and thirty year-olds. Recognizing the power of contemporary music, the new assemblies will be instrumental . . . A soft keyboard beneath an altar call, the sound of a cello during communion service . . . I am convinced instrumentation reaches hearts . . . We feel it is wise to use this tool." Note his absence of Scriptural authorization for this change. For change agents "feelings" trump Scripture when it gets in the way.
* In an interview in the **San Antonio Express-News** (9/6/03), Vic King, Oak Hills' minister of missions, said "Oak Hills' core values are similar to those of other **evangelical churches**." He continued, "Oak Hills also believes that salvation doesn't come through baptism, but that baptism is the initial step of obedience after salvation." .
* Their core values were said to be like the "Evangelical" churches. In "lay" terms, this refers to Baptists, Reformed Churches, Assemblies of God and other "conservative" denominational bodies.
* Bro. Lucado also said, "Our Lord called us to be a force for unity among San Antonio Churches. We, for the first time, 'swapped pulpits' with Trinity Baptist Church."

Now I ask those who preach and those shepherd our churches: Can you see the wolf? Yes, Bro. Lucado is gifted and an effective, successful writer. Yes, he has had far greater acceptance among those outside our brotherhood than any other writer. Yes, he did attend Abilene Christian University. Yes he once was a missionary and a preacher of truth and righteousness. Please, take off the blindfold, remove the earplugs and see the sad and ugly truth. This brother and the church he serves have abandoned New Testament Christianity for the appealing fields of "Evangelical" Protestantism. Like Hymenaeus and Alexander, they have made shipwreck of the faith (I Tim. 1:19-20). Given his high visibility, his popularity and success Bro. Lucado will influence many young men to emulate his example.

As unfortunate as this case is, Bro. Lucado and Oak Hills congregation are but one example of scores of others who have done likewise. A tidal wave of error is sweeping across the face of our brotherhood. It will eventually reach your congregation. The time to prepare for this invasion and protect your flock is ***now***! Ours are not premature or unfounded warnings. The wolves are already within the fold. Many casualties have already been suffered. For the sake of the Lord Jesus and his holy church, rise up and be the faithful watchmen and shepherds God expects you to be!

88. WHEN THE WALLS CAME DOWN

We all know the story of ancient Jericho, how the strong walls of that fortified city crumbled and fell before the children of Israel (Josh. 6:20-21). Those walls were brought down by God. Today we are witnessing other walls crumbling and falling, the result of the preaching, writing and teaching of certain brethren who fancy themselves sufficiently wise to change the faith, worship and practice of the Lord's church.

I. The ancient wall between the Lord's one true church and the hundreds of man-made denominational churches is crumbling and already down in many places. The Book of God makes it crystal clear that Christ has only one church (Eph. 4:4-5; 1:22). It also plainly condemns divisions into contending religious factions (I Cor. 1:10-15; 3:1-4). For two thousand years our brethren have preached and called men into the church founded by Christ and opposed denominationalism as contrary to God's will. Today a new breed of preachers and professors blush not to say that we ourselves are but another denomination and that other denominations are equally acceptable to Christ. With all their vaunted learning, they are unable to see the distinction between the real and the counterfeit (Lev. 10:10).

II. The wall between truth and error is crumbling before the false teaching of relativism and subjectivism that is emanating from several of our universities. The fact is, God's Word is truth (John 17:17). We have that on the highest authority; Jesus! It is objective truth, neither relative nor subjective. It is a solid, reliable standard that exists separate and apart from man, churches, schools of thought and educational institutions. "The word of Jehovah is right" (Ps. 33:4). It is "perfect" (Ps. 19:7). It is "settled in heaven" (Ps. 119:89). It will "never pass away" (Matt. 24:35). It is God-given (II Pet. 1:20-21). It will judge us in the last day (John 12:48). If every last believer in Christ with all their schools, books and papers perished, the Word of God would still stand, true and dependable. If all the world of Christendom embraces skepticism and denigrates and denies the Word, it will still stand and judge them in the last day! For 200 years our brethren have believed and taught this fundamental truth. Today our "agents of change" are hammering away at this wall.

III. The wall between God-ordained worship and "will-worship" based on emotion and popular opinion is crumbling. The worship which God expects of us must be "in spirit and truth" (John 4:24). It is sincere and heart felt and it is as he has ordered in his divine Revelation. His worship is simple and unadorned without pomp and pageantry. It needs no cathedral or vast throng to validate it. True worship, of necessity, is based squarely on the New Covenant of Christ (Matt. 28:20). We cannot look to Moses or David for our authority (Matt.17:4-8). We dare not look to uninspired teachers and theologians of the denominational world!

The most notable changes proposed by our "change agents" are in the realm of public worship of the church. They want acceptance of instrumental music, choirs and solos. They want women allowed a leadership role. They want drama and skits. They want emotionalism and excitement. Paul calls such "will-worship" (Col. 2:23).

IV. The wall between Bible preaching and emotion-driven entertainment and story telling is crumbling. For 200 years our preachers operated under the mandate of Christ to "preach the gospel" (Mk. 16:15). They felt obliged to "speak as the oracle of God" (I Pet. 4:11), and to preach the whole counsel of God (Acts 20:27). Faithful elders knew that it was through the "foolishness of the preaching" that God ordained to save men (I Cor. 1:21). Today, many young preachers, groomed and trained in "Christian" universities, much prefer "story-telling" and emotional hoopla to Bible preaching. The wall is already down in some quarters.

V. The wall between the Biblical plan of salvation and human ideas about how to be saved is breached. From the beginning of our back to the Bible movement, our brethren have understood and preached salvation as a free gift of God's grace (Eph. 2:8-9) that required faith (Heb. 11:6) repentance and baptism (Acts 2:38) on the part of those wishing to receive that salvation. Now a new kind of preacher moves among us telling the lost that salvation is by grace alone or by faith alone and thus denying the message of the author of eternal salvation (Heb. 5:8-9). Bro. Rubel Shelly says, "My salvation is on grace alone, Not by anything I've added to it." "The one step of salvation is faith . . . " "It (baptism) is not the fifth step (in the plan of salvation)." (Quotes from Shelly's recorded sermons, cited in **Change Agents and Churches of Christ** by William Woodson, p. 36).

VI. The wall between heaven ordained male leadership for the church and the human doctrine of female leadership is pierced. God's position is clear: "as in all the churches of the saints, let the women keep silence in the church: for it is not permitted unto them to speak, but let them be in subjection (I Cor. 14:33-34). Although churches of men have long ignored heaven's decree, our brethren have honored it; that is, until the "change movement" emerged among us. Now we have teachers and professors preferring the authority of the feminist leaders over Christ and agitating for women to serve in church leadership roles. The elders of the Church of Christ in West Islip, NY have proudly published the fact that Katie Hays serves their congregation "as a minister in the fullest sense of that calling... This includes preaching from the pulpit" (**Christian Chronicle** on line, September, 2002)! Having gone beyond the doctrine of Christ, they have not God (II John 9).

VII. The wall between a verbally inspired and inerrant Bible and a fallible, human document, uncertain in origin, unreliable in content and impotent in authority has been broken. For two centuries our brethren have observed this flagrant unbelief among our denomination neighbors. Many of those who abandoned the Old Paths last century for instruments of music and missionary societies eventually embraced this low view of Scripture. But our men stood strong, until recently. From the classrooms of our universities a trickle of unbelief in the inerrancy and authority of God's Word has grown to dangerous proportions. In days past, our preachers and teachers encountered this skepticism only when they enrolled in denominational seminaries or secular schools of higher learning. Now our sons come face to face with it in some of our schools.

It was an act of God, for the benefit of his people when Jericho's walls came down. It is an act of Satan for the harm of the church when the walls mentioned above are breached.

89. HEROES WHO PAVED THE WAY FOR US

In my 47 years in the brotherhood of Churches of Christ I have been privileged to meet, hear and know many of the men who proved themselves heroes of the faith. They loved God, they served Christ wholeheartedly, they led thousands to the Savior. They built up the churches in which we now serve. While this list is not comprehensive, it is representative of what preachers of the church of which we are part believed and did in their labors for the Master.

B. C. Goodpasture preached until his death in his 83rd year. He served as an elder in the Hillsboro church in Nashville. For upwards of 50 years he edited the **Gospel Advocate**, the most influential gospel paper ever published among us. He loved the church. He believed that we need to keep our ties with those who had preceded us in the kingdom. He published scores of great books by our pioneer preachers so we could understand how the church began and grew here in America and the message they preached.

Gus Nichols preached for the Sixth Ave. Church in Jasper, AL for most of his life but his influence was felt throughout the Southeastern part of the nation. He was a great evangelist and led several thousand to salvation in Christ. He planted numerous congregations in North Alabama. Not only was he a great preacher, he was a great debater, often defending the faith against the teachers of error. He was humble as a little child.

James D. Bales was a towering scholar among us. Most of his career was spent as a professor at Harding University. He wrote over 100 wonderful books. He conducted numerous debates, especially with unbelievers. His knowledge of God's Word and related subjects was legendary.

Batsell B. Baxter devoted most of his years to teaching at David Lipscomb College. In addition, he preached for the great Hillsboro congregation. For years he was the featured speaker on the Herald of Truth radio and T. V. broadcasts. He was known, respected and loved for his loyalty to Christ, his masterful preaching and his humility. The outreach of his preaching was greater than any man among us.

Guy N. Woods spent most of his years conducting evangelistic meetings. He was the most effective debater of his generation. He was a masterful writer and logician and in later years served as editor of the **Gospel Advocate**. He wrote adult Sunday School materials for years. For some 20 years he conducted the Open Forum at the Freed-Hardeman College Lectureships.

L. O. Sanderson was the most prominent songwriter and editor of hymnals in his generation. For years he served the Gospel Advocate in the preparation of their several hymnals. Being a gifted writer, teacher and leader of music, he worked diligently to see that the songs in our hymnals reflected truth and not error in their lyrics and that they actually contributed to the worship experience of those who sang them.

Otis Gatewood was the best know missionary of the post WWII period. He had proven himself in his mission work in Utah's Mormon country where he converted many and planted several congregations. Following the war, he led a group of dedicated young missionaries into Germany. Many of the churches we now have in Europe owe their existence to his wonderful influence. He refused to allow the Iron Curtain of Communism to keep him out of Eastern Europe and Russia and at great risk to himself he led the way in planting the church there as well. He was a scholar as well as a great organizer and leader. He was honored by the governments of Germany and Russia.

All of these heroes of the faith believed that the church of which they were part was the church of Christ revealed in the New Testament. They believed that denominationalism was wrong. They viewed the New Testament of Christ as the only rule of faith and practice for God's people. They all preached that salvation by grace was available only to those who in faith, repented and were baptized for the remission of their sins. They all taught that in worship, we are to sing without instrumental accompaniment and that we are to commune each Lord's Day. They were committed to the principle of restoring the original faith and practice of the apostolic church. They were unwilling to compromise with religious error. "Remember the days of old, Consider the years of many generations: Ask thy father, and he will show thee; Thine elders, and they will tell thee" (Deut. 32:7). May we learn from these great heroes.

90. MORE HEROES WHO PAVED THE WAY

Churches of Christ are scattered across the nation and around the world because dedicated men of God devoted their lives to evangelizing and planting churches in generations past. It has been my privilege to know many of these soldiers of the cross whose memory is blessed. We are indebted to them inasmuch as they cleared the path over which we now travel. They helped to remove the obstacles and build the bridges we now use. Lest we forget them and the contributions they made, I share with you a few brief memories of them.

Marshal Keeble was the greatest preacher among our Black brethren. The child of former slaves, he grew up in poverty and with limited education. Yet he became a highly capable preacher of God's Word and led upwards of 20,000 to the Lord. He helped to plant well over a hundred congregations across the nation. He founded and directed **Nashville Christian Institute** that trained and sent forth hundreds of leaders for the African-American churches. His humility was as legendary as his preaching.

J. C. Bailey was a Canadian and spent most of his preaching years in his home country. Many of our congregations in Canada owe their beginning to his labors. At age 68 he went to India and God crowned his final labors with success he could have never dreamed of. It is estimated by some that as many as 100,000 turned to Christ through that old man's labors. He continued to visit India until he was in his 80s.

Jim Massey was a missionary. He spent many years in Nigeria and led several campaign groups to that and other foreign lands. Jim was a gifted writer, a tireless worker and utterly fearless. Thousands will be in heaven because of his labors. He taught for many years at International Bible College in Florence, AL. He blessed a generation who knew him.

Bob Hare went to Germany with Otis Gatewood following WWII. Most of his adult life was spent working there and in Eastern Europe. He was brave beyond words, risking his freedom and even his life, to smuggle Bibles to the slaves of Communism and to preach the saving gospel to them. Our many churches in Eastern Church sprang from the work of Bro. Hare.

John Hardin was a longtime missionary to South Africa. He went first, just to assist the preachers who were laboring there, but soon emerged as a leader of the workers in that nation. He taught and trained young preachers, he planted churches throughout southern Africa.

Ira North preached for the largest church among us, the Madison church near Nashville. God gave him uncommon ability to organize, plan and accomplish great things for Jesus. At his death he left behind a flourishing childcare home, a home for elderly Christians, a flourishing Christian Camp, a nationwide T.V. ministry and a congregation of some 6,000. For years he taught at David Lipscomb College and for a while edited the **Gospel Advocate** magazine. He loved the church and held fast to the faith. He knew you could have a flourishing church and still be faithful to the teaching of Christ.

All of these heroes of the faith lived and served under the conviction that Christ has only one church. They believed that we were God's people and were not ashamed to preach that all who were saved would be part of the church of Christ. They believed that all things we believe and do must be anchored in the authority of the New

Testament of Christ. They all believed that it was our sacred duty to commune each Lord's Day and to sing our hymns without instrumental accompaniment. They were willing to stand alone rather than compromise with denominational error. They loved the brotherhood. They cherished the memory of those who went before us. "Their works do follow them" (Rev. 14:13). We are their debtors. May we be worthy of the bequest they left us.

IX.
IF WE ARE TO SURVIVE THIS ASSAULT

91. A CLARION CALL TO THE SOLDIERS OF CHRIST

The church of our day is facing an unprecedented challenge. A wave of apostasy is challenging the integrity and existence of our congregations such as has not been seen since the end of the 19th century. Large numbers of our younger members and significant numbers of congregations appear ready to embrace these false prophets of change. Several of our Christian Universities are already in their camp and some of their professors are among the most vocal spokesmen for the digressives. Our largest gospel paper is now a sounding board for their champions and their innovations. A call is being sent across our great brotherhood for volunteers who are willing to do battle to save the church of Christ from the forces of apostasy.

* We must raise up an army of men willing to publicly stand in opposition to these agents of change. We need no summer soldiers or fair-weather patriots. We need courageous men who are set for the defense of the gospel (Phil. 1:16), no matter how long the struggle lasts. Likely, many of us will finish our course before the church is delivered from those who have set out to make a denomination of her.
* We must be willing to devote our energies to fighting a common enemy rather than each other. Of course we will disagree on some points, some methods and strategies. Brethren always have. But we must not lose sight of whom the real enemy is. The change agents are counting on us being so consumed with internal strife and bickering that we will not be able to mount an effective resistance against them. Such distraction has

neutralized strong armies in the past.
* We must mount an offensive campaign rather than waiting for the promoters of change to attack our positions. Remember the old military maxim, "A strong offense is the best defense." Too long too many elders and preachers have waited until the enemy was within their gates before they responded. Even if they manage to force them out, they almost certainly will lose some members and suffer damage.
* We must build a defense perimeter around and protect our own congregations, but we must also accept responsibility for defending the kingdom at large. If we save our local congregation but the rest of the brotherhood is swept away we will have suffered a terrible loss.
* We must promote the common good. Important as are our personal projects and local works, we must not neglect the welfare of the kingdom of God throughout the world. We must encourage every good work done by faithful brethren wherever they may be.
* We must be willing to help each other in the combat we will be facing. Such spiritual conflicts sometimes leave a man in a lonely, isolated position. We must lend such good men every possible encouragement. Two men fighting together can usually accomplish more than each standing alone. The Duke of Wellington attributed his victory over Napoleon to that fact that he had the good fortune to lead a "band of brothers" in combat.
* We must not allow old loyalties and friendships to silence us. The fact that we once attended a school or enjoyed a friendship is not an acceptable reason to stand with muted voice if they now are working to harm the church of our Lord.
* Each of us must be willing, without shame or hesitation, to recruit as many soldiers as possible to our holy cause. We call them not to our party or clique. We call them to be "good soldiers of Christ Jesus" (II Tim. 2:3). The "change people" are busily recruiting young men to their "new" faith and practice. Each man of sound faith and conviction must use his influence to win his neighbor to the Savior's side in this conflict.

* We must be willing to discriminate. Do not lend the least aid or comfort to the enemy. He who would place unholy hands on the faith and worship of the Lord's church should find no welcome among us. Don't promote their projects or their personnel. Such can only bring harm to the Cause we love. Do not contribute to their projects. Do not recommend students to attend their schools.
* We need to know our friends as well as our enemies. Lend your aid, support and encouragement to every brother who is faithfully serving in his post of duty. Count him your ally and stand shoulder to shoulder with him in battle.
* We must whet our sword and repair our armor lest we meet the enemy unprepared (Eph. 6:13-17). Read the books of the false teachers so you will know first hand what they are saying. Read the books written to refute them. Attend lectures and seminars addressing these issues. Subscribe to good papers that will keep you posted on what is happening and provide you valuable ammunition for the battle. Fill your quiver with the arrows of truth that will put to flight the agents of change.
* We must consult with one another about strategy and coordinate our efforts lest we duplicate or counteract one another, or lest we allow another a good soldier or congregation to be overrun by the opposition. Use your phone, the Internet or mail to keep in touch with your fellow-soldiers. Share information; help each other to be informed and encouraged.
* The future of churches of Christ in America depends on the loyalty of her men of arms. Where do you stand?

92. HOW IMPORTANT IS THE PRESERVATION OF CHRIST'S CHURCH TO YOU?

The church of our Lord Jesus is under a massive attack throughout the nation. This is no ordinary, run of the mill problem such as we have faced in times past. Not since the great apostasy of the late 1800s have we encountered a problem of this magnitude. After years of quietly infiltrating our schools and congregations, what has come to be known as the **"change movement,"** has now burst forth in full blossom. At least two of our most prominent schools and dozens of congregations, including many of the largest among us, have already been swept into this new heresy. Under attack is **the very nature of the church** (Are we truly the Lord's church or are we just another human organization?); **the nature and essence of our worship** (Shall we worship with instruments of music and shall our communion be part of a common meal?); **the leadership of the church** (Shall women be allowed to preach and teach over men?); **what constitutes one a Christian** (Is baptism an essential aspect of one's salvation or are we saved by grace through faith alone?); **the nature and extent of our fellowship** (Should we stand apart from churches founded by men or should we embrace them as Christian brethren?).

It takes no genius to understand that if these ideas finally prevail among our people we will have completely lost our identity and will cease to be in any sense the church of Christ. Clearly the threat is enormous. We know that there are many who want to see the above agenda successfully imposed on all our congregations. Without doubt there are thousands who are appalled at the temerity of those who would hold and teach views so diametrically opposed to the revealed will of God. The question is just how badly do we want to save the church from apostasy? Are we willing to pay the price necessary to accomplish this? Consider the following:

* Do you care enough to pray fervently every day that God will protect his church, that he will discomfit those who would harm her, that he will raise up a faithful band to defend her walls and lead the way in restoring her to prosperity (II Cor. 11:28)?
* Do you care enough to invest your time energy and money in opposing this change movement and in promoting faithfulness to God's Word? Are you willing to put your hands to the task and work to help salvage those around you (II Cor. 12:15)?
* Do you care enough to spend time educating and informing

yourself and the brethren where worship? This is especially pertinent for those who preach.
* Do you care enough to write, preach, teach and talk to every person exhorting them to hold fast the faithful word (II Tim. 4:2)?
* Do you care enough to speak up and speak out against the false teaching and error when someone promotes it in your presence? Too many sit tongue-tied and mute while others espouse these concepts in Bible classes, sermons or conversations.
* Do you care enough to work with others in combating the error? One soldier here and one there can easily be overrun, surrounded or driven from his post. But standing together, we become an unmoveable force that can block the incursions of the enemies of the faith (Eccle 4:9-12).
* Do you care enough to tolerate the imperfections and different approaches of good men who uphold the sound doctrine of Christ, and varied opinions on lesser matters, in order to win the greater victory over the true enemies of the church (Phil. 1:16-18)?
* Do yo care enough to help reclaim, restore and rebuild those disciples and congregations who have been led astray (Gal. 6:1)?
* Do you care enough to reject those who are determined to abandon the Bible way (Rom. 16:17-18)? We cannot keep them in our midst and expect to keep the church loyal to the Master's will.

The way you respond to these questions will reveal just how much you really love the church for which Jesus died. I urge you to let your love and loyalty be manifested by your diligent service on behalf of Christ's church in this hour of crisis.

93. A NECESSARY INGREDIENT OF VICTORY

As I assess the condition of our churches in this new millennium, I see a missing ingredient that has left us vulnerable to Satan's wiles. We have lost the sense of brotherhood we once had. I am 65. I remember when all congregations in an area knew each other, supported each other's efforts, cooperated in good works, and helped in planting new congregations. We rejoiced at the victories of others and mourned their losses. We had gospel papers that helped us keep in touch with each other. We thrilled to read of victories in distant fields and lifted up prayers when fellow-Christians were in need. Preachers we had never seen, we knew by name and by their teaching. We felt free to call on them for advice and assistance. They were willing to give it. Back them people were not so much interested in where a man went to school, only if he were a faithful preacher of God's Word. We honored men who were faithful proclaimers of the gospel and were proud to call them our brothers. Churches respected the membership of sister congregations and did not try to recruit them in order to increase their own numbers.

We all loved the Church of Christ and were proud to be members of it. There were not nearly so much doubt and suspicion about each other. We loved our fellow-Christians like family and called them brother and sister. Sadly, this spirit of brotherhood has been neglected and largely disappeared over the last 30 years. To regain our strength as a people, we must work to rebuild and restore that sense of brotherhood (I Pet.4:17).

94. BROTHERHOOD

All Christians are children God by faith in Christ Jesus, having been baptized into Christ (Gal. 3:26-27). Being children of a common Father, we frequently refer to fellow Christians as brothers and sisters (II Pet. 3:15). Our relationship in the church is set forth under the analogy of a family. While tied together by blood, members of a common family may live in separate places. Although sharing common parents, brothers and sisters can be strikingly different in appearance, height, and size. Their taste in style and dress, customs and manners can vary greatly. The costliness and style of their housing and furnishings can be noticeably diverse. The same differences are seen in the church. Christian brothers and sisters are scattered around the earth. They are of different racial and national origins and speak different languages, yet all are "one man in Christ Jesus" (Gal. 3:28).

All Christians are members of the one church which Christ built (Matt. 16:18; Acts 2:47), but as a family we have different levels of maturity, occupations and skills. Our differences are seen in numerous areas. We range from primitive to highly cultured, from uneducated to highly educated, from poor to wealthy, weak to powerful, employees to employers, and from young to old. An ongoing problem that nags the church is our inability to understand and tolerate such differences, to appreciate our spiritual kindred, hold them in high esteem and to treat them as beloved brethren.

Being members of the brotherhood of the saints of God there are certain expectations incumbent upon us.

I. Brotherly Love. "Let brother love continue" (Heb. 13:1). Agape love is our new commandment (John 13:34). Without brotherly love we cannot love God (I John 4:20). Such love worketh no ill to his fellow Christian (Rom. 13:10). "Love suffereth long, and is kind; love envieth not; love vaunteth not itself; is not puffed up, doth not behave itself unseemly, seeketh not its own, is not provoked, taketh not account of evil, rejoiceth not in unrighteousness, but rejoiceth with the truth . . . " (I Cor. 13:4-7).

II. Brotherly Concern for Each Other. It is the common expectation that brothers and sisters will manifest genuine concern or each other. There should be concern for those who suffer, whether it be mental or physical. This will be readily seen in solicitous care and attention, visiting those sick and afflicted and bearing their burdens (Gal. 6:2). It will be demonstrated in sharing with brethren who are in need. Some may be in perpetual poverty, others in financial distress because of sickness or disaster. We who are blest will give to those in need (Eph. 4:28) and gladly do so. Our love will reach out to encourage the fainthearted and discouraged (I Thess. 5:14). We will by all means rally to the side of the brother or sister persecuted for righteousness sake (Phil. 2:21-30).

III. Brother Consideration. Children of the same parents must exhibit consideration for each other if the family is to be happy and remain intact. There must be allowance for individual thought and opinion in a family. Brothers should feel free to ask their questions (John 14:5-9). Treatment of other members must be fair and equal (Matt. 7:12). Members must be honest in their dealing with each other (Eph. 4:25). Advantage must not be taken of ones siblings. In a happy and peaceful family there is patient allowance for the weaknesses and shortcomings typical of humanity (Eph. 4:2). All of these considerations are of vital importance to the well-being of God's spiritual family.

IV. Brotherly Cooperation, Fellowship and Support. Among the most visible and admired aspects of family life is the cooperation, support and fellowship of loving, loyal brothers and sisters. In olden days when most families farmed for their living this was especially evident. When one member was bothered by an adversary, he had the support of his brothers. If there was a large or difficult task to be done, all would lend a hand. Even when the children were grown, with families of their own, they eagerly looked forward to those family reunions where all the brothers and sisters could be together. Oh how this spirit is needed in today's church. We are brothers, not competitors, not antagonists, not enemies to be destroyed. We must never knowingly hinder another brother's work for Christ (Phil. 1:15-18). Paul pleads with us to be tenderly affectioned, one for another (Rom. 12:10). With such care and concern we can evangelize the world for Christ, drive Satan from his conquered lands and build up the kingdom of Christ as never before. Without it we are doomed to failure.

V. Brotherly Correction. A loyal brother will tell you when you are wrong. He cannot stand silent while you do wrong or bring harm to yourself. Jesus tells us, "If they brother sins, rebuke him; and if he repent forgive him" (Lk. 17:3). It was brotherly concern that prompted Paul to withstand Peter when he gave way to social pressure and shunned the Gentile brethren (Gal. 2:11-14). At times this will entail the painful duty of public censure and disfellowship (I Tim. 5:20). Yet even then, we must "count him not as an enemy, but admonish him as a brother" (II Thess. 3:15).

In a day when the church is as a city under siege, as a pilgrim band in a hostile wilderness, we desperately need to understand and meet our duties to our brothers and sisters in Christ. A scoffing, unbelieving world delights to see us fragmented and at war within. Lost sinners need to see a demonstration of the family of God into which they are invited to come. A family filled with angry bitterness will turn them away. Our young people and new converts need the loving care and strength that a strong spiritual family can provide. Without it many of them will be discouraged and lost.

Let not a single day pass without giving thanks for your spiritual family. May we all walk worthily of our holy calling lest we bring hurt and embarrassment to our family (Eph. 4:1).

95. LOVE THE BROTHERHOOD

Across the country and around the world upwards of two and a half million souls are members of the Church of Christ. Each is a child of God (Gal. 3:26), and as such, all are brothers and sisters in Christ (Matt. 23:8-9). Peter calls this Christian family, "the brotherhood" (I Pet. 2:7). All of us who have been in the church more than 20 years remember when the expression "the brotherhood" was a staple of our spiritual vocabulary. Today among a certain portion of our preachers and writers that terminology has been retired in favor of "our fellowship."

The change grew out of the Unity Meetings between some of our preachers and those of the Christian Churches. Following the earliest meetings, our brethren came home speaking of "our fellowship." It did not take long to perceive the reason for so doing. If the Christian Churches were acceptable to God, then they too were part of Christ's brotherhood. To avoid offending them and to gently reshape the thinking of our people to accept other religious groups as our spiritual equals a new vocabulary was needed. "Our fellowship" implies that we are but one segment of the great church of which Christ is head. That of course is the very meaning of denominationalism; one church divided into many segments, each with a different denomination or name. The pronoun "our" implies that we have a denomination of our own making just as the others about us have. Not surprisingly after a few years some of those folks began to openly speak of the church of Christ as a denomination. Of course Scripture condemns the concept of denominationalism in no uncertain terms (I Cor. 1:10-12). In days past, our brethren had a very useful slogan, "Call Bible things by Bible names." It would be a blessing to our people if all would restore the terminology which God chose to give us.

That said, we need to be reminded that God expects us to "love the brotherhood" of which we are part. This we should do because:
* The brotherhood consists of God's children;
* Each member thereof is our relative in the family of God;
* The members thereof are, over all the finest folks in the world. They are like Christ;
* We all have a mutual interest in the progress of the church, or kingdom of Christ;
* We have a common task to engage our interest and energy . . . evangelizing the world for Christ;
* We all have a common destiny. Faithful to death, we will receive a crown of life (Rev. 2:10);
* It is God's will that we do so.
* Because we love the brotherhood, we should be jealous for the safety and well-being of the church. Paul wrote to the church in

Corinth, "For I am jealous over you with a godly jealousy ... But I fear ... lest ... your minds should be corrupted from the simplicity and the purity that is toward Christ" (II Cor. 11:2-3).
* Loving the brotherhood, we should resent, resist and reject any individual or group that seeks to do harm to our spiritual family (Tit. 3:10).
* Because we love the brotherhood, we should join hands and hearts with every other member of our spiritual family to protect and defend it.
* For the sake of our children and grandchildren, we must love the brotherhood and see that it is kept safe and intact for them and others who come after us.

96. GOD'S REMNANT

Scripture teaches that God has always had a faithful few in the earth who served him. That small group is described as a remnant, i.e., "A small fragment; an end of a bolt of cloth of good quality but small in size."

* In Noah's day the remnant consisted of Noah and his family, just eight souls (Gen. 6:5-10).
* In Sodom and Gomorrah the remnant was only four souls (I Pet. 2:6-7).
* In the days of the Exodus, of those adult Hebrews who escaped Egypt, only Joshua and Caleb were counted faithful to enter the promised land (Num. 14:29-30).
* Throughout their history, the great majority of the Hebrews refused to walk in the paths of God. In Elijah's day God had only seven thousand who had not bowed unto images of Baal (I Kings 19:18). Isaiah told his generation that there was only "a very small remnant" who were faithful (1:9). Just a remnant survived the Babylonian Captivity to return home to Canaan (Ezek. 6:8).
* Jesus never expected the vast majority of people to follow him.

"For narrow is the gate and straitened the way, that leadeth unto life, and few are they that find it" (Matt. 7:14). "Many are called, but few are chosen" (Matt. 22:14). Paul affirmed that today there is "a remnant according to God's election of grace" (Rom. 11:5).

It is the faithful few who always have and always will carry the Cause of Christ forward.

One is not predestined or programmed to be part of the remnant. It is a matter of personal conviction, based on teaching and guidance. When we preach the gospel, those who believe and choose to be baptized are saved (Mk. 16:15-16). Like newborn babes they must long for the sincere milk of God's word (I Pet. 2:2). To receive the reward for the remnant we must be faithful unto death (Rev. 2:10).

Only God knows for sure if a brother or sister is truly part of his remnant. Only He can discern the thoughts and intents of the heart (Heb. 4:12-13). We can only judge by the fruit they bear if they are part of God's remnant (Matt. 7:16-21). Each of us must examine ourselves to see if we are part of the faithful remnant (I Cor. 11:28).

This truth presents many lessons for us today.
* A large church is not necessarily a faithful church.
* That a body of people is small is no reflection on their standing with God. "It is the remnant that shall be saved" (Rom. 9:27).
* That the majority of people may believe a certain doctrine is not proof it is acceptable to God. It may be just the opposite.
* That the wealthy, highly educated or powerful do not embrace a particular teaching is no proof it is not a true principle of the Christian faith. Many prefer the broad gate.
* We must not expect everyone to follow Jesus. We should not be discouraged when the majority turns its back and only a remnant chooses to follow the Master.

We cannot expect everyone who makes a profession of faith to be wholly committed to Christ to the end. They never have and never will.

97. WHO WILL LEAD THE REMNANT?

Like a toxic cloud, apostasy is settling over significant numbers of our congregations and schools. One need not be a prophet to predict that where this occurs, a separation is inevitable. Faithful Christians, who love the church and respect the authority of the Scriptures, will not be able to stay and be part of a congregation that has cast aside the Will of Christ and determined to chart a new course. God always has, and always will, have a faithful remnant who will be true to His will and way (Rom. 9:27). Because they remain faithful, they will be saved. The question is, who will provide the leadership to rally those brethren who refuse to be led into denominationalism?

Four options come to mind.
* Without strong leadership, they will be left as sheep without a shepherd to wander aimlessly until they are finally scattered and lose their identity.
* Some will be left to seek fellowship in non-institutional churches (They used to be called anti orphan home and anti-cooperation churches). They are far more conservative than many of our congregations. Some of them have moderated their approach on their issues over the last few years. Visitors will find their preaching and worship very much like ours before agents of change appeared on the scene.
* Some will be tempted to follow those ultraconservatives brethren that for years have been railing against anything and anyone they did not personally have a controlling hand in. There is a sprinkling of these preachers and congregations across the country. Yes they are conservative, and they reject the new currents of change, but they have one wheel in the ditch and history demonstrates that they will never provide leadership that will give the church growth and victory.
* Hopefully, wise and good men, sound in faith, conservative in commitment, level-headed and able to discern and avoid either extreme of liberalism or legalism will rise up. Only such men can

provide the Biblical leadership to help us restore the church of the 21st century to a solid Biblical base.

A little historical background will make this point clearer. In the years following the Civil War our brotherhood experienced an upheaval and apostasy almost identical to that we are experiencing today. Those determined to change the church styled themselves "progressives" while those who sought to maintain the Biblical faith called them "digressives." So effective were the digressives in promoting their views and so naive and complacent were many good men that before the dust had settled they had swept away some 85% of our churches and most of our schools. The issues then were: how can we determine what God allows, man-made organizations to do the mission work of the church, instrumental music in worship, placing women in roles of leadership, fellowship with denominations, classifying the Lord's church as a denomination, choirs, soloists and other similar things. There was a significant circle of well-educated preachers who espoused the theological liberalism popular in that day. Among other things, they questioned the inspiration and authority of the Bible.

The digressives had two primary camps. J. H. Garrison led the theological liberals. They had a large influence in the Christian schools that were taken. Isaac Errett through the **Christian Standard**, led the moderates. They promoted all the agenda except the flagrant liberalism of Garrison's followers. Among those who opposed the digressives, David Lipscomb was the most prominent leader. He led moderates who wished to maintain the Restoration Movement on its original Biblical course. Through the pages of the **Gospel Advocate** paper and the Nashville Bible School (Now David Lipscomb University), he was able to keep his followers on a steady course that avoided extremes. Daniel Sommer of Indianapolis pursued a radical approach that not only opposed the digressives but Lipscomb and the moderates. Sommer's legacy has been a seed bed for an unending cycle of "ultraconservative" splinter groups.

Those preachers, congregations and schools that followed the leadership of Bro. Lipscomb prospered and multiplied in a phenomenal way. By the 1960s our churches had spread to every state in the Union and in more than a hundred foreign nations. Brethren conducted numerous schools, providing educations for our children. Scores of good works were undertaken, providing care for widows, orphans, unwed mothers, the aged. We had numerous gospel papers all of the centrist view and several publishing houses that provided good, dependable literature for our people.

Today we have already lost much of what we had gained. Some of our Universities and Colleges are under the influence of the new digressives. Many of our gospel papers have either been discontinued or have suffered serious decline in circulation. The international radio and television outreach that we once were proud of is no longer a distinctive voice for the New Testament church. Many campus and youth programs have weakened rather than strengthen the faith of their young charges, leaving them vulnerable to the sirens of change. From every quarter we heard of churches pursuing a new course, and the conflicts that pursuit causes.

Our liberal digressives have their leaders. The question is who will lead the surviving remnant? Will faithful leaders arise soon enough to save the greater number of our churches? Or will we tarry and hope until major losses are inflicted? Our current agitation is not going to be a year long or a five year tussle. Such changes within religious groups take years to run their course. The conflict mentioned earlier spanned well more than 50 years and resulted in a divided brotherhood. The digressives emerged as the Disciples of Christ/Christian Churches. Those clinging to the Old Paths continued as Churches of Christ.

Granted, no man, editor or school can appoint themselves to be leaders of our people, nor can any group elect them to that position. Granted, every congregation is autonomous and independent. But now as in the past, men will arise to provide leadership, be it good or bad, others will voluntarily follow. Our liberals are providing their leadership in a most successful way. We have a radical reactionary group eager to lead those who reject liberalism. What we desperately need is for wise men, rooted and grounded in God's Word, faithful and loyal to the New Testament Church, to step forward and issue the cry to arms. Only that kind of leadership will save the day. We need not one, or a dozen but thousands, of loyal soldiers of Christ to lead us in this hour of crisis.

98. AN APPEAL TO PREACHERS AND ELDERS

A war is raging. The enemy is working day and night to undermine the authority of Christ's Word and impose their ideas on His church. Many of our soldiers seem unaware of the fact. They go about their business as if all was rosy in the kingdom; seeing no threats of danger at all. Others are trying to avoid the conflict like the draft dodgers who fled to Canada during the Viet Nam War. If the church is to survive for generations yet to come, the soldiers of Christ must arise.

Arm Yourself. "Put on the whole armor of God, that ye may be able to stand against the wiles of the devil" (Eph. 6:11). Christ considers his preachers and elders to be soldiers in the army of heaven. They are not peacetime soldiers with weekend duty. They are involved in a mortal struggle with the prince of the powers of the air (Eph. 2:2). Daily they must face his hosts of wicked spirits (Eph. 6:12).

Take Your Place in the Lines. Christ's expectation is that we be good soldiers (II Tim. 2:3). He expects us to "fight the good fight of faith" (I Tim. 6:12). There is no place for slackers, dodgers, malingerers, deserters or onlookers in the army of Christ. We are on active duty with a lifetime enlistment (Rev. 2:10). We must faithfully march forth with the King of Kings (Rev. 19:14). One of the great problems facing today's church is that many preachers and elders have not the will, the desire or the sense of loyalty to their

King to take their place in the lines against the forces of evil.

Use Your Sword. To be of any significant value in war, a soldier must have a weapon, know how to use it and have the courage to engage the enemy. Christ has provided us a powerful and effective weapon, "the sword of the Spirit which is the word of God" (Eph. 6:17). Not everyone that owns a Bible is prepared to use it effectively. Not every soldier has the fortitude to stand in the gap and defend the kingdom against her enemies (Ezek. 22:30). Read your Bible, teach it and wield it effectively against every false teaching that appears before you.

"Quit Ye Like Men." These words of Paul (I Cor. 16:13), remind us of the serious nature of our conflict. Christianity is not in debate club or child's play. Neither is our war a game. It is a titanic struggle for the souls of men; for the heart of a nation. It is a mortal conflict with the devil and his angels. It is a war for the heart of our civilization, our culture and the church. At stake are the minds and hearts of our children. Faith and courage are essential elements in good soldiers.

Never Surrender. Victory is our only option. As Paul wrote these lines, he had in mind those Roman soldiers who enabled Rome to rule the civilized world of his day. They were invincible because they were trained to never surrender. If defeated today, they were trained to regroup and fight again tomorrow. In every war there is a problem keeping the fighting spirit of the troops at high level. Surveying our Christian soldiers, it is evident that some have grown weary of the strife. Some are discouraged by the success of our enemy. Some have been wounded, or have grown old in the conflict. As it was during the Viet Nam conflict, some have been persuaded that to continue the battle is wrong, useless or hopeless. In the dark dreary days of World War II, courageous Winston Churchill addressed the students of his alma mater. His subject was the war, which at that time was going badly against England. The eloquent leader summed up his speech with these stirring words, "Never,

never, never surrender." So it must be for those of us privileged to serve in the army of Christ. There are thousands of foes without, arrayed against us with deadly intent. Sadly there are traitors and turncoats within the church. They are devoting their energies to undermining the authority of our King. They are subverting the faith, worship and practice of the church by sowing discord among the citizens of the kingdom. In the face of all these enemies, of our Lord we must "Never, never, never, surrender."

99. WISE LEADERSHIP NEEDED IN THE CURRENT CONFLICT

A struggle is underway for the heart and soul of Churches of Christ. A small band of well-trained and highly motivated agents of change are challenging preachers and elders of churches of Christ for the leadership of their flocks. While the champions of change likely cannot claim over three hundred congregations under their banner at this time, they do control some of our most prestigious churches and schools. Thus they are in position to shape the thinking of a multitude of young people, including young preachers, who will soon be taking their new ideas into more congregations. In too many cases, leaders of local congregations are failing to meet the challenge of these false teachers.

The following ideas on leadership are especially relevant to today's situation.

I. "Two things, well considered, would prevent many quarrels; first to have it well ascertained whether we are not disputing about terms rather than things, and, second, to examine whether that on which we differ is worth contending about" (Cotton). There is considerable difference in holding and teaching a doctrine that is false and simply using non-traditional vocabulary. In every generation the young devise new ways to express their thoughts. Paul warns against striving over words (II Tim. 2:14) But he also condemned those whose teaching and conduct were contrary to sound doctrine (I Tim. 1:10). There are scores of insignificant things in the Bible text about which we may disagree with no damage done. But when it comes to the fundamentals of the faith regarding our faith, worship and practice we must be united.

In waging successful warfare, a wise general will be very careful in choosing the battles to which commits his troops. A hundred hills maybe of no strategic value but one may be of absolute importance. For that one piece of ground he will fight. So it must be in our fight of faith. The big issue is not new hymns, nor is it the use of projectors. It is not, how long we extend the communion service or how short the sermon is. The issues worthy of contention are those involving principles essential to being acceptable to God. Among those issues we must address are things that have to do with salvation. Is man saved by grace through faith, before and without obedience in baptism? The Scripture plainly says that sins are washed away when we are baptized (Acts 22:16). The Lord adds to his church those who have been baptized (Acts 2:38, 47; I Cor. 12:13). The way in which we approach God in worship is an essential matter. Worship based on human traditions is vain, useless and unacceptable (Matt. 15:6, 9). Thus when men tamper with our singing, our communion and the nature of our public worship (by turning it into a charismatic style) then we must take our stand. A major shortcoming in our response thus far has been the many skirmishes fought on matters that are nonessential.

II. "Fortunate is the person who has developed the self-control to steer a straight course toward his objective in life, without being swayed from his purpose by either commendation or condemnation" (Napoleon Hill). Every preacher and elder must be committed to leading his people in the straitened and narrow way of Christ. When he teaches the truth of the gospel without fear or favor, when he reproves and rebukes error (II Tim. 4: 2), when he contends earnestly for the faith (Jude 3), there will be some who flay him. If he speaks smooth words that sinners love to hear, there will be those who flatter him (Is. 30:10). To successfully resist the pressure to compromise the faith and drift with the tides of change; a man must be fully persuaded in his own mind and resolved long before the challenge appears. Only then well he be able to stay the course even if he must travel alone.

III. "The ability to keep a cool head in an emergency, maintain poise in the midst of excitement, and to refuse to be stampeded are true marks of leadership" (R. Shannon). In the months and years ahead a thousand battles will be fought as faithful Christians find their congregations being infiltrated by those who wish to lead them away from the path laid out by Jesus. It will not be enough just to know God's will on the points of contention. Only leaders with "cool heads" and spiritual wisdom will be able to excise the problem without disrupting and harming the body. Rash decisions and actions can be as destructive as that caused by the promoters of change. If any man "lacketh wisdom, let him ask of God, who giveth to all liberally" (Jas. 1:5). Leaders of even temperament will not despair, nor will they overreact. They will not resort to unethical methods. Nor will they sacrifice truth for tranquility. They will not be stampeded into unhealthy change nor stubbornly refuse to accept that which is right and beneficial for the congregation. May God grant such wisdom to all who lead his people.

100. FIGHTING THE GOOD FIGHT OF FAITH WITH A PROPER ATTITUDE

As we survey the damage done to the Cause we love by ruthless change agents, and as we realize the detestable objective they have in mind, it is easy for us to become embittered and to reflect that bitter spirit when dealing with them. Such bitterness is counter productive and must not be allowed to take hold in our lives.

Paul wrote of false brethren who were creating havoc among the churches of his day, I "tell you even weeping, that they are enemies of the cause of Christ" (Phil. 3:18). So we should view these departures with heavy hearts. We must try to snatch all that we can from the fire (Jude 23). We must find no pleasure in the unpleasant work we must do in exposing and reproving those who have left their first love. The liberal change agents like to paint those of us who do not go along with their agenda as narrow, negative, hateful, ranters who have nothing positive to offer. We must live our lives, do our work and conduct ourselves in such a way as to refute that libelous charge. "For so is the will of God, that by well-doing ye should put to silence the ignorance of foolish men" (I Pet. 2:15). We must pray for ourselves and them: for ourselves, that we will be faithful, no matter what the future holds, that we will have a right spirit, that we will continue to love the brotherhood; for them, that they will see the error of their way and repent and return to the Master's fold. Satan is rejoicing today. Our Lord is sorrowful. We must be faithful unto death (Rev. 2:10) and we must at all times have the mind of Christ (Phil. 2:5) "who, when he was reviled, reviled not again" (I Pet. 2:23)

101. LET'S DISARM THE ENEMY

Change agents have landed many successful blows by accusing those who oppose them of certain failures in their teaching, worship and practice of Christianity. The effective use of this strategy has been the reason large numbers of brethren have allowed these false teachers to stay and function in their midst, even though they really do not agree with their philosophy and call for change. The change agents present themselves as pleasant, kind, caring and tolerant and since they emphasize practicing the principles of Christ in daily life, these brethren tolerate them.

To disarm and neutralize these accusing invaders we must live our lives and do our work in such a way as to put the lie to their accusations. I challenge every preacher among us to consider the following suggestions which will effectively disarm them.

* When we preach, let the truth be presented in love (Eph. 4:15). Away with harsh, hateful proclamations that insult and offend even good people. Away with sarcasm and ridicule in the pulpit. "Let your speech be always with grace, seasoned with salt, that ye may know how ye ought to answer each one" (Col. 4:6).
* When we have to correct a brother, let us do so with love and compassion, in a spirit of gentleness (Gal. 6:1). Treat the erring brother or sister as you would wish to be treated were you in their place (Matt. 7:12).
* Let us never be quarrelsome and factious in our attitude and conduct. Agents of change really make an issue of the quarrels and divisions that disgrace our congregations and many of our preachers. God has no use for the factious man, nor should we (Tit. 3:10-11). Be peace makers (Matt. 5:9). Give "diligence to keep the unity of the Spirit in the bond of peace" (Eph.4:3). If division must come, let it clearly be at the hands of the agents of change!
* Let us live out our sermons in everyday life with deeds of service, care and compassion for those about us (Gal. 6:10). Greatness is in service not in position or recognition (Matt. 20:26-28).
* Let us work to make our worship services truly meaningful so that no one can complain that they are dry, boring and lifeless. We all know the difference between singing and preaching that is uninspiring and that which is. Where worship and lessons are uplifting and inspirational, change agents are powerless.
* Let us be less critical and judgmental of our brethren and seek the good they do and dwell upon it. If we are honest, each of us falls short of the glory of God (Rom. 3:23). All of us are limited in some areas of our knowledge. All of us desperately need mercy if we hope to be saved (Tit. 3:5). All of us have been wrong is some areas of our thinking and had to make adjustments as we learned better. Hence we need to be patient with each other and slow to attack, condemn or reject a brother with whom we differ. We should receive each other as Christ received us when we first came to him (Rom. 15:7). Such an attitude is "to the glory of God."

* Let us be true students of the sacred book. Change agents shame and ridicule us as mere pikers who know only the outer wrappings of the word of God. Spend the necessary hours in your books, searching the Scriptures and verifying your information so that when you preach and teach, you can do so with authority (Matt. 7:28-29). Thus prepared, no man can gainsay your message (Tit. 1:9)!
* Be interested in young people. Where they are neglected they will either leave the church or gravitate to those who show interest in them. Change agents allure them into their silken web and their apostasy.
* Be flexible in all areas where God has not legislated. Many things in our life and society change for the better. We have modern buildings, creature comforts such as air-conditioning, cushioned seats, carpeted floors. Such things will continue to improve and we should be not resistant to them. Be firm in the essentials of the faith but flexible in all other areas. Such things as length of services, new hymnals and song books are matters we must not quarrel about.
* Be evangelistic. Don't allow yourself to be consumed with fighting error. Be a soul-winner. Support missionaries. Build up the cause rather than use all of your time and energy shooting at those who have gone astray.

Follow these suggestions and you will create an environment where change agents cannot succeed. Their calls will fall on deaf ears because you have disarmed them by your wise conduct.

102. IF WE ARE TO WIN

A spiritual war is raging within the brotherhood of Churches of Christ. On one hand are those who love the church and are committed to maintaining the Bible-based faith, worship and practice that our fathers observed. On the other is a group of younger men who feel they have outgrown such an old fashion approach to Christianity and are busily engaged in trying to introduce a broad array of changes into our congregations. While we slept, the agents of change took the offensive and have made a broad and successful sweep through our brotherhood. Our two largest schools are already in their hands, as are dozens of congregations, including some of the largest among us.

I am convinced that we can successfully block the spread of this destructive movement and recover some of what has been lost. With Paul we can be confident, "If God is for us who is against us?" And we can be more than conquerors through him that loves us (Rom. 8:32,37). But if we are to be victorious there are some things that are absolutely essential.

* There must be an awareness of the magnitude and seriousness of our problem. At this point, far too many of our brethren are totally unaware of the danger that is upon us. They seem to be living in blissful ignorance while the enemy is besieging our walls. Remember that Paul says, "I would not brethren, have you ignorant" (I Cor. 10:1). Every preacher and elder should feel duty bound to inform himself regarding this divisive movement then share that information with their congregation. Ignorance will bring defeat. With knowledge we will get the victory.
* There must be a sense of urgency. The danger is such that we cannot wait till tomorrow to think about it or to make preparation to protect our flocks from it. Delay can only bring disaster. Weak leaders tend to think that by ignoring, or postponing response, maybe it will go away. Be assured the change movement is not going to disappear after a few months! It is already too deeply entrenched and successful.
* There must be a sense of love and appreciation for the church of Christ. Only those who truly love the church will make the necessary effort to save her from her enemies. We sing "I love thy Kingdom Lord . . . the church our dear redeemer saved with his own precious blood." Love is demonstrated by actions. A man who loves his wife will not stand by idly while she is

maligned, threatened or attacked, nor will those who love the church. They will stand up and bravely fight for her honor and welfare.
* There must be a sense of commitment to invest the necessary time, energy and money to secure the victory. Our nation planned to spend $95 billion to defeat Saddam Hussein's regime. Without that degree of investment, the operation might fail. Every Christian and every congregation should gladly be willing to help in this warfare. Money is needed for tracts, for gospel papers, for special speakers, for lectureships and forums. Such efforts take time and energy to successfully develop and implement.
* There must be a sense of brotherhood. We will never win unless our vision and interest transcends the local church where we serve. Good people with limited vision might save their own congregation while others about them are swept away. With brotherly concern they might have helped save them from apostasy. Brotherhood implies mutual concern and assistance for fellow Christians in other congregations.
* To successfully address this challenge and win the victory we must have a sense of our history. Those who have not learned the lessons of history are doomed to repeat the mistakes of history. What is transpiring in our generation happened to us before between 1865 and 1925. Christian churches and Disciples of Christ that you see in your neighborhood are the fruit of that former change movement. You need to read Homer Hailey's **Attitudes and Consequences of the Restoration Movement** or Earl West's **Search of the Ancient Order**. When you do so you will understand what is happening today, and the danger it poses.
* There must be a sense of personal responsibility. We cannot assume that someone else will see to this problem. We have kingdom duties and responsibilities that cannot be ignored or avoided. We cannot sit back and expect someone else to fight the battle for us.
* There must be a sense of outrage at the harm being inflicted on the church. We should be filled with righteous indignation when we

read or hear them ridicule our forefathers in the faith. We should be stirred to anger when we observe their hateful criticism of the Lord's church while at the same time they have nothing but praise and adulations for other religious bodies. We should be unhappy with those who question the inerrancy of God's Word, and deny its authority in the life of the church. Those who, with unholy hands, try to change the faith, worship and practice of Christ's blessed church are enemies of the cross of Christ (Phil. 3:18). They must be seen and treated as such.

103. THE CONVICTION IT TAKES TO WIN

Before this generation passes one of two things will have occurred:
* The change agents will have been met, defeated and routed, or
* They will have prevailed and the church we love will be left a broken and scattered remnant.

The victory will not be easily won, nor will the conflict be won by armchair soldiers. It will only be gained if a courageous and dedicated band of Christian soldiers commit themselves, without reservation, to their Lord and the welfare of his kingdom.

When the patriot fathers launched the revolution that gave birth to this nation, they pledged their "sacred honor, wealth and lives" to that cause (Declaration of Independence). It will take that same degree of dedication and commitment to save the church from the juggernaut of error that now threatens to destroy her.

Paul was willing to spend and be spent for the Cause he loved (II Cor. 12:15). Christ loved the church and gave himself up for it (Eph. 5:25). To win this battle that spirit must take hold of our hearts.

* Truth must take precedence over error, no matter how popular the error may be.
* Loyalty to Christ must take priority over loyalty to men and

institutions, no matter how strong the bands of friendship and affection may be.
* The authority of Scriptures must preempt the will of men in all matters relating to our faith, worship and practice (Gal. 1:10). To preach, to accept, to tolerate another gospel is more than a simple choice it is to be alienated from and anathema to God (Gal. 1:8).
* The kingdom of Christ must be cherished more than jobs, brotherhood recognition, popularity and worldly success. If we are "striving to please men (we) should not be servants of Christ" (Gal. 1:10).
* "The old paths" of Scripture must be valued more than the new paths of the "change agents" (Jer. 6:16). The old came from Christ; they are plainly set forth in Scripture. They can be followed in full confidence. The new paths of the professors of change have as their authority the uninspired assertions of men who aren't sure about the inerrancy of God's Word (See **God's Holy Fire**, By K. L. Cukrowski, M. W. Hamilton and J. W. Thompson of Abilene Christian University, pub. By ACU Press, pp. 39-44). Nor are they sure of the primacy of the new Covenant of Christ over the Old Covenant of Moses.

The battle being thrust upon us will be intense. It will result in the rise and fall of many in the Israel of God. False teachers who have already attained positions of power and influence are not likely to meekly surrender and walk away. It will require spiritual warfare on a large scale to dislodge them. As in Gideon's day, many will have no stomach for the conflict. The outcome will depend on a Gideon's band of 300 brave men to meet and rout them. The most pressing question of the day is where will you be found in the day of battle?

104. DISCERNING THE ISSUES

Those who lead God's people must be men of discernment, able to recognize the difference between truth and error, between the holy and the common and to teach and lead the saints in righteous paths. (Ezek. 44:23). To protect the infant church the Holy Spirit endowed some leaders with the gift of "discerning of spirits" (I Cor. 12:10). As the church of today is confronted by a host of false teachers who are clamoring for drastic changes in our faith, worship and practice we desperately need wise men who can discern what the real issues are.

* **The issue is not new songs**. All songs were once new. Every generation of Christians has learned new songs. Many Christians have written hymns that were introduced to our people. Some proved acceptable and appealing and found a permanent place in our hymnals. Others did not. The choice of songs belongs to the elders and the congregation who use them in worship; certainly not to university professors. It becomes an issue when a few seek to impose their choice of hymns on the whole church and are willing to press their preference to the point of division. Faction and division are sinful (Tit. 3:10).
* **The issue is not short songs with few words or songs not printed in our hymnals**. All hymns, save the Psalms, are the products of uninspired men. Two hundred years ago no hymnals had musical notations and harmony lines.
* **The issue is not songs that originated among other faiths**. Most of the great hymns we sing were written by poets of other churches. The issue is the content of the songs. Do they convey Biblical truth? If they express true worship and do not promote error they are acceptable.
* **That lyrics of songs are projected on a screen is not the issue**. Remember, song books for each member are a fairly modern convenience. I have worshipped with churches in Africa where only the song leader had a hymnal. They were a luxury the rest could not afford.
* **Having a group skilled singers sitting together or having microphones is not the issue,** not so long as the singing is congregational. Back in the 50s some congregations, in order to improve their singing, encouraged their skilled singers to sit

together near the front of the auditorium. But when the group becomes a choir performing as others listen that is an issue to be met.

* **Having more than one song leader stand before the congregation at the same time is not the issue**. The Bible says nothing about song leaders, one or more, standing before the congregation and leading the singing. I have seen two and even three song leaders standing before a church in mission fields where there were no trained and accomplished song directors. They needed the help and reassurance the others could lend them. If they sang different songs at the same time that would cause confusion. If they were there to perform for the entertainment of the audience, whether a solo, duet or trio, that would be an issue. Worship is not entertainment.

* **The issue is not casual dress worn at church**. God does not prescribe a fashion standard for his worshipers. We have a cultural and even religious tradition of "Sunday dress" for worship. Such is neither scriptural nor unscriptural. I prefer to dress up for church, but not everyone shares that preference. In the ancient times, when many slaves were brought into the church, I suspect they did not have the option of dressing up for worship. So long as our dress is modest (I Tim. 2:9), and appropriate for Christians assembled before Jehovah, customs and conventions of the age and place will having a bearing on the degree of formality. **The real issue is having a casual attitude toward the church, the Word of God and his worship**. God rebuked the prophet-preachers of Israel who were "**light**" and treacherous (Zeph. 3:4). Proclaiming the gospel and worshiping Jehovah is serious business, and should be approached with proper solemnity. Preachers should leave the comedy routine to the comedians.

* **The issue is not rasing the hands in prayer**. Ancient Christians sometimes lifted up holy hands when praying (I Tim. 2:8). A similar reference is found in Ps. 134:2. But if someone thinks by such outward actions we can generate a superior spirituality, they deceive themselves. Lifting up of hands is an outward

posture in prayer just as kneeling, standing or falling on ones face. It has no special spiritual value. **An issue occurs when a preacher or praise leader calls on the congregation lift up their voices in simultaneous prayer,** (such as I recently witnessed). With many praying aloud there was confusion. That is an issue since God is not the author of confusion (I Cor. 14:33). He wants all things to "be done decently and in order" (I Cor. 14:40).

* **The issue is not whether or not to have Sunday evening or midweek services.** Those are wonderful practices; edifying, educating and exhorting those who attend. But God does not command three services per week. He ordained that we assemble on the first day to break the bread (Acts 20:7). Other classes and services are options that elders may use or not use. Many churches, operating in less favorable circumstances, such as mission areas, do not have them. Many of our churches in days past, when transportation was more difficult, did not have them. The issue is what do the leaders do or not do when their people assemble. Do they honor God by obeying His will to the very best of their knowledge and ability?

***The real issue is not which translation a preacher, teacher or congregation uses.** A false teacher can promote his error from the King James Version as well as from the New International Version. All translations are the products of uninspired men. All have strengths and weaknesses. All stand in need of wise teachers to explain their meaning; even the tried and true KJV. It is the doctrine they teach that is the issue. Is it true to God's revealed will or contrary to it? That is the issue.

* **The issue is not, were some of our earlier preachers limited in their education or unpolished in their methods?** Of course some of them were. They were human, men of their generation. Some of them had few talents and opportunities to improve them, but the used them in a remarkable successful way. But others had advanced education, were true Bible scholars and were polished orators. **The real question is, do today's change agents have the love and respect for God's Word,**

and his church that those pioneers had?
* **The issue is not, have we have too much division and strife within the church?** The answer is yes. But such problems are not unique to churches of Christ. All other religious bodies have their problems as well. Even one division is too much, especially if I am the one responsible for it. The question is who has been responsible for the divisions of the past? It is unfair to blame the wife whose abusive husband beats her for not maintaining peace in her home. Likewise it is unreasonable to blame the Lord's church because ambitious, misguided, carnal, contentious brethren fomented strife and division. They bear the blame, not the church which suffered from their abuse.
* **The issue is not, shall we adjust to face our changing society and culture**? We have always adjusted in areas where Christ left us free to do so. We don't dress like our 19th century forebearers did. We have modern buildings. We have adjusted our methods for evangelism. We don't have 2-3 hour sermons. We have all the modern conveniences such as electricity, air-conditioning and indoor plumbing. **The issue is the kind of changes the change agents wish to impose upon our churches**. They wish to touch those things sacred and holy; such things as worship, how we are saved, the role of women in church leadership, the unique and separate nature of Christ's church. That God does not allow, nor can we stand idle while they profane that which is holy.
* **The issue is not, are there some radical, vituperative, ultraconservatives among us?** Yes there are. There have always been such folks. The church in general does not endorse, approve or support their methods or narrow views. **The real issue is are the change agents any better than those on the far right?** In dishonest fashion, they hold these radicals up as typical of all who oppose then. God's truth always lies between the extremes of legalism and liberalism, between radical conservatives and liberal change agents (Prov. 4:26-27).
* **The issue is not change.** Faithful brethren have and will always welcome changes from bad to good; from the mistaken to the

correct; from unscriptural to scriptural; from poor methods to better ones; from ineffective means to effective ones that advance the Cause of Christ according to his will. **The real issue is the kind of changes the "change agents" would have us make.** They propose changes from the Biblical way to non biblical ways; changes from Christ's authority to that of the multitude; changes from the sacred to the worldly; from the apostolic pattern to that of our secular culture; changes from the teaching of men appointed by Christ (the Apostles) to men appointed by themselves to remake his church.

Only when we understand what the real issues are will we be able to deal with them in an effective way. May God give us preachers and elders who can discern between the "holy and the common, and between the unclean and the clean" (Lev. 10:10). Without them we will be overrun by those who are enemies of the Cause of Christ.

105. DANGERS CONSERVATIVES MUST AVOID

We are locked in a mortal struggle for the hearts and minds of the members of the Churches of Christ. Liberals are determined to reshape the doctrine, worship and practice of our churches into an acceptable denominational image. Conservatives are just as determined to resist and defeat their efforts and preserve the church in its purity. There are dangers that we conservatives must avoid, lest we hinder our efforts and give the enemy the advantage.

* There is **the danger of a closed mind**. We must never close our minds to a Biblical point that is raised, even if we have not previously thought of it. An open mind is an honest mind. Remember how the Jews covered their ears at Stephen's message and attacked him (Acts 7:57). Truth is truth, no matter who speaks it.
* There is **the danger of overconfidence in our knowledge and understanding of God's Word**. This is closely kin to the above

point. While we must have absolute trust in the Scripture and its authority, we must be modest about our knowledge. Overconfidence is a special temptation to the young preacher. That is why God placed the leadership of his church in the hands of elders; i.e., men who are older and more experienced in the way of righteousness. The older and wiser one becomes the more he becomes aware of the vast amount of information he has yet to master.

* There is **the danger of assuming that ones opinion of a matter is the equivalent of God's Will on the subject**. That I or even my parents and grandparents have always believed something is no proof it is God's will. We must always operate by the rule, "To the law and to the testimony! If they speak not according to this word, they have no light" (Is. 8:20 NIV).

* There is **the danger of impatience with those not as wise or perceptive as we.** We see parents who are impatient with their youngsters and teachers impatient with their pupils. We also see preachers who have had the time, means and opportunity to study a given issue, who are very impatient with those not so blessed. They may be just as loyal, and devoted to Christ, his word and his church as their critic, but they are still uniformed. God's man must be patient and filled with brotherly kindness toward them or he will be shortsighted and unfruitful for Christ (II Pet. 1:6-8).

*There is **the danger of arrogance**. Occasionally we see a brother, full of knowledge, sound in convictions but arrogant in spirit. He is proud of his knowledge, proud of his soundness, proud that he is not like others who are not so fortunate. He is like the Pharisee of Luke 18:9-12.

* There is **the danger of being harsh and cruel in dealing with those in error**. Jude teaches us to have mercy on those who are in doubt as we try to snatch them from the fire (Jude 22-23). Our goal must be to salvage every possible soul, including those preachers and professors who are harming the Cause we love. Each case of harshness and cruelty is held up as the reason why folks should listen to the liberals' gentle message.

* There is **the danger of assuming everyone who loves God must agree with us on every point relating to God's Word**. Only those who live alone and preach only to a recorder will experience 100 percent agreement from their audience. There are many reasons why we have varying understandings of the many truths of God's Word: ignorance of the whole of it; different levels of achievement in sacred knowledge; different social and cultural backgrounds; differences in age and experience, etc. There are fundamental truths on which we must agree and other points in which we must tolerate each other's differing points of view. Otherwise, your brotherhood will include only you and your two or three disciples who will allow you to do all of their thinking for them. We can disagree on many items and yet both love God and his Word with equal devotion.
* There is **the danger of thinking ones knowledge of primary and fundamental matters make him a scholar in more complex or technical matters.** We have all known the brother who is well informed and sound on the basics of Christianity and thinks that makes him a Greek or Hebrew scholar. We smile as he seeks to prove his technical point with his interlinear and Johnson's Notes. An old proverb rightly says that "a little knowledge is a dangerous thing."
* There is **the danger of loving controversy and a good fight**. I went to school with boys who thoroughly enjoyed fighting. Because they generally were bigger, tougher and more experienced, they usually won. Usually they were at fault. They had become bullies. Some preachers exhibit this same weakness. To them fighting is more important than serving others; personal victory is more to be desired than saving the soul. They do not help our cause. God's man must love the brotherhood (I Pet. 2:17).
* There is **the danger of not discerning between the fundamentals which are unchanging and nonnegotiable and expediencies and traditions which can be revised, changed or even discarded at our convenience**. The latter we

must not fight over.
* There is **the danger of being, or appearing to be, anti-intellectual when opposing liberalism**. The fact is most of our liberals are men with advanced education. But so are many of our great conservatives. Having a doctorate should not make a brother suspect. It is his teaching and practice that determine his loyalty or lack thereof. When we attack a man on the basis of his education, we leave ourselves open to charge that we are really jealous of his attainment, or intimidated by his superior knowledge.

We have a war to wage, a battle to win. Our cause is sacred. The future of the kingdom of Christ is at stake. Every soldier must resist those dangers that will interfere with our gaining the victory.

106. MISPLACED LOYALTY

Loyalty or fidelity is a blessed and noble attribute to possess. Those without it can never be good friends, good citizens or good Christians. God places a high premium on fidelity in the lives of his children (Gal. 5:22). But loyalty has its priorities.
* Our first loyalty must be to God and his Son (Matt. 22:37-38; 10:37).
* We must be loyal to Christ's church and his sacred Word.
* There is loyalty owed to our mates, children and extended family.
* There is a loyalty owed to friends and comrades with whom we associate in life.
* There is loyalty we owe to our employer and our nation.
* Our loyalty is cultivated by the schools we attend, especially those of higher education. It is cultivated by those who administer the schools as an essential base for future financial support, student referrals and general support. Schools have offices of alumni affairs, with employees to keep the fires of loyalty glowing.

It is a misplaced loyalty to allow ones loyalty to the lesser relationships of life take precedence over our obligations to those that are higher. It is wrong when our loyalty to our job or career overshadows our loyalty to our family. It is wrong when our loyalty to a church surpasses our loyalty to Christ and his Word. That is the sin of denominationalism. It is a misplaced loyalty that places things of the world above ones loyalty to the Cause of Christ. It is a serious mistake when Christians allow their loyalty to a school, even a Christian School, to surpass their loyalty to Christ, his word and his church.

Today, churches of Christ are under a nationwide siege from those who have espoused the agenda of the change movement. The stream of that system is flowing from some of our Christian Universities. This puts a strain on those Christians who are graduates of those schools. For they must choose between loyalty to the Lord's church or to a school which is undermining and damaging the church by their promotion of the change agenda.

It is a strange phenomenon among our people that Christian Schools often enjoy greater loyalty from some Christians than does the church, her Head and his Word. The reason can be seen when we think how schools work to create loyalty in their students, and continually cultivate that loyalty through mailings, campus events such as lectureships, and honors bestowed on graduates. The church has none of these promotions, it can only offer us the fact that Christ died for her, that she is the home of the saved on earth, that her saved ones will be with Christ in eternity. The day is now upon us, that some of our schools are standing on the side on those who are ravaging the church we love. As it was in Joshua's day, alumni of those schools will have to choose which they will serve; the God who gave his Son for them and gave us the church, or the Schools who want our loyalty and support even as they do harm to the bride of Christ. May none of us allow our loyalties to be misplaced in this struggle.

107. CONCESSIONS WE MUST MAKE

In their effort to capture the hearts of young and naive disciples, the champions of change lay a constant barrage of criticism against the Lord's church. In so doing they aspire to cause sufficient discontent that brethren will turn to them for leadership. Also they would like for us to deny obvious problems so that we would appear, stubborn and intransigent. The fact is, some of the things they cite are true in part or in whole. They certainly are not the first to make these observations.

* *Yes, there are too many divisions among us. Even one division is an evil thing. Whether it is local, within a congregation, or general, affecting the whole brotherhood, division is bad (Rom. 16:16). A distinction however must be made between those who "cause divisions" and those who are the victims of it. Interestingly, many churches have experienced division because of the work of the change agents!
* Yes, we do have some traditions. Some are biblical and must be observed and preserved (II Thess. 3:6). Others are quite harmless and in most cases, beneficial. Some congregations have traditions that no doubt hinder them. The latter we must constantly work to eliminate.
* Yes, we do have some "sectarian-minded people." But we do not excuse them or glorify them. We try to show them a more excellent way, the way of loyalty to Christ, rather than to men or opinions. But we also have some "denominational-minded people" among us. They are those who have readily embraced the change movement. They see the church as a denomination. They see nothing wrong with denominationalism in contrast to the religion of Christ.
* Yes, some of our churches do have lackluster worship services. The cure is to call them back to worship that is truly "in spirit" as well as in truth (John 4:24); to teach them to love God with all their hearts, souls and minds (Matt. 22:37). To provide them exciting services based on the doctrines and commandments of

men (Matt. 15:9) is certainly not an acceptable antidote!
* Yes, some of our churches are not as evangelistic as they should be. Changing our ways of worship, our beliefs, our church government or the nature of the church, will not change this. If all our neighbors who believe in Jesus are saved already (as many change agents believe), there certainly is little incentive to teach and try to win them, is there?
* Yes, some of our congregational leaders are not as effective as they should be. Some are too old, some too old-fashioned, some too cautious and some are out of touch with the flock. Such men need to grow in the grace and knowledge of Christ (II Pet. 3:18). They need to educate, inform and improved themselves so they can lead effectively. Some should step aside and make room for more capable leaders. Interestingly, the same complaint can be made against many preachers. The one thing we don't need to do is throw away the Biblical standard for qualified "men" to lead and save our churches and elevate women to these places of leadership; not if we wish to continue as Christ's church (III Tim. 2:8-3:1).
* Yes, Alexander Campbell, Barton Stone and their Christian peers did launch the American movement to restore New Testament Christianity. But they did not found the church. Christ did that (Matt. 16:18). They simply planted the gospel seed of the kingdom (Luke 8:11) and it brought forth on our continent the same kind of church that it produced in Jerusalem and the Mediterranean world of the first century.
* Yes, many of our preachers are not learned university men, but it is precisely this type of men who have evangelized, planted most of our churches, and built them to their present level of strength. We appreciate the attainments and contributions of those scholars who were loyal and faithful to Christ, his Word and his church. But the fact is, many of our problems have originated with those who put worldly scholarship about the authority of Christ's Word.
* Yes, our fathers were slow to speak out against racial segregation. But their sons and daughters have done so. They chose however

to deal with that issue as a moral, spiritual matter than as a political issue and have avoided posturing thereon.
* Yes, we all are part of history's stream and yes, our culture does influence our thinking, values and behavior. But we are committed to honoring God's Word as an objective standard, superior to all of those worldly influences. We do not always perfectly reach our goal, nor do we always understand the Word as well as we should, but we never cease trying. We keep our minds open to any new insights or understandings we may have missed. We are ever ready to make any necessary adjustments that we may be conformed to the image of Christ (II Cor. 3:18). The promoters of change are likewise subject to these historical, cultural influences.

Having made all of these concession, we ask our agents of change, "What does this prove?" Such is the case with every generation of Christians in every society, and so will it be for every generation yet to come. We are the human side of the church; weak, frail, imperfect. We are always a work in progress. There is also a divine side of the church, perfect as Him who founded it. That is the eternal, unchanging kingdom of our Savior, Jesus! By the way, do the changes agents think that they have somehow risen above the weaknesses we have conceded? "Wherefore thou art without excuse . . . for wherein thou judgest another, thou condemnest thyself; for thou that judgest dost practice the same things" (Rom. 2:1).

108. SOME THINGS WE CANNOT AFFORD

As we stand locked in mortal battle with teachers who would destroy the church of Christ we know and love, there are some things we in the army of Christ cannot afford.

We cannot afford **morbid suspicion of other brethren in the army of Christ**. We must not allow ourselves to sink to the low level of assuming that every brother is unfaithful until he proves himself to our satisfaction. "To his own Lord he standeth or falleth" (Rom. 14:4). If a man is a fellow-Christian, if he is fighting the good fight of faith and resisting the devil, I should welcome him as my comrade in arms. This is the lesson Jesus taught in Mark 9:38-40. I should respect him as such until he demonstrates otherwise. If I only trust and count as faithful those whom I personally know, then my army will amount to a handful at best.

We cannot afford **to listen to the whispers of gossips that would try to set us one against the other**. In war, one branch of the military pursues psychological tactics. They spread disinformation, rumors and other methods of confusing the enemy and turning them one against the other. Satan has used this ploy to great advantage in our day. "A perverse man scattereth abroad strife; and a whisperer separateth chief friends" (Prov. 16:28).

We cannot afford **to demand perfect agreement on every jot and tittle** before we can stand with a brother in the battle against the change agents. It is inevitable that there will be matters of judgement on which we disagree. There will be some scriptures we don't understand the alike. There will be methods or strategies that one will use that the other will not pursue. But remember we all are fighting for a common cause, the precious church of our Lord Jesus. That I am not comfortable with one method or strategy of battle does not mean it is wrong. Fundamental and clearly revealed doctrine we do not negotiate on, but there are many other items wherein we can tolerate each other for the greater Cause we serve.

We cannot afford **a narrow, shortsighted approach in this warfare**. The battle for the heart of the church is far wider and much more than just the congregation where I preach. While that is surely vital and important, the church of Christ is the Lord's family around the world. If I can help to advance the Cause or to defend it in another city, state or nation, it is my duty to do what I can. Sometimes we see a man whose only interest is in protecting the church from whence his salary flows. Such is not a proper attitude for a noble soldier of the cross.

We must not **spend our powder and shot on our fellow soldiers**. There is a misguided view in some quarters that by blasting away at a fellow-preacher we are preaching the gospel and defending the Cause of Christ. They care not that he is serving God to the best of his ability; faithfully preaching the truth of the gospel as he understands it. While we shoot at each other, or defend our backs, the enemy gains the victory by default. How tragic! Paul warned, "if ye bite and devour one another, take heed that ye be not consumed one of another" (Gal. 5:15).

We cannot afford **a mean hateful spirit** if we wish to win the hearts and confidence of our brethren and keeping them from following the pipers of "change." The change agents have capitalized on that very attitude to persuade many that those who oppose them are narrow, sectarian bigots whom no one should heed. Even in a pitched battle, we must "speak the truth in love" (Eph. 4:15). Our speech must be with grace, seasoned with salt (Col.4:6); that is if we are serious about winning.

We cannot afford **a scorched earth policy**. Gen. Tecumseh Sherman brought the South to her knees in the Civil War but the destruction he visited on the people made his name a hiss and a by word for a hundred years. It created a spirit of sullen hostility toward the victors that lived on for much of a century. Some preachers seem to operate by this principle. They are unwilling to exercise patience; not interested in salvaging a brother, a good work, a congregation; just to destroy them if they have imbibed or tolerated some error in this conflict. Such victories can cost us the war, if disciples refuse to hear us because of that attitude.

Paul knew that some brethren needed to be corrected because they oppose themselves (II Tim. 2:25). May we not be guilty of that mistake?

109. OUR CHALLENGE

To win in our struggle against the liberal forces at work among us we must find a way to enlist every available man who shares our basic loyalties and is willing to stand strong. Most folks can easily see the dangers of the extreme liberals or the radicals on the right. Either camp is still relatively small in number. Between those extremes are several thousand congregations and preachers whom we must try to salvage and save. Large numbers of them are clearly tilted to the left and will likely go that way if we are not able to reach them with a clear and cordial message that will help them see the problem and inspired them to stick with the Book of God.

While the two extremes mentioned above have done their damage, our ability to hold the center has been greatly weakened, even crippled, by an unfortunate tendency to demand total agreement on every detail from our fellow-workers and an unwillingness to work together. This attitude has been seen primarily among those who are the conservatives of the middle group. The tendency to attack rather than reason, to write up and write off those who don't see the details as we do has weakened our forces. It has also provided powerful ammunition for the liberals to use against us. By painting us as narrow, factious and hateful they have convinced many younger, weaker, more moderate brethren that they offer the only reasonable alternative

Is there any way we can arrive at a simple understanding of basic truths that must be mutually held if we are to be able to work together against a common foe, without writing a creedal statement?

The following items are being challenged by liberal brethren. They are central to our being New Testament Christians and the church of the Bible. If we are in agreement on these points how tolerant can we afford to be on other issues that occasionally arise?
1. The verbal inspiration and thus inerrancy of the Bible.

2. The full and final authority of the New Testament of Christ in the faith and practice oft the church.
3. The ability of the common man to arrive at a correct understanding of the word of God.
4. Belief in the nature and status of the contemporary church of Christ of which we are members as the church which Christ purchased with his blood; that it is not a sect or denomination founded by humans?
5. That denominationalism is unacceptable to Jehovah?
6. The fact that the Lord's church is separate from the other religious bodies founded by men. Hence we can have no fellowship with them.
7. Loyalty to the concept of restoring Christianity to its original faith and practice.
8. Loyalty to the items and kind of worship set forth in the New Testament: Weekly communion, on the First Day as a memorial; Acappella music; Prayers; Offerings and Scripture Studies.
9. Congregational leadership that is limited to male Christians.
10. Only men to be "preachers, ministers and evangelists."
11. No name but that of Christian for individual disciples and only Bible names for the church.
12. Commitment to the sufficiency of the church to do its work of evangelism. (Here we must be careful not to drift into a position like the non-institutional brethren did). The liberals would like very much to brand us as just a new brand of "anti-ism." We clearly have a bevy of organizations soliciting the funds from our churches to do their work of evangelism in the same way that the missionary societies did a century ago.
13. Baptism by immersion as an essential prerequisite for remission of sins and membership in the church.

We will sink or survive on our ability or lack thereof to maintain a united front in the face of our enemy. The big question is can we find a common ground on which to stand and fight our common enemy?

110. PRINCIPLES FOR CHRISTIAN SOLDIERS

Among the many metaphors the Holy Spirit uses to describe Christians is that of soldiers. Paul exhorted Timothy to "suffer hardship with me as a good soldier of Christ . . . " (II Tim. 2:2). Christians in Ephesus were told to "put on the whole armor of God, that ye may be able to withstand the wiles of the devil" (Eph. 6:11). As in carnal war, so in our spiritual warfare, there are certain principles that are indispensable to victory.

I. **We must know our friends and our enemies**. We should "know them that labor among (us) and are over (us) in the Lord . . . and esteem them highly in love for their work's sake" (I Thess. 5:12-13). In the present conflict with those who are determined to "change" our faith, worship and practice, it is crucial to know if a brother is sound in his faith or a promoter of error. This should be determined before any man is invited to be a local preacher, to conduct special services and before any man is appointed an elder, deacon or teacher. We need to know the proponents of error, lest we inadvertently invite them in and suffer for so doing.

II. **We must reject the factious man or woman** after appropriate admonitions (Tit. 3:10). No church is under obligation to keep a factious preacher in their employment; a factious elder or deacon in his office; a factious teacher in a Bible class; or a factious person in its membership. As a secular army cannot endure the man who sows discord in the ranks, neither can the army of Christ. In the military, it means court martial and dishonorable discharge, in Christ it means to exclude them from fellowship.

III. **We must mark them that cause divisions and occasions of stumbling** contrary to the doctrine (we have) learned" (Rom. 16:17). This means we are to take note of their troublesome teaching and practice. It means we care to "turn away from them. For they serve not our Lord Christ, but their own belly" (Rom. 16:17). Neither should they be allowed to infiltrate other congregations without warning.

III. **We must understand our enemy**. Many a battle has been lost because an army's leadership failed to understand the tactics, the zeal, the determination and the strength of the enemy. To effectively combat the "apostles of change," we must understand them and their message. To do this we must take the time to read their books and publications. We need to know their background and training. While they wear the uniform and insignia of Christ, their orientation is thoroughly denominational. Their allegiance is not to the church of Christ, but to a newly emerging denomination that seeks to supplant the Lord's church. Their strategies have been learned in denominational seminaries. Their methods are based on emotionalism, excitement and popularity. They promise their target churches rapid growth and wonderful renewal. They hide their true intent under the guise of superior knowledge learned in the divinity schools of the great secular universities. Paul warns us "Let no man beguile you . . . " (II Thess. 2:2).

IV. **We must defend the gospel and the church against these predators** (Phil. 1:16; Acts 20:28-31). One is impressed at how often the liberal teachers say we should not defend scripture or church. They like to say, "Scripture has lasted for thousands of years without our defending it"(**God's Holy Fire**, p. 44). Of course their logic is, if we are persuaded we should not defend these sacred things, they will be left to their schemes without opposition.

V. **We must contend for the faith once delivered** (Jude3). We must take the battle to the enemy. The ancient military strategy says, "a strong offense is the best defense." We cannot afford to sit passively waiting until these folks attack our local congregations. Ours is a brotherhood-wide conflict. One side or the other will prevail. Clear-thinking dictates that we take the battle to their door step and rout them from our midst.

VI. **We must be steadfast and unmovable** (I Cor. 15:58). The battle will be long, costly and hard fought. There must be no compromise with error; no accommodation with enemies of righteousness. When our forefathers were faced with the liberal ancestors of our "change agents," the battle raged from 1850 to 1925. The issues then were virtually identical to those we face today.

VII. **We must be victorious**. There is no substitute for victory! Not only is the faithfulness of our congregations, schools, mission-outposts at stake, in each of these there are souls, precious to Jesus, who will either remain faithful to him or be swept into apostasy. Only those faithful unto death are promised the crown of life (Rev. 2:10).

VIII. **We must be properly armed**. An unarmed or ill-equipped soldier has little chance of success in battle, no matter how sincere or noble he may be. Only Christian soldiers who are well-armed can prevail in this conflict. Most of the champions of change are highly educated men. But the David with Scripture in his sling can bring down those Goliaths with their weaver's beam degrees. But only if our Davids are prepared.

IX. **We must be strong in prayer at all seasons** (Eph.6:18). With God's help we will prevail, without it we will surely fail. The effective soldier of Christ is truly a spiritual man, devoted to prayer and holy living.

111. AN APPEAL TO THE ADMINISTRATORS OF OUR CHRISTIAN SCHOOLS

Dear Brethren:

The stability of the Lord's church all across the nation is being threatened by an element of our people who are working to introduce major changes into the faith, worship and practice of our

brethren. In numerous cases this has resulted in division of congregations and the discouragement of those involved. I am confident that you are aware of the changes being promoted:
* A new way of viewing the world. **Postmodernism** denies absolute truth, promotes pluralism and subjectivism and prefers the new over the old.
* A new view about the authority of the Scripture in the life of the church. They deny that the New Testament should be viewed as a pattern for us to follow.
* A repudiation of the commitment to restore the faith and practice of the early church.
* A new hermeneutic. They propose a method of interpreting the Bible that has the effect of making every man a law unto himself as he subjectively decides what the Scriptures mean to him.
* A new way of viewing the church of Christ. They deny that the church of Church is the one true church that Christ built. They view it as just another denomination founded by men.
* A new way of worship. They teach that our rejection of instrumental music in worship is without a Biblical basis, thus nothing more than our tradition. They are willing to accept and fellowship those who use instruments in worship and are open to the practice themselves.
* A new way of viewing the Lord's Supper. Some of them are teaching that rather than a solemn memorial feast it is to be observed in conjunction with and as part of a fellowship meal of common food.
* The Biblical prohibition of women in the leadership of the church is being challenged. They argue we unduly restrict them and they should be allowed to publicly lead the church in worship. Some already are using women preachers.
* They are promoting the idea that we should open our fellowship to those of the denominational world, accepting them as our brethren in Christ.
* Some are ridiculing our use of the name Church of Christ and proposing that we drop that Biblical name from use.
* Other points are also being promoted but these are sufficient to

point out the seriousness of the problem we face.

It would be very helpful to elders, preachers and parents if you would issue some sort of statement or affirmation, letting the brotherhood know the position of your school in reference to this push for change. Parents want to send their children to a school that will fortify and strengthen their faith, not undermine it. Church leaders want to recommend schools that will help, not harm their students' faith. In days past leaders of our Christian Schools worked hand and hand with the church to uphold the Biblical standard of faith, worship and practice. It would be beneficial both for your school and the churches if you could publish something in this regard.

112. HANDMAIDEN OR MISTRESS

The Bible knows nothing of Christian Colleges. But as expediencies to help the church do her work, they have played a significant, but not always a salutary role in the history of our Restoration Movement.

In the early days, the founders and promoters of Christian schools saw them as handmaidens to the church. Their mission was perceived to be that of assistants to the church in fulfilling her mission here on earth.
* They provided a wholesome, quality education for the children of church members within a strong Christian environment. Teachers were expected to be faithful members of the church and campus life was to be shaped by Christian values.
* Christian schools provided an environment where young Christians could meet and find mates who shared their faith in Christ.
* They educated young Christians and provided them skills necessary for success in business. The graduates, as they pursued their vocations, provided strong, well-trained and

faithful leadership in local congregations.
* The schools provided training for young men who desired to serve as gospel preachers. With solid, dependable Bible instruction, they would go forth and bless the church by their faithful teaching and leadership. It was understood that the doctrines imparted by the schools would be thoroughly Biblical and reflect the broad general convictions of the brotherhood on all essential points.
* They trained and encouraged young Christians to take the gospel of Christ to mission fields where the good news had not yet gone.

For these valuable contributions, Christians and congregations gave thanks and encouraged their young people to choose our Christians schools for their education. Thousands of Christians provided financial support for our schools and some congregations lent support especially to their Bible departments and mission programs.

A Shift In the Relationship Has Occurred

Since the 1960s a new spirit has evolved within the leadership of some of our schools. No longer do they perceive themselves as handmaidens to render service to the Lord's church. While not formally announced, the shift is seen in their actions. They now see themselves as the superior mistress to supervise, lead and guide the fumbling, unprofessional churches. Their behavior suggests that congregations exist to serve the schools by providing them students and the funds needed to maintain and further enlarge their institutions. The principal interest of the academics that control many of these schools is to gain the approval, respect of their educational peers in the broader secular and denominational realms.

Today an eldership cannot safely assume that a graduate of some of our Christian schools will hold doctrinal views consistent with New Testament principles. In fact they must be very careful that he does not hold views contrary to Biblical standards. Parents can no longer assume that all teachers in those schools hold views that will strengthen the faith of their sons and daughters.

Rather than serve the church, many administrators and professors look upon the typical elder and preacher as obsolete and out of date in their understanding of spiritual matters. Hence they (the school men) have taken it upon themselves to reshape the beliefs, worship and practice of our churches. With an elitist air, they have launched their uninvited program of change for our people.

Looking back a hundred years, we see the same scenario was played out among our people in that day. The Christian schools led in the apostasy that divided our people then. We did not learn from the mistakes of the past. The problem has surfaced again in our day and we suffer for our folly.

If there are to be Christian Schools among us, those who direct them must never forget their proper position as handmaidens to serve and benefit church of the Lord Jesus.

(The author appreciates those schools that have faithfully served the church and continue to fill their role in the work of the Lord).

113. INOCULATING YOUR CONGREGATION AGAINST THE CHANGE DISEASE

Sooner or later every congregation of God's people will be confronted by someone wishing to promote the agenda of the "change movement." Rather than wait until the dangerous moment arrives, we need to act now to inoculate our members so they will recognize the symptoms and reject it upon sight. The following suggestions will help to immunize your congregation beforehand.

* Your preacher needs to present an extended series of lessons on the fundamentals of the faith. He needs to touch on all points of

faith, worship and practice that are being challenged by the promoters of change. Such lessons should be repeated on a yearly basis.
* Lessons need to be presented that remind brethren of the danger of false teachers and false doctrine.
* Elders could plan a retreat for the men of the church where the dangers of the change movement could be pointed out and the specific errors of it discussed.
* Elders might wish to invite a guest speaker who is informed on this issue to come and spend a week end with the congregation. It would be most important that he be a faithful man of wisdom, experienced in dealing with error, lest he do more harm than good.
* Each year a quarter of Bible Classes should be devoted to studying the distinctives of the church revealed in the Scripture.
* A series of tracts should be purchased that address the many points under attack by the promoters of change. Each week each family should receive a copy and be asked to read it. It could then be the basis of the Bible class or sermon the following week.
* A mature sister whose faith is strong and whose understanding of the Word is substantial should be assigned to teach a course for the Ladies' Bible Class on God's plan for women in the church. This should address the challenges of those who wish to place women in leadership roles. The same materials should be presented in any other classes for women from highschool and up.
* Books addressing the errors of the change movement and others setting forth the Biblical basis for our faith, worship and practice should be purchased and placed in the church library. Notice of these should be placed in the church bulletin and perhaps mentioned in the announcements. In larger congregations several copies of significant books should be ordered.
* The elders should have a sit-down discussion with their minister and other staff members, especially youth and campus workers making it clear that they do not accept the agenda of the change agents, nor will they allow it to be introduced into the life of the

congregation.
* A similar session should be conducted with deacons and all Bible class teachers.
* A statement from the elders should be presented to the congregation, preferably in person on Sunday morning stating their position and determination to not allow the change program to be brought into the church. This should be printed in the church bulletin or mailed to each family of the congregation.
* It should be made a matter of policy that no one will be considered for work with the congregation who is sympathetic with the change agenda.
* The same rule should apply to anyone considered for an invitation as a guest speaker.
* Elders must stay on high alert for the foreseeable future. Such movements take years to run their course. The fact that a church was rock solid ten years ago is no guarantee that it will be so ten years hence.
* No brother should be added to the eldership who is unsure of his convictions on this crucial matter. A divided leadership will eventually be a defeated leadership.

Elders, remember that they who hesitate or procrastinate may well lose that which is most precious to them.

114. UNPLEASANT TRUTHS

Not all truths and facts are lovely and pleasant. It is not pleasant to learn you have cancer or that your house has termites. Yet to deal with the problem you must come to terms with such unpleasant truths. In the church, as in private life, most of us hate to face unpleasant facts. It is easy to turn ones head, close ones eyes and hope the unpleasant things will go away. Unfortunately it just doesn't work that way.

* It is a fact that there is such a thing as false teaching. Peter wrote of men who will privily bring in "destructive heresies . . . " (II Pet. 2:1). Paul warned of teachers who like grievous wolves would attack the flock of God "speaking perverse things" (Acts 20:30).
* It is a fact that false teaching is spread by false teachers. There are men who march in our ranks as fellow-Christians but who teach a gospel different from that which the apostles preached (Gal. 1:7-9). Their teaching is a perversion of the true gospel.
* It is a fact that some brethren who once stood with us in the Lord's service, have departed from the faith once delivered (I Tim. 4:1; Jude 3). They have made shipwreck concerning the faith (I Tim. 1:19).
* It is a sad fact that some congregations that have left their first love as did the church in Ephesus (Rev. 2:4-5).
* There are some people yet in the fellowship of the church who are as dangerous as jagged rocks hidden under the surface of a placid harbor (Jude 12). They wait to inflict a devastating injury to the church when least expected.
* There have always been folks who circulate among Christ's people, "teaching things which they ought not for filthy lucre's sake" (Tit. 1:11).
* There are men who "in covetousness . . . with feigned words make merchandise of" God's people (II Pet. 2:3).
* There are men who cause divisions among God's people (Rom. 16:17).
* In every generation there are those among God's people who chaff under the limitations of the Word of God and thus choose to go out from among them to find the freedom to teach different doctrines and introduce new and different practices (I John 2:19).
* To prevent the church from being ravaged and destroyed by false teachers, God tells us to reject the factious teacher (Tit. 3:10) and to mark them that cause divisions contrary to the teaching of Christ (Rom. 16:17). We are to reject them and give them no encouragement or fellowship (II John 9-10).

* It is a fact that those who continue to support and encourage men who have departed from the faith become partakers with them in their evil works (II John 11).

While these truths are not pleasant, they are absolutely essential for the survival of the church. Those who ignore them or defy them, not only will bring grief into the life of their congregations, they will have to answer to Christ in judgement for rejecting that part of his will they did not find pleasing to them (John 12:48).

115. PAINFUL AND UNPLEASANT, BUT NECESSARY

Those who have had to deal with cancer or other serious health issues know that the treatments are often painful with unpleasant side effects. Yet they are necessary if the patient hopes to survive and find renewed health.

Today a cancerous situation has developed within the Lord's church. The symptoms of this malady are a rejection of the faith, worship and preached in the past; an overwhelming desire for change in all aspects of church life and a willingness to embrace virtually anything new and different in the practice of their faith. Those smitten generally have their spiritual eyesight damaged so that they cannot discern the difference in Biblical Christianity and the counterfeit versions of religion that flourish around us.

If the church of Christ is to survive as a recognizable body, drastic action must be taken to excise the cancer of error that is rapidly metastasizing throughout the body.
* Painful as it is, we must talk about the problem. Ignorance and denial are deadly in the face of this affliction. Brethren must know of the danger they face.
* We must begin treatments immediately. Each day treatment is delayed might mean souls lost, even entire congregations lost to the Lord's Cause.

* We must deal with specific symptoms, teachings and practice. Vague generalities will not cure the disease.
* We must change our diet; No more study materials written by change agents; no more invitations for them to come, lest they spread their disease among us; no more bland diet of sweet words that do not address the real problem we are up against. We need sound, healthy doctrine (Tit. 2:1); strong meat (Heb. 4:14) that will strengthen our faith and convictions if we are to be able to resist this invading illness.
* We must cease to promote or patronize their colleges, lectures, seminars and books. We must not lend aid nor comfort to those who would destroy that which is sacred to us (II John 11).
* We must not send our young people to their schools, camps and workshops lest they be infected with their virus.
* We must first isolate and then remove the malignant growth from each congregation, school and all other brotherhood activities.
* We must post a clear warning to all lest they be overtaken by the disease.
* We must inoculate every member young and old against this plague.
* We must create an environment where change agents cannot flourish. Those who are physicians of souls should make sure that the environment in their congregations is so thoroughly clean and healthy that carriers of the change ailment will have to flee to other bodies or be driven out. Most of them could readily find a home among the Christian Churches, Baptists or Lutheran bodies.

Granted this treatment is both painful and unpleasant but it is absolutely essential if we are to survive.

116. PREVENTIVE MEDICINE FOR YOUR CONGREGATION

When an epidemic breakouts out in a community, public health officials encourage everyone to be pro-active in order to prevent the spread of the disease. We have an epidemic of error sweeping through the brotherhood of churches of Christ. It is commonly known as the "change movement." It is most often spread by preachers but sometimes by young adults recently out of Christian schools and student centers, or by means of religious books and journals promoting this ism. It is a terrible mistake for elders and preachers to think, "If it ever shows up here we will make sure it does not spread among us." Chances are by the time you find out you have the problem it will already have gotten into the hearts of some of your members. We must inoculate our members by informing and instructing them before hand. We offer four suggestions that will help you prevent the problem.

1. Beginning immediately, plan and deliver a series of lessons that address the specific challenges the change agents pose. Ideally these will be presented on Sunday morning when most of your members will be present. These lessons can be approached both positively and negatively by showing what we believe and why on a given subject or by pointing out the error of those who want to change our faith, worship and practice.
2. A curriculum of Bible class studies should be instituted that will cover the same materials. They should be offered to all classes from high school through adults. The advantage of the class presentation is that there could be interaction and discussion. No less than one and perhaps two quarters should be devoted to this study. Ideally it should be repeated every two years.
3. A series of tracts could be purchased that address the areas being attacked by the change agents. Enough should be purchased that each family could be given a copy. Each week they should be distributed to all present with the elders encouraging all members to read it that before the next Lord's Day. For a catalog of available tracts call Haun Publishing Co. 1-800-231-9709.
4. A monthly bundle of **Christianity: Then and Now** could be ordered and a copy placed in the hands of each family with the

encouragement to read it. That will place some 48 lessons in their hands in a year's time . . . all devoted to dealing with the challenges of the change movement. Copies mailed in bundles are .20 each.

The following areas of our faith are under attack and should be addressed:
* The authority of the Bible for all we believe and do as a church.
* The priority of the New Testament of Christ over the Old Testament for the faith, worship and practice of the church.
* How to correctly interpret the Bible and determine how it authorizes things.
* The relationship between God's grace and man's faith and obedience to it,
* The necessary role of baptism to salvation by faith.
* The nature of the church of Christ: its oneness, its importance and its relation to man's salvation.
* The sinfulness of denominationalism.
* Why we do not share fellowship with denominational preachers, churches, institutions and events.
* Why we do not observe holy days such as Easter and Christmas.
* The Lord's Supper, why we observe it as we do and why only on the first day of the week.
* Our praise to God, why we have no choirs, solos or instrumental music.
* The use of drama and singing groups in our worship.
* The nature of Christian worship; that it is not an entertainment experience.
* The kind of preaching and teaching God expects of his leaders.
* The reign of Christ and his kingdom. Why we do not accept the premillennial doctrine.
* The Scripturalness of the name church of Christ.
* Why we do not have women in positions of public leadership in our churches.
* What it means to restore New Testament Christianity.
* The role of pioneer preachers like Alexander Campbell and Barton

Stone in the church. That they are not our founders and their teachings are not our standard.
* The sufficiency of the church to do its work of evangelism without human organizations.
* The various kinds of traditions that exist in churches, noting those which are good, bad or of no consequence.
* The possibility of preachers, congregations and schools departing from the faith and becoming apostate.
* When, how and why we ceased to be in fellowship with the Christian Churches/Disciples of Christ.
* How we should deal with those who depart from the faith of Christ.

As the right medicine can prevent many diseases from getting a grip on a human body, so the right kind of teaching can keep a congregation from being overcome by the false teachings of the change agents.

117. LESSONS FROM OUR SOUTHERN BAPTIST NEIGHBORS

Over a period of years liberals gradually insinuated themselves into the leadership of the Southern Baptist denomination. They infiltrated their universities and seminaries and spread their pernicious doctrines through them. Thousands of youngsters were indoctrinated and took their liberal agenda back to the churches where they worshiped. They also captured control of their publishing houses and most other denominational agencies. Even though the majority of their churches and preachers were conservative in their faith, the denomination was being herded into the camp of liberal Protestantism.

When conservative leaders finally awoke to the seriousness of their problem, they organized and coordinated their efforts and quickly took control of the situation. The liberal element did not voluntary abdicate their seats of power when they saw that the majority of the members stood against them; nor did they surrender without a hard fought battle. The liberals protested that they were not really liberals, even though their handling and interpretation of Scripture and their views on moral and social issues were those of theological liberals. They protested that they were really moderates and those who opposed them were radical reactionaries who would destroy their church if successful. They found enthusiastic support and comfort from the secular media which consistently painted the liberals as poor, mistreated and abused moderates and the conservatives as radicals

The conservatives were careful to pick their battles. The major battle was waged on the inspiration, inerrancy and authority of God's Word. Only by dogged determination did the conservatives prevail. When the liberals finally realized their cause was lost, they began to separate themselves and find consolation with others whose liberal faith they shared.

There are valuable lessons for us to learn in this bit of contemporary religious history. Can we; will we observe, learn and profit therefrom or will we sit idly by while a band of liberal preachers and university professors capture the minds and hearts of our people? It is safe to say that it is not the average member in the pew who wants to introduce "changes" into his congregation. The push is coming from a handful of theologians and preachers at the top. My God help us be "good soldiers of Christ Jesus" (II Tim. 2:3) and withstand this harmful trend with steadfast faith (I Pet. 5:8-9).

118. GOOD RIDDANCE

I recently heard that a Muslim cleric left America for his Middle-Eastern place of origin. He was unhappy with our government's efforts at homeland security following last year's attack by Muslim terrorists. I did not anguish over his departure nor beg him to stay.

In fact, I was glad to hear the news. He was not a loyal sympathetic American. His values were not ours. He despised the great principles of freedom and liberty we cherish. He had neither part nor lot with us. America is better and safer now that he is gone.

Just two weeks ago I read that a professor/preacher of the change movement had left the Church of Christ and assumed a ministerial post in a denominational church. Sad as that may seem, the published writings of this brother indicated that he did not share the essential, basic, fundamental faith of those known as churches of Christ. He was a denominationalist at heart and in his theology. Among us, training our young people, he would only do harm to the Cause we love.

There are many more like him: men who have made shipwreck of the faith (I Tim. 1:19), who are yet working among us. They labor not to build up and strengthen the church but to shame and ridicule her past, her former leaders, her ancient forms of worship, her sacred doctrine. The sooner they are recognized and rejected; the sooner they too depart, the better it will be for the Lord's church.

Faced with the departure of some of his brethren, the apostle John wrote, "They went out from us, but they were not of us: for if they had been of us, they have continued with us: but they went out that they might be made manifest that they all are not of us" (I John 2:19). Weep not brethren, when such folks make their exit, rather thank God that they are gone. May the Lord hasten the day when church is free of all such men who no longer cherish the old paths of New Testament Christianity!

119. OUR POST WAR STRATEGY

As America contemplated war with Iraq, President Bush and his advisors were developing a post war strategy to help rebuild that nation and hopefully instill a love for freedom and democracy in the hearts of the Iraqi people. As we in the church do battle with the forces of the change movement, we too must be thinking of a meaningful postwar strategy.

It will not be enough just to win. If God is with us and we block the advance of this destructive movement; if the agents of change flee to the denominations which they so admire, what will our condition then be? Our mission must be bigger and broader than just defeating the enemy among us. There is a positive and constructive side of Christianity that must be pursued. Preachers or people who have no greater goal than doing battle with their own errant brethren have failed to understand our reason for existing.

We must not be content to save the status quo of the last 40 years. The church is in dire need of renewal by the restoration of scriptural emphasis on all things related to her life and work, her faith and worship.

* For 30 years our growth has been stagnant. We must renew our commitment to aggressive evangelism. The great commission is still our primary mission (Matt. 28:19).
* A lost world still languishes for the simple gospel. We must send forth a new wave of missionaries Even as Americans grow cold and indifferent to the gospel, millions in other nations are begging for the bread of life.
* American families, including many within the church, are being ravaged and shattered by the corrupting influences of our modern culture. We must provide teaching and training to prepare young adults for lasting marriage and to strengthen those already wed.
* Our children are being corrupted by a decadent culture. Schools have been captured by humanists and are being used to undermine their faith in God and his Word. Corrupting music, television and movies are blurring their sense of moral judgment. We must renew our approach to educating them, rooting and grounding them in the faith of the gospel (Prov. 22:6).

* Our members, generally, are deficient in Biblical knowledge. This has left thousands of them vulnerable to false teaching such as that of the change movement. We must do a better job of educating and indoctrinating them in the fundamentals of the faith.
* The change agents have captured and spoiled some of our major schools that heretofore have provided advanced education for our young people and training for young preachers. Those lost to their clutches should be abandoned and the surviving faithful schools must be supported and encouraged to greater service.
* Many preachers have lost their faith in the authority of God's Word and the need to restore the original facets of the faith and practice of the church. Such men are no longer of useful service to the church. They must be rejected and in their place a new generation of faithful men must be encouraged to take up the work of preaching and be trained for true and loyal service.
* We must rebuild a sense of brotherhood. Those who are older can remember the sense of love, loyalty, concern and cooperation that existing among our brethren prior to the 1960s. Somewhere, somehow, that sense of brotherhood has been allowed to wither and atrophy. We must reverse this destructive trend. This sense of congregational isolation has contributed to the success of the change agents who have been able to prey on a given congregation while others ignored the danger of their brethren.

This conflict will be years in resolving. With God's help we will defeat those who have turned against the church they once loved and served. The big question is, "Are we committed to a workable postwar strategy?" Without such a strategy, the victors will eventually wither away.

120. "WE BESEECH YOU ON BEHALF OF CHRIST"

Paul penned these words to the Corinthians, some of whom had become alienated from the head of the church (II Cor. 5:20). Within our brotherhood we see turmoil and confusion as the result of a self-appointed band of change agents who are pressing for unscriptural changes to our faith, worship and practice as the body of Christ. In the face of this challenge, which has the potential of doing great harm to the church, the author extends the following appeal:

I. To you who are elders of God's church: I beseech you to be faithful shepherds; to diligently protect the flock of God among you (I Pet. 5:2-3). Please don't allow agents of change to gain even the smallest foothold among your people. They are truly wolves in sheep's clothing (Matt. 7:15). They will promise you great things; numerical growth, an influx of young families and revitalization, but their prescription will actually bring death. It may well divide and scatter your people. It most certainly will change your congregation by leading you away from the clearly taught principles of the gospel into the world of unauthorized human ideas and opinions. Even if you gain the advantages which they promise, you will lose the favor of God and be rejected. What a terrible price to pay.

II. To you who stand before God's people to preach his word: I beseech you to preach Christ (I Cor. 2:2), but do not neglect his teaching regarding his doctrine and his church. To do so will leave your hearers weak and anemic in faith and vulnerable to Satan's deception. Preach the whole counsel of God, including warning your people against cunning false teachers who will lead them astray from the paths of God (Acts 20:26-31). Take time to inform yourselves regarding the message of the change agents, invest the time and energy to prepare yourselves to answer them and to defend your people from their error (Phil. 1:16). Then use your classes and sermons to make sure your brethren are properly taught and inoculated against this pernicious error. Should the agents of change appear in your congregation or even in your city, be bold and courageous to speak out against their pernicious program of change.

III. To you who work with young people: In most cases the change agenda finds early acceptance among youth workers and their charges. Please understand that your job is more than just providing entertainment and fun for the precious young people of your congregation. They are young and immature, but you are older. Children don't always know what is best for them or good for them. You are there to help them discover that. While many of your peers have eagerly embraced the call for emotionalism, excitement and entertainment in worship, please don't follow them in that error. I beseech you to be faithful to God's standard. Recognize this pattern he has provided us and follow it (II Tim. 1:13). Do your work in such a way that when those boys and girls are grown they will be faithful members of the Church of Christ and not likely to be lured away into denominational bodies.

IV. To you who are young in years: I beseech you to always be faithful to Christ and his church. Take heed to the teaching and guidance of your elders in the faith. Remember it is God's will that "ye younger, be subject unto the elder" (I Pet. 5:5). Please remember that what your friends like and enjoy may not be what God wants from us in our worship. Respect the authority of God's Word. It will judge us in the last day (John 12:48). Do not allow vivacious and charismatic young teachers to lead you away from the faith of your fathers. The church was here long before you were born and will be here when Christ returns. We must take heed that we stay faithful to it.

V. To our sisters in Christ: I beseech you to remember that God who created you said, "Your desire shall be to your husband and he shall rule over thee" (Gen. 3:16). In his divine wisdom he ordained, "Let a woman learn in quietness with all subjection. But I permit not a woman to teach, nor to have dominion over a man, but to be in quietness" (I Tim. 2:11-12). He gives you his reasons for so doing. "For Adam was first formed, then Eve; and Adam was not beguiled but the woman being beguiled hath fallen into transgression . . . "(I Tim. 2:13-14). Understand that this restriction is not simply a matter of custom, culture or tradition. The Holy Spirit directed Paul to tell us, "As in all the churches of the saints, let the women keep silence in the churches: for it is not permitted unto them to speak; but let them be in subjection, as also saith the law" (I Cor. 14:33-34). In our generation you have been liberated from virtually all the limitations that culture and social convention placed upon your predecessors. For some this has been a blessing for others it has brought a catastrophe. But remember that no matter what the social reformers may say, or regardless how liberated your peers may be, you are still under the restrictions that Christ our King has placed upon you. You cannot be his faithful child and rebel against his revealed will. Even if people arise within the church urging you to ignore those prohibitions and aspire for public leadership roles in the church, please don't heed them. Reject them as false teachers whose message will lead you astray. To be with Christ in glory, we must abide by his will in this life (Matt. 7:21).

VI. To all fellow-Christians: I beseech you to be faithful unto death (Rev. 2:10). Observe the old paths of Biblical truth. They are unchanging and totally reliable. Stand up for Jesus! For his church and his Word! "Mark them that are causing divisions and occasions of stumbling among our people and turn away from them" (Rom. 16:17). When the change agents come knocking, do not open the door and give bid them welcome. "They are enemies of the cross of Christ" (Phil. 3:18).

X.
WE MUST AVOID BOTH EXTREMES

121. AVOIDING THE DITCHES

The highway of holiness has dangerous ditches on both right and left-hand sides. Whether we wreck on one side or the other is of little consequence. The results are fatal in either case. Moses warned Israel, "Ye shall walk in all the way which Jehovah your God hath commanded you, Ye shall not turn aside to the right hand or to the left" (Deut. 5:32). From the earliest ages, God's people have been plagued with the extremes of liberalism and legalism. The great challenge of every Christian and congregation is to maintain a balanced position between these two perversions of God's way.

What is Legalism? Legalism is an unwholesome attitude toward religion. It is a blind zeal for law with no thought for the spirit or intent of it. Paul was a minister of the "new covenant, not of the letter, but of the spirit; for the letter killeth, but the spirit giveth life" (II Cor. 3:6). Legalists have a greater concern for rules than for people. When Jesus healed the poor invalid at Bethesda, the legalistic Jews showed no sympathy for the man. Rather, they persecuted Jesus because he broke their uninspired rules about Sabbath keeping in so doing (John 5:1-18). He reminded them that, "the Sabbath was made for man and not man for the Sabbath . . . " (Mark 2:27). Legalists worship the law more than the Lawgiver. Traditions are gradually elevated to equality with God's law in the legalistic mind. A legalist is obsessed with details and numerous insignificant matters, while casually overlooking serious matters of major importance. Pharisees, who were legalists, were scrupulous to tithe even their garden herbs; mint, anise, and cummin. Yet they had little interest in weightier matters of the law such as justice, mercy and faith (Matt. 23:23). They majored in minors while minoring in major things. With the legalist, there is always the disposition to make additional rules to reinforce what they perceive to be God's law. The Pharisees of Jesus' day were classic legalists. They bound heavy burdens and grievous to be borne, and laid them on men's shoulders; but they themselves would "not move them with their finders" (Mat. 23:4). James tells us that "One only is the lawgiver and judge, even he who is able to save and destroy" (4:12). When man sets himself up to criticize and judge his brother, he has ceased to be a doer of the law and is condemned.

What is Liberalism? It too is a mistaken attitude toward Christianity. The liberal has a low view of Scripture. More extreme liberals deny the miraculous element of the Bible. They question the full, complete inspiration of God's Word. Especially do thy reject the Bible as the final authority in religious matters. In liberalism there is always a willingness to place human wisdom above the revealed wisdom of God. Liberals feel that they can select the portions of the Bible which they choose to accept and follow. We are describing a frame of mind that does not feel obligated to do all that God says to do. We definitely have an element of liberalism in the Lord's church today. It is a movement away from doctrinal preaching. It substitutes subjectivism for objective Biblical authority. It shows a willingness to fellowship denominations. It compromises truth with error. It is unhappy with simple New Testament worship. This spirit has always found fertile ground in Christian Universities. The Sadducees of Christ's day were liberals.

The departure of our "non-institutional" brethren in the 50s did not end our problem with legalism. From then till now we have had a small but a noisy band of "ultraconservative" brethren who have carried on a belligerent agitation against all who would not heel to their demands. Lacking a significant organ of communication and champions who commanded wide respect, they have not succeeded in forging their own independent fellowship, though for years many have tried to do so. Like a thorn in the foot, this legalistic element has imposed a decided limp on our brotherhood.

Today while we endure the legalism on the right, we are faced with a much greater threat from a wave of liberalism on the left. This assault is originating primarily from those associated with our Christian Universities and their proteges. Most of them are men with high educational credentials and a following among the young adults of our churches and schools. They are having marked success in many of our large city churches that have younger memberships. While few of these "liberal teachers" would openly question the miraculous events of the Bible, or the inspiration of the Word, by their words and deeds they demonstrate that they do not respect the authority of the Bible in regulating the faith and practice of the church. They are working to broaden our fellowship to include that of denominational bodies. They especially chaff at having to sing without instruments, choirs and soloists. They wish to move women into roles of public leadership. They think they have found a new way of interpreting the Bible that will allow them to do all of this and still claim to be New Testament Christians. If they cannot capture and lead our brotherhood into their liberal camp their future will be with the Christian Churches and Disciples of Christ who have long trodden the same path. Either of the ditches described herein will wreck and destroy a congregation. God's way is the Biblical way that stands between these two extremes. May God grant us wisdom to clearly see his way and the courage to walk therein. Only by so doing can churches of Christ survive the current crisis.

122. LABELS

A few days ago a visiting Christian inquired, "Are you liberal or conservative?" Fifty years ago no one ever had to ask that of a gospel preacher. Today the question is quite relevant. These and other labels have become common in our generation. Labels are slippery, uncertain things. One man's liberal is another man's conservative. To an "agent of change," I am a conservative, even a radical. But to a brother who styles himself "non-institutional," I am a liberal. I see myself as a faithful Christian, loyal to Christ, honoring his Word, today just as I did 47 years ago.

In order to communicate clearly we need to attach specific definitions to the terms we use. Those of us who occupy the traditional position of churches of Christ in America, see ourselves as conservatives who occupy the middle ground between liberals on the left and radicals on the right of the spectrum. We respect the Bible as the inspired and inerrant Word of God. We regard it as the absolute and final authority in all matters relating to the faith and practice of the church. We thus recognize Christ as founder, head and savior of the church. All the words and deeds of Christ are true and reliable. He is coming again to judge the world according to this Word (John 12:48). We are still committed to the concept of restoring the faith and practice of the church as it was in the beginning (Jer. 6:16).

The term "liberal" has various shades of meaning. In modern Protestant theological circles, a liberal rejects the notion of the Bible as a supernatural book, inspired of God. He does not view it as having full authority over the lives of Christians and the church. He rejects such items as the virgin birth of Christ, his miracles, the resurrection and ascension. To a liberal truth is relative, not absolute. Thus to him the beliefs and practices of the church can and should change with changing times

The liberals at work among us are not generally of this extreme stripe. Ours would never openly question the inspiration of the Bible, although they do hold a low view of its absolute authority for the church. They spend much of their time and energy knocking their predecessors and contemporaries in the faith who are determined to cling to the old paths of New Testament Christianity. They are constantly pushing the limits, embracing changes without too much concern whether they are biblically approved. Like rebellious youth, they are eager to abandon the past standards of their spiritual ancestors. As youngsters are wont to do, they are always seeking something new or different. Like young adults away at college they have embraced exotic ideas and can hardly wait to get back home and show them off to the unenlightened folks on the farm.

Two areas that are red flag issues for our brotherhood liberals are their willingness to accept, or at least to tolerate, the use of instrumental music in worship and the assumption that the church of Christ is really, not the church of the Bible, but only a denomination. That being the case they are ready to extend the hand of fellowship to other religious organizations, which in their thinking are of equally value with us.

Radicals stand to the right of us. We share with them all the basic assumptions about Scripture, the miraculous and the Savior. The difference is in attitude and emphasis. Where the conservative tries to preach the truth in love (Eph. 4:15), the radical presents his message in a harsh, and often hateful way. The conservative loves his fellow-Christians, even those who are drifting toward liberalism or radicalism. Thus he will be patient in trying to correct them and win them back. Conservatives are slow to withdraw fellowship from those who are going astray while radials seem eager to break fellowship. Conservatives are quick to welcome home the brother who has gotten into the ditch. Radicals tend to be unforgiving and very slow to let the prodical come home. Conservatives regret having to do battle with fellow Christians, preferring to make war with enemies of the faith who are outside the family. Radicals seem eager to take the sword against a brother with whom they disagree.

Radicals eventually grow so disenchanted with the brotherhood that they separate themselves, claiming to be the only true representatives of the Lord's church. Over the last century, four such separations occurred.

While labels are unfortunate, they are part of our vocabulary of communication. Even the apostles labeled certain men as false teachers, false prophets and enemies of the cross of Christ (I John

4:1; Phil. 3:18). Our daily prayer should be that God will open the eyes of our hearts (Eph. 1:18) and enable us to discern between the good and the bad; between those teachers and writers among us who are faithful and loyal to Christ, his church and his Word and those who are radical or liberal (Lev. 10:10). Truth will always be found in the middle ground between those two extremes (Prov. 4:25-27).

123. DEADLY ENEMIES OF THE CHURCH

While on earth, Christ was confronted with enemies who wished to destroy him and defeat his mission. Having conquered death and ascended back to the Father, he left his church on earth to take the message of salvation to the world for which he died (Mk. 16:15). From her inception, the church of Christ has been besieged by foes within and without. Paul and his helpers were harassed by hostile Jews and angry Gentile who resorted to violence to silence the great missionary. The disciples also had to cope with opposition from misguided Christians. Some Jewish disciples devoted themselves to harassing the apostle and imposing their Jewish customs on Gentile converts. Listen to his plaintiff words, "Our flesh had no rest, but we were troubled on every side; without were fightings, within were fears . . . " (II Cor. 7:5 KJV). Others corrupted the faith and led disciples astray with teaching that was contrary to the divine message of Christ (II Tim. 1:15). Well did Francis Schaeffer observe, "The devil never gives us the luxury of fighting on only one front, and this will always be."

Today the church of Christ is besieged by foes both within and without. From without we are under attack by a hostile culture, militant unbelief, pagan religions, hundreds of counterfeit churches, an antagonistic media. These enemies alone are enough to occupy every soldier in a never-ending struggle with the forces of evil.

From within we are faced with enemies as well. We have those who are corrupting the church and spreading strife and division by disregarding the precepts and principles set forth by Christ to govern and regulate his people. Jesus said, "Whosoever therefore shall break one of these least commandments and shall teach men so, shall be called least in the kingdom of heaven" (Matt. 5:19). They fancy themselves theological scholars and call themselves progressives or workers for change. We call them **liberals** and false teachers. They are descended from the Sadducees of first century Judaism. But as we contend with those who are subverting the faith, we face another problem within our ranks. On the opposite hand are hostile, angry, vindictive preachers who are lashing out in attack against everyone in the church who does not conform to their perception of things. Even those who are standing rock-solid on the Word of God and waging the good warfare against the proponents of liberalism, they blast with their missiles. It is a sad situation when a Christian's foes are they of his own spiritual household (Matt. 10:36). These brethren hold a faulty attitude about the faith. It is known as **legalism**. The legalists are spiritual grandchildren of the Pharisees of Jesus' day. They profess a great love for the law of God and his church, but they have little love for the people of God. They are quick to divide the body, and place a low premium on the unity of the church. They often delight more in making war on fellow preachers than in warring against the enemy without. They are to the church as bounty hunters are to the law. They discourage weak members and drive them away. Liberals are grateful for legalists. They hold them up as examples of all that is wrong in the church and imply that all who do not buy their package of change are like them.

Thus contemporary soldiers of Christ stand with their backs to the wall, trying to fend off liberal change agents, while legalistic brethren are snapping at their heels like snarling dogs. Satan is shrewd. He knows that every hour soldiers of Christ spend in fighting enemies within and without is time lost for evangelizing and saving the lost and thus building up the Cause of Christ

John, in his Revelation, depicts the victorious Christ, defeating all of his enemies (Rev. 19:11-21). Those vanquished will drink the bitter cup of wrath on the day of judgment, whether they are enemies within or enemies without.

XI.
IF CHANGE AGENTS SURFACE IN YOUR CONGREGATION

124. OPTIONS FACING KINGDOM CITIZENS

The time is rapidly approaching when many members of the church of Christ will have to make some hard, painful decisions about their spiritual life and place of worship. The pressure that will force these decisions is being applied by a number of preachers and professors who have appointed themselves to introduce and implement revolutionary changes within our churches. The zeal and determination already manifested by those promoting change make it evident that the pressure surely will increase in days ahead. Each unchallenged step, each victory, makes them bolder and more aggressive. When the problems surface in your congregation, and they surely will, each disciple will have to decide which way he or she will go. Among the options are the following:

I. One can go with the change agents when they infiltrate and capture your home congregation. For some, whose faith, conviction and commitment are anemic and shallow, this will pose no problem. For such, one church is as good as another, it really does not matter what one believes. They are not choosing between God's will and men's will, for them the choice is just a matter of personal preference. We can only pity those whose faith has so little substance to it. They ignore the clear warning God provided them (Acts 20:28-29).

II. Those with strong faith and deep convictions cannot follow the above course. If they are unable to convince their brethren to remain faithful to Christ's Word, they will have to leave a congregation that has left its Biblical roots and seek out a sound congregation that is holding fast to the faith once for all delivered to the saints (Jude 3). Some will be fortunate to find a good church nearby. Others will have to drive a distance. Even though such a commute imposes some hardships, the consolation of worshiping and serving with those of like precious faith, makes it worthwhile.

III. Some who are strong in faith and not easily discouraged will fight to save their congregation from the hands of those interlopers who would capture it. Every new faction that emerges always makes a grab for the property and facilities of existing congregations. The tactics used are sometimes unscrupulous. To go out and start a new congregation from scratch; to purchase their own property, is too big a task so they make a grab for the property someone else built and paid for. One should never be ashamed of, nor apologetic for, resisting those who like wolves have invaded the sheep fold (Matt. 7:15). If anyone is to leave, let it be those who want to have a new and different faith and practice.

IV. If the forces of change succeed in capturing your congregation and you are unable to salvage it, a faithful Christian will bid them a sad adieu. More important than friendships, past memories and even family ties is ones loyalty to king Jesus. There will doubtless be cases where faithful disciples will be forced to plant a new congregation that is loyal to God's Word and begin again the work of winning the lost and building up the kingdom of God. They will seek out the faithful remnant and go to work. Perhaps they will have to meet in a private home until growth allows them to do better. Those who commandeer the old congregation will likely accuse them of splitting the church; call them a faction or a splinter; try to turn others against them by ridicule and misrepresentation. But God will bless their efforts and like a scion from a fine old fruit tree they will take root, grow and bear fruit for Christ. This is exactly what our great grandfathers had to do a century ago when the progressives among them (Disciples of Christ/Christian Churches) abandoned the old faith and set about to reconstruct the faith and worship of our brethren.

V. Some will no doubt turn away from the church in disgust and discouragement. So deep will be their wounds and disillusionment that they will turn away from Christ altogether and drift back into a life of sin. Others will seek fellowship in some denominational body where at least they can worship in peace, free from disruption. How tragic such a situation will be, but be certain it will occur. Those whose insistence on change drives these souls from God's church will stand before the Master, guilty of the blood of those they have turned away from the Master's fold of safety.

125. WHEN THE ENEMY APPEARS AT YOUR DOOR

Across the land, agents of change are actively seeking to impose unscriptural changes on the Lord's church. These changes will destroy the Biblical identity and purity of congregations and transform them into denominations whose faith and practice are the products of men rather than of Christ. Given the extensive nature of this movement it is inevitable that every preacher and elder will eventually have to face and deal with those agitating for these changes. The following suggestions will help you be successful in protecting your congregation and in routing the enemy from your gates.

* **Don't go into battle unprepared.** Every preacher and elder owes it to himself and his congregation to inform himself of the issues at hand and the leaders of the change movement. He needs to develop a proper biblical response to their assertions. Preparation should begin immediately. "Put on the whole armor of God, that ye may be able to stand against the wiles of the devil" (Eph. 6:10).
* **Innoculate your sheep ahead of time** so the virus of apostasy cannot invade them. Don't wait until the error has raised its head among you and then try to warn folks against it. By that time the damage will have been done and some will surely be lost ... or you may be driven out. Thus did Paul (Acts 20:28-31).

* **Don't allow the enemy's agents in** to do their subversive work in your congregation. You are under no obligation to open your pulpit or classes to those who would harm the church. Let them know up front that they are unwelcome in your midst and that they will be given no opportunity to spread their views (II John 10-11).
* **Never make the mistake of assuming the proposals of the change agents are innocent and harmless.** While one suggestion may seem innocuous in itself, it is but the nose of the camel in your tent. One by one, demands will be made until the congregation is overwhelmed and swallowed up in an accumulation of error.
* **Don't try to defend our flaws and failures.** The agents of change nearly always preface their proposals by pointing out some failure among our brethren. Of course we have failed to measure up to the perfect standard of Christ. So have the change agents (Rom. 3:23). Gladly admit those legitimate charges and go to the heart of the matter; their desire to change the faith and practice of the church to a new non-biblical kind of religion.
* **Don't defend a tradition as a divine essential.** The enemy often points to some of our practices that are traditional ways of doing things and tries to justify his program of changes. Traditions of men that make void the word of God are wrong (Matt. 15:6-9). Traditions of the apostles are righteous and should be observed (II Thess. 3:6). Some traditions are harmless, such as the time of our assemblies, the length of them, the hymnals we choose, the kind of buildings we build. Never try to defend such things as divine obligations. Their proposed changes are clearly traditions of men!
* **Be totally honest with those whom you must challenge.** In the heat of combat it is easy to exaggerate the failures of your enemies and to distort their teaching to your advantage. It is easy to deny your own shortcomings and mistakes. Perceptive people will see the slightest hint of dishonesty. Often they will give the change agents a free pass to do their mischief because they were misrepresented by a preacher or elder who opposed

them. Don't give them that advantage.
* **Never resort to vicious, un-Christian personal attacks against the promoters of error**. Let the Spirit-given Word of Christ convict them (John 16:8-9). Let the facts of the case paint them as the heretics they are. Resorting to harsh, hateful attacks will cost you credibility with those whom you are trying to save. Speak the truth in love (Eph. 4:15).
* **Don't compromise with the enemy.** When change agents realize that they are not yet able to capture a congregation, they will propose a compromise. They will push for an alternative service so that the stubborn traditionalists can worship in the same old tired way, and the enlightened ones can have a super-service that will meet their felt needs without hindrance and limitations. It is only time before the gangrene spreads and divisions does its destructive work.
* **Don't trespass upon the autonomy of other congregations**. God created his church so that each band of Christians is independent and answers only to him. This has numerous advantages but also the limitation of allowing a church that so wishes, to embrace error and practice it. Autonomy means they have the right to do that and then answer to God for the mistake they have made. Often in our zeal to protect the church, we are tempted to meddle in the affairs of another congregation of which we are not members. Resist this temptation (I Pet. 4:15).
* **Don't walk away from the battle.** In every war there are some soldiers, who because of cowardice, or weariness, or because the battle is not progressing as they wish, will abandon their position, leaving it to the enemy. We see this in some of our Christian soldiers. The agents of change have no right to invade your congregation. They have no right to the hearts and minds of the flock. They have no right to claim for their use, church buildings others, who did not share their perverse views, built and paid for. Let them do the leaving. Hold your ground. "Be ye steadfast, unmoveable... forasmuch as ye know that your labor is not vain in the Lord" (I Cor. 15:58).

126. WHEN THE AGENTS OF CHANGE COME TO YOUR CONGREGATION

History is a great teacher. The history of our Restoration Movement teaches us that innovators will always be lurking among us, looking for an opportunity to introduce their new doctrines and practices. It also shows us that innovative movements are like leaven. In their early stages they work silently and invisibly, but all the while they are multiplying until they affect the whole body: local congregations, educational institutions and eventually the entire brotherhood. This was most visibly illustrated in brotherhood events between 1850 and 1925. Reading the history and biography of our people during that momentous period, one can see how innovators proceeded and the disaster that resulted when faithful brethren were asleep, naive, undecided and without strong leadership. By the end of that period, a new denomination was born; the Disciples of Christ/Christian Church. Its beginning membership was composed of brethren led astray from churches that once had embraced the plea to restore New Treatment Christianity. No less than 85 percent of the movement was lost at that time. The likelihood of the same kind of disaster occurring among our churches today is very high, almost predictable.

Today a vigorous and widely scattered element of preachers and college professors among us are promoting changes for our churches. Most notably, they would change the way we view and interpret the Bible; the way we view church (i.e., that it is only a denomination); the way we worship (i.e., that we should be tolerant of those who wish to use instrumental music in worship) and the role of women in the church. What should faithful disciples do when promoters of change appear within their congregation? Long before they come, wise elders and preachers will have been at work, making their members aware of the potential problems. They will fortify them with teaching that affirms the biblical basis for our faith and practice. They will make them aware of the errors being promoted and the methods used to advance them. Sermons, classes, bulletin articles, appropriate tracts and guest speakers will be used to vaccinate the congregation, making them immune to the sweet-speaking sirens of change.

In most congregations, calls for change will most often come from youth ministers and campus ministers. They tend to catch the virus while pursuing their education, or at workshops and seminars which have a long history of featuring speakers that "push the envelope" for change. Another source is from move-ins. It will generally be young adults who have imbibed this spirit elsewhere, especially while attending some of our Christian Universities or campus programs. They may try to introduce changes into your congregation.

Before any moves have been made to introduce changes, watchful elders will sit down with youth workers, campus workers and those who work with young adults and make it crystal clear that such attempts will not be tolerated.

Great care must be exercised in employing preachers and other workers for the congregation. Carefully screen all applicants with the current problems in mind. Look beyond their references. Everyone has a friend or a relative who will assure you this fellow is an angel. In interviewing a potential employee, set forth in no uncertain terms, where you stand and what you expect from him. Ask pointed questions. Leave no room for vague, double entendre answers. False teachers do not readily reveal their faith or agenda. Be doubly cautious with prospects who are recent graduates from our large Christian Universities. Some of these schools are fountainheads for the changes surfacing among us. Any student trained there will almost certainly have been exposed to fuzzy thinking about the authority of Scripture and changes to our faith and worship. Many will have been infected with this virus.

Wise elders will be good watchmen (Acts 20:29-30), alert day and night for any efforts to inject false ideas and unscriptural practices into the life of the church. If such an attempt is made, it should be dealt with swiftly, kindly, with a proper Christian attitude of love, but with a firmness that does not yield to compromise and pleadings for tolerance. Those employees who do not heed the correction should be terminated forthwith. These are extraordinary times and they demand extraordinary measure.

If you are in a congregation whose elders and preachers are unaware of the problems before us, or are hesitant to act, ask to visit with them and explain the dangers we are up against. It would be helpful to have good materials in hand to share with them. Be kind, considerate, respectful and humble. Good leaders are sometimes uninformed.

If you see corrupting practices being introduced, first try to discuss the matter with your leaders or those involved in trying to corrupt the church. Go with knowledge of scriptures in hand. Jot down your thoughts so you won't forget or get sidetracked. Again be kind, respectful and humble but be firm. If the leadership will not respond and the changes make it impossible for you to worship and serve God as the Scriptures teach, it is time to leave. Find a congregation that is faithfully worshiping and serving the Lord. There may be others ready to leave with you. If numbers are sufficient, start a new congregation where you can worship the Lord in spirit and in truth. It is never wrong to refuse to worship in an environment of error. Nor is it wrong to plant a faithful church where an unfaithful one exists.

127. BEFORE YOU INVEST IN A NEW THING, CHECK IT OUT

Folk-wisdom is a wonderful thing. Without the advantages of higher education, our forefathers learned valuable lessons of life and encoded them in wise sayings. "Don't buy a pig in a poke," i.e., don't make a purchase without first inspecting the item. There is a certain risk in ordering merchandise from a catalog. The actual product is often not the quality that the picture implies.

Those progressive-minded elders, preachers and members, who are taken with the proposals for change being promoted by some of our university scholars, really need to check out the actual product before they buy the package. What sounds exciting in a religious journal or a book may appear quite different in a real life setting. They owe it to themselves and the church to visit a Disciples of LChrist congregation. There was a time (125 yrs. ago) when these folks were one with us in faith and practice. They chose the road now being promoted in a flurry of books being produced and circulated by faculty members of Abilene Christian University and endorsed by the president of that institution. To see the end results of the "drive to introduce change" in our brotherhood, "go and see." Then you can make an informed decision whether or not to proceed.

* In a Disciples Church you can see the "new hermeneutic" at work. Their seminaries have been instilling in their students this approach to the Bible for a full century. One's approach to the Bible plays out in the faith and practice of the congregation.
* You can see the kind of music the agents of change will bring into your worship assemblies. When the question of instrumental music in worship is no longer a "faith or salvation issue," you get not only the pipe-organ, the piano and the chorus, but the rock band as well.
* There you can see first hand what the talk about "freeing our women to serve God" is really all about. They have women preachers and elders.
* You can see how replacing the search for Bible authority on questions of faith, practice and morals with the "story telling" approach can lead to gay membership and ordination.
* You can see for yourself the real meaning of, "we are Christians only, but not the only Christians." There you will find participation in the Billy Graham type of crusades, membership in the ministerial alliance, acceptance of the unimmersed as

fellow-Christians and membership in the World Council of Churches.
* You can see how "we can do anything the Bible does not condemn" plays out in the practice of a church. First they rejected the idea of "the law of silence" that says we can only do what the Scripture authorizes us to do. They then abandoned "book chapter and verse" Bible preaching. They now have no trouble embracing things clearly forbidden and condemned by Scripture.
* You will see the fruit of theological liberalism in the life and teaching of a church. Many of their theologians and preachers blush not to lay their sinful hands on the sacred text of the Bible and question if it is even legitimate.
* You can see a full blown denomination. With its national governing body, headquarters, presiding officers. They now proudly acknowledge that they are truly a denomination.
* You can see the kind of preachers it genders; reverend pastors whose preaching has been reduced to the level of cold water.
* You can see a dying church. For half a century the Disciples have been declining in membership. Standards have been lowered to the bottom notch. Entertainment has replaced worship. Every new social fad of liberalism has been embraced, still they are dying.

Please, Christian leader, before you buy the "change" package being promoted among us, make the visit; check it out. Is this where you really want to go? Once you invite the change-makers in, the likelihood of restoring the Biblical faith and practice of the past is almost nil.

128. IF YOUR CHURCH LEAVES YOU

We are accustomed to hearing the sad news of a member or a family leaving the church. Today members of churches of Christ in America must face the possibility that the congregation of which they are members is in the process or has already **left them**! If it is your sad lot to face this painful experience, please consider the following thoughts.

* If your church is leaving you and God's Word, please **don't close your eyes and pretend it really isn't happening.** We see this sad phenomenon all across the land. Some elders can't believe their preacher really means what he says in his classes and sermons that question the ancient truths of God's Word or promote unscriptural changes. Some members close their eyes and ears to activities in their congregations that would not have been tolerated in days past. Some watch as youth programs are clearly leading young people away from the ancient gospel. We must face the hard fact that a deadly apostasy is presently at work in our midst and unless stopped it will destroy the church we love.

* If the preacher and elders of your congregation abandon the Word of God for the program of the "change agents," **refuse to go with them**. They are unfaithful shepherds (Jer. 50:6). You are personally responsible for your soul (II Cor. 5:10). The gospel you obeyed, you learned from God's Word. The church you were added to was the church Christ built. The worship you offered was that you found set forth in Scripture. Don't give up the solid ground of truth for the shifting sands of popularity, emotionalism and promotionalism.

* If your congregation departs, **don't grow discouraged and quit the Lord and his church**. When this long struggle is over, there will be three losing parties. 1). Those who follow the pied pipers of change will be lost in apostasy. 2). The faithful survivors who held fast to God's standard will be greatly reduced in size and strength. 3). Those who grew discouraged and left the church for some denominational body or to live without fellowship with God's people will stand condemned as well. They were not faithful unto death, they will not receive the crown of life (Rev. 2:10).

* Should your church start down the broad road of departure, **pray** that God will give you the wisdom to understand the problem

and the information you need to fortify yourself and help others; that he will give you the courage to be strong in the Lord and in the strength of his might (Eph. 6:10); that he will use you to help his people.

* If your church is leaving you, **take your stand for the Lord Jesus and His holy Truth**. Don't be timid or ashamed of the gospel (Rom. 1:16). Like Paul, be "set for the defense of the gospel" (Phil 1:16). If you love the church don't stand idly by while unfaithful disciples ravage and ruin her.
* If such is your fate, then **rally other like-minded souls together**. Confront your leaders, if they are unresponsive and determined to abandon the old paths, then;
* **Find a faithful congregation where you can indeed worship God** in spirit and in truth (John 4:24); where you can serve God with a good conscience (Acts 23:1). Seek out a church where you can invest your energy and finances in work that truly glorifies Christ and honors the church for which he died . . . rather than promoting unfaithfulness and apostasy.
* If no faithful church is close at hand, invite those who love God and wish to be simple New Testament Christians to join hands with you in **starting a new congregation dedicated to faithful service to our Master**.

Would to God that every Christian was privileged to live and die in a strong, faithful congregation where godly shepherds keep the wolves driven from the door and loyal preachers boldly proclaim the unsearchable riches of Christ. Unfortunately, for many of us this lovely wish will not be realized. That being the case, we must gird up our loins and be mentally and spiritually prepared should the evil day come.

XII.
THOSE WHO FAIL TO DEFEND CHRIST'S SACRED CAUSE

129. HAVE YOU KEPT THE FAITH?

At the end of his long and illustrious life, Paul could truthfully say, "I have fought the good fight, I have finished the course, I have kept the faith..." (II Tim.4:7). Every Christian, and especially every man who preaches God's word, needs to review his record and ask himself, "Have I kept the faith?" This question is especially pertinent in this day of change when an army of men are at work among us to implement changes that will alter the very nature of the faith we hold and the church of which we are members. In coming years every member of the church of Christ will feel the pressure to join the clamorous crowd that is pushing for change. Conflict will be forced upon us. Preachers will be faced with accommodating the demands for change or having to seek a new job. Members will have to choose between compromise and conflict, going along with or going out from the congregation where they have long worshiped and served God. Many will face the agonizing choice of staying with their loved ones in an apostate congregation or leaving them behind out of duty to the Lord who died for them. To my fellow preachers I pose the following points for pondering:

* Have you kept the faith in the materials you have presented in your classes and sermons? It is so easy to preach what the worldly crowd wants to hear. Isaiah was faced with those who demanded, "Prophesy not unto us right things, speak unto us smooth things, prophesy deceits..." (Is. 30:10). A man can preach for a church 20 years and teach only truth and no error. Yet he can be guilty of failing to teach the "whole counsel of God" (Acts 20:27). Fidelity demands that we do more than just speak the truth, we must give our hearers those truths that they need to hear at this moment of time. It means that we address those volatile, unpopular issues that folks may not wish to hear. It means we must be willing to risk our jobs and financial security to deliver God's message to those who have embraced error. It means we be willing to endure the criticisms and insults of those who are determined to impose their new ideas of faith and worship on the congregation. To fail to meet this challenge is to fail to keep the faith!

* Have you keep the faith by refusing to endorse, to lend your approval to those popular teachers, schools and papers that are promoting the agenda of change. So serious is the current threat to the integrity and well-being of the Cause of Christ that we cannot allow those promoting change to operate among us unchallenged. No longer should we recommend that our young people chose a Christian school that is aggressively promoting the doctrine of change. Nor should we recommend that our brethren subscribe to journals that are advocating unscriptural changes for our people. No invitations should be extended to men who are agents of change. Materials written by those who wish to change our faith and worship should not be purchased and used in our Bible classes. No missionary should be supported who is not unquestionably sound in his faith and fully committed to maintaining the ancient gospel of Jesus. Why should we support a work that will produce only a denominational church and teach sinners that they can be saved by faith alone?

* Have you kept the faith by speaking up when you are in the presence of fellow-preachers and church leaders? Some men faithfully teach the truth in their home setting. Yet they are strangely mute in the presence of their preaching peers who sing the praises of those who are obviously enemies of God's church. We do not say you must be obnoxious, self-righteous, or disorderly. But there is a time and a place to openly declare your faith; to speak up and let it be known that you want no part of the change movement; that you are prepared to do battle for the Master!

* Have you kept the faith by using your time, energy and resources to defend the greater Cause of Christ against her enemies? Some men will fight valiantly to protect the church where they are employed from false teachers. Yet they show no interest when apostates are ravaging a congregation across town. They seem totally disinterested in what is happening in other cities or states. Thus Satan is able to capture the hearts and minds of disciples in mission fields and areas where the leadership is weak, because good men, who could and should come to their defense, refuse to do so. It is not true faithfulness if we only are stirred to defend that from whence our salary comes.

* Are you keeping the faith in the face of today's challenge? Many men fought valiantly and bravely when the forces of error arose in days past. They took up sword and shield and conducted themselves as good soldiers should. But today, many of these veterans are sitting quietly, observing the strife, but not responding. In the army of Christ we don't get too old to do battle. There is no retirement age. Often the old warrior is the best because of his wisdom and experience. Only when the mind and body fail can we lay down our weapons.Brethren, the day is fast approaching when each of us will stand before Christ and give account for our conduct in this life (II Cor. 5:10). When you stand there, will you be able to joyfully and truthful say to your Lord, "I have kept the faith?" May God grant that it be so.

130. DANGEROUS ASSUMPTIONS CAN BE DISASTROUS

When Naaman, the Syrian leper, was told to wash in Jordan and he would be cleansed of his disease, he responded, "Behold I thought, He will surely come out to me and stand, and call on the name of Jehovah his, God, and wave his hand over the place, and recover the leper" (II Kings 5:11). His plaintiff words, "Behold I thought" have been the basis for thousands of sermons. They are most appropriate for the church at the beginning of the 21st century. These words of Naaman reflect a *mistaken assumption* on his part that could have caused him to die a leper. Among contemporary churches of Christ such mistaken assumptions could also result in irreparable damage. Powerful and influential men and schools among us are working feverishly to impose changes on our churches that are neither scriptural nor helpful. These changes have to do with the name we wear, the doctrine we hold, the worship we offer to God, the role of women, the way of salvation, the authority of the Bible and numerous other matters. When folks read or hear of the work of these change agents some make dangerous assumptions.

* **Some assume it is no big deal**. How wrong they are. These changes, if accomplished, will destroy the very foundation on which the church stands. The rubble that will survive will not be a church of Christ but a denomination.
* **Others assume it involves just a few young preachers**. Wrong! The changes are being championed by a bevy of professors associated with our Christian Universities. The problem has already spread throughout the country and affected several of our largest churches. It is found in virtually every large city in the country. It is safe to say that several hundred preachers are already committed to this program, maybe more.
* **Some assume it will go away if left alone**. Wrong again. Error works like leaven and if left alone it will soon affect the entire brotherhood (I Cor. 5:6). It is like a deadly virus. Once turned loose in a church it will not cease until it is driven out or until it has conquered its host. It also spreads from church to church especially through youth groups and campus activities attended by young Christians.
* **Others assume that no one will listen to them**. Already a significant host of our people has embraced the clamor for change. Large audiences at some Christian university lectureships stand and applaud the outlandish pronouncements of such speakers
* **Some assume it will not affect us.** This is a tragic assumption

which can have destructive results. No congregation is immune to the possibility that someone will try to bring in this heresy. Members can however be inoculated before hand by sound teaching and proper warning. If done they will not be vulnerable to the erroneous message.

* **Still others assume that someone else will rise up and squash the false teachers**, therefore I need not inform myself or address the issue. The church is more vulnerable today than in years past. We have no David Lipscombs, G. C. Brewers, Guy N. Woods, or Thomas Warrens prepared to do battle with the false teachers among us. We are an army of soldiers with few brilliant, courageous generals among us. Each of us must prepare himself and fight the good fight of the faith in our own community (I Tim. 6:12).

* **Many assume that God won't let it happen to his church**. Wrong! It happened a hundred years ago when digression swept away 85 percent of our congregations and people, all of our schools, most of our mission work. Look around you and see the Disciples of Christ and Christian Churches. They are proof that such has happened and can happen again. We must learn and heed the lessons of history lest we repeat the mistakes of the past.

Naaman escaped from his leprosy only because he abandoned his false assumption and did what God instructed him to do. So it will be for the church of our generation. We must stand fast, we must resist every effort to subvert the faith, we must contend earnestly for "the faith" of Christ revealed in the New Testament (Jude 3). We must take note of them that are causing divisions among us and turn away from them (Rom. 16:17-18). Dangerous assumptions can be disastrous to those who hold them.

131. SOME QUESTIONS FOR PREACHERS AND ELDERS

* Is the faith you hold worth contending for (Jude 3)?
* Is the gospel you preach worth defending (Phil. 1:16)?
* Is the church of which you are a member worth dying for (Eph. 5:25)?
* Is the Cause of Christ worthy of preservation and protection (I Sam. 17:29)?
* Are there ordinances and commands which must be honored by those who desire to please Christ and see heaven (Matt. 7:21; Heb. 5:9)?
* Is there a way of worship that is heaven ordained and God-given (John 4:24)?
* Are their false teachers who lead disciples astray and do great harm to the Lord's Church (I John 4:1; Jude 17-19)?
* Are we to resist such false teachers steadfastly in our faith (II Pet. 2:1-2; I Pet. 5:9)?

If you answer the above questions in the affirmative, then we must ask just where do the promoters of the change movement fit into God's scheme of things? They deny the gospel revealed by Christ and long preached by our brethren! They dispute the faith we have long contended for! They ridicule, shame and despise the church of which we are members! They discount and change plain commands and ordinances of Christ! They corrupt the worship and practice Christ prescribed for us! They are rending and dividing the body of Christ. Every man who truly loves Christ, his word and his church should be incensed by the arrogant assertions of these agents of change. His blood should be stirred to oppose and resist these false teachers with all his strength.

If you answer these questions in the negative, then the likelihood is that you will either join the change movement or else stand by in cowardly silence while the enemies of Christ ravage the church for which He died.

I urge every reader who loves the precious Cause of Christ to take his stand as a faithful soldier of the Lord Jesus (I Tim. 6:11) and resolve that he will make a commitment to Christ to follow and defend the right and resist the wrong til God calls him home.

132. IF WE DO NOTHING

Powerful winds of change are blowing across the landscape of the Lord's church. Criticism and speculations that would not have been tolerated a generation ago now go unchallenged. Schools that once were bastions of faithful teaching now ring with uncertain sounds. Champions of the faith that formerly stood in the breaches to turn away proponents of error, have now finished their course and await the Lord's return. Today such giants in the faith are hard to find. Looking around we see in their place too many preachers who either do not know the fundamentals of the faith, or how to defend it. Worse still, there are some who do not hold those sacred truths. In the last twenty years those who no longer believe in the restoration of New Testament Christianity have grown bolder and now openly speak and write things which they would only have whispered in private in days past. To those timid souls who cannot find it in themselves to address the issues before us I raise the question, "What will happen to the church of Christ if nothing is said or done to preserve her from those who are daily working to change her into something new and different?"

Some no longer feel obliged to look to the New Testament as the sole authority for their faith and practice.
Some are experimenting with new concepts of leadership for congregations.
Some are creating their own organizations to do the work God commissioned his church to do.
Some are willing to open the leadership of the church to women.
Some are ready to embrace the use of instrumental music in worship and denominational ideas regarding the Lord's Supper.

Some are ready to embrace other religious bodies in Christian fellowship, even though they do not wear the name of Christ nor respect his holy Word.

Some are anxious to convince us that the church is nothing more than a denomination like those around us.

Some feel superior to those saints who went before us and hesitate not to belittle them and the work they did.

Some thirst for an emotion-based worship like they see in the electronic churches of the tel-evangelists.

Some have embraced a humanistic code of human conduct and come to terms with the sinful world.

We are truly engaged in a great struggle for the heart and soul of the church and her members. The problem is, only one side is doing much fighting. Those whose job it is to contend earnestly for the faith (Jude 3) and to fight the good fight of the faith (I Tim. 6:12) are often found sleeping, playing, running or encouraging those who are enemies of Christ's Cause. If we do nothing, those who would reconstitute the church will win by default. They will train our preachers, they will write and publish their corrupting message. They will influence our children in the colleges we have built and sustained. Their disciples will fill our pulpits and the day will come when the church of Christ that we have known and loved will cease to exist. Do not deceive yourself by saying such could never happen. All one needs to do is look at our religious neighbors. Bodies that once were pillars of conservatism are now sink holes of liberalism that bear little or no semblance to their past.

Fellow preachers and elders "quit ye like men" (I Cor. 16:13). Get to work today fortifying the souls of those in your charge. Teach them the fundamentals. Take nothing for granted. Provide good sound tracts that explain what we believe and why. Recommend dependable Christian journals. Use your church bulletins to set forth simple lessons on every truth we hold. Let your pulpits ring with solid, timely lessons that do more than build self-esteem. Teach your brethren why we are what we are. Explain the problems facing us and show their fallacies. If you are so fortunate that these problems have not yet come your way, prepare you brethren so they will be alert and set to resist them when they do appear. Pray mightily unto God that He will help us successfully defend the walls of Zion so that we can pass the true faith of Christ to the generation that shall follow us.

133. SEEDS OF SELF-DESTRUCTION

It is a common phenomenon for institutions, business, teams and even churches to fall into patterns of behavior that result in self-destruction. The church will survive or fall on the leadership provided by her elders and preachers. This article addresses the role of preachers in this unfortunate type of experience.

The seeds of our self-destructions are sown when the following things occur:

When preachers would rather fight against their fellow preachers than against a common enemy who would destroy them both. This is a common occurrence. A preacher sees some flaw in the life or teaching of a fellow-soldier; forgetting the greater danger posed by the enemy, he spends his time and energy attacking the brother on his side of the battle line. Common sense dictates that if this becomes a widespread practice the body will suffer more wounds than it can stand and destruction will follow. The enemy will win by default.

When preachers will not take time to inform themselves of the dangers that threaten the church. Some are like the proverbial monkey who hears no evil and sees no evil as they sit with their eyes closed and ears plugged. Of course it is not pleasant to read about destructive heresies. It is time-consuming and laborious to prepare oneself to respond to them, but such must be done if the body is to survive. Some seem to think they will be excused or exempted if they can say they "just don't know about these things." They serve the church in the same misguided way some American leaders serve the nation by refusing to consider the threat of Islam.

When they see no need to engage the enemy. Granted, preaching is more than fighting error. But make no mistake about it, we are to arm ourselves for battle against the host of spiritual wickedness (Eph. 6:12). We are to fight the good fight of the faith (I Tim. 6:12). There are false teachers whom we are to resist steadfastly in our faith. The preacher who refuses this important aspect of his work is unfaithful to his duty. He leaves the church at great risk of subversion and overthrow. Given time, the forces of change will manifest themselves and a defenseless church will easily succumb.

When elders and preachers fail to provide needed information and indoctrination to their congregation, the seeds of self-destruction are being sown. One cannot wait until the enemy is at the gate to arm the citizens. When change agents have infiltrated a congregation and gained a foothold, it may well be too late to try to save the flock from digressions. Today is the day of salvation, not only for lost souls, but for the saving of the church from apostasy. A few good sermons addressing the problems beforehand will serve as an inoculation when the proponents of error appear. Well-written tracts, covering the points being raised by change agents, placed in the hands of each family, will fortify their faith and guard them against the sirens of change. A guest speaker who can inform the flock of the nature, extent and danger of the change movement might be an effective road block to future incursions.

May it never be said of us that as preachers or elders we sowed the seeds of the church's self destruction.

XIII.
PARABLES FOR A DAY OF CHANGE

134. PARABLE OF THE CHRISTIAN FAMILY

Some years ago Joe and Mary Christian scraped and saved and finally got enough money to fulfill their dream and make a down payment on a dairy farm. By hard work and sacrifice they made a success of their investment, the farm prospered. They were able to build a lovely home, with a barn and outbuildings on their property and their dairy herd grew. God truly blessed their labors.

Joe and Mary were blest with four sons and a daughter. When they grew up, the kids went off to college and studied agriculture and business. Upon graduation they came home to help Joe run the farm. But while at school they picked up some new ideas about farming. They saw no future in dairy farming. They preferred a diversified approach. They wanted to plant some of the land in corn, some in soy beans and raise pigs and chickens instead of dairy cattle. When they could not convince Joe of the need to change to their program, they grew restless and fretful. They became critical of their father's efforts and predicted he would soon go out of business. The situation became intolerable. Since the young folks had married and had children, they now numbered 15 to the two parents. They turned their attention to Mary and persuaded her that they were right and that Joe was just being stubborn. After a while the situation grew ugly and the children told their dad that they were going to farm the way they learned in school and if he did not like it he could leave. The question is who should leave and go else where? Poor Joe, who by sacrifice and hard work bought and developed the farm, or the children who had not put a penny into the operation? I think I know what you would say. Well, consider the following scenario:

If a congregation was established, its property purchased and meeting house built and paid for by members of the church of Christ who firmly believed:

* That Christ established and recognizes only one church (Matt. 16:18-19);
* That in the church, worshipful praise should be offered with voices alone, with no instrument other than the heart (Eph. 5:19);
* That the Lord's Supper is a sacred memorial of the death of Christ and not part of a fellowship meal with meat and vegetables (I Cor. 11:20-22);
* That women are forbidden by God to fill public leadership roles in the church, specifically that they are forbidden to teach and have authority over the men (I Tim. 2:11-12);
* That the Bible is the infallible inerrant will of God (Ps.19:7) and that it is a divinely given pattern for us follow (Heb. 8:5; II Tim. 1:13);
*That God saves sinners by grace through faith when their faith leads them to obey Christ, in particular, in baptism for the remission of sins (Acts 2:38).

If that congregation has worshipped and served God according to these standards for years then a new preacher, new elders, and/or younger members decide that they wish to introduce serious changes into the faith, worship, practice of that congregation that conflict with their past beliefs and practices, what shall the older members do? The two approaches are certainly incompatible. There is no way the two can worship together in peace and harmony unless those who hold to the original standards go contrary to their consciences. Amos said it well, "Can two walk together except they have agreed?" (Amos 3:3). A separation is bound to occur. The question is who should be the ones to leave and go elsewhere?

* Honesty says that those who built and paid for the facility should not be expected to leave!
* Those who hold to the faith of the founders and past leaders of that congregation should not be expected to surrender their property.

* Even if the majority have been seduced into the camp of the change agents, they have no right to the property that was built and paid for by brethren who obviously did not share their new found faith.
* The interlopers need to leave. If they want to worship like their neighbors in the Christian Churches, they should go there. If they want to be an independent Community Church they should start their own. They have no right to wrest away the property of those whose faith they have rejected. Honest people would do this. But it seems when people abandon the doctrine of Christ they prefer to take someone else's meeting place rather than go and build their own. This is yet another reason why such should be rejected (Tit. 3:10-11).

135. PARABLE OF THE UNHAPPY HUSBAND

When Jim married Betty he thought she was the sweetest girl in all the world. Through the eyes of love, all she was and all she did was beautiful.

But after a few years, Jim's love began to wane. He began to see flaws in Betty he had not seen before. There were those extra pounds, strands of gray sprinkled in her hair, and that mole on her cheek. Her hair style was not very attractive and her taste in clothing left much to be desired. Her cooking was mediocre and her housekeeping no better. It eventually reached the point that nothing Betty did pleased him. Other women were much more appealing, much better suited to be his wife.

Jim had two choices. He could make a clean break and leave Betty or he could stay and in his misery devote himself to criticizing her alleged shortcomings. Maybe he could force her into becoming like other women he admired. Jim wrestled with his choices. To leave would be embarrassing. What would family and friends say? It would cost him a bundle! So he elected to stay. In his misery he devoted himself to criticizing poor Betty's every move. He told his friends, neighbors and co-workers what a sorry wife she was. The more he put her down, the better he felt about himself. How could a man of his qualities and attainments have gotten saddled with such a poor wife?

Does this story sound vaguely familiar? Jim is a type of disaffected preachers who work among churches of Christ. They have become infatuated with the denominational churches they see about them. Betty represents the Lord's church. Like Jim, those unhappy preachers won't leave the church, so they dedicate themselves to belittling and badgering her hoping to change her so she will be like those denominational churches they so admire. They are as sorry preachers as Jim is husband, unworthy of the churches that employ them.

136. PARABLE OF THE FIREFIGHTERS

The city of Churchville had three fire stations. All the fire fighters were members of the local Fraternal Order of Firemen. Jim Williamson worked at station 1. In station 2 were some firemen he had known for years. In days past, a couple of them had been suspended for misconduct. After their suspension they returned to their station, chastened and sober. One day the alarm sounded and the men in station 1 donned their suits and sped to the scene of the fire. It was the Christian Manor Home for Seniors where Jim's mom and dad resided. When the other trucks arrived, Jim spotted the two fellows who had previously been suspended. Being the principled man that he was, Jim refused to be associated with men who had embarrassed the city's firefighters. In fact he insisted that they should not be allowed to help put out the fire; that they be sent back to the station. While he argued with the fire captain, the flames raced through the structure. Others, including those two men with blemished pasts, desperately struggled to evacuate the patients. While Jim stood by his principles, the building was a total loss.

Several patients were lost in the smoke and flames.

If something in this story sounds vaguely familiar, it might because something akin to this is seen within the church. Some preachers have drawn the circle of their fellowship so close that they are uncomfortable working with other fellow-Christians, even in saving the church from devastating apostasy. This is especially the case if the others happen not to be as perfect in life and understanding as they imagine themselves to be. There is a four-alarm fire raging out of control among the churches of Christ here in America. The problem is more commonly known as the "change movement." Like arsonists, the agents of change are moving from church to church igniting flames of discontent and demands for changes that are contrary to God's Word.

A few firefighters are working to try to put out the flames and salvage the church for future generations. Some brethren who are engaged in fighting the flames are critical of other firefighters who happen not to have their approval. So principled are they that they spend much of their time and energy trying to keep the others from helping. They encourage brethren not to allow them to help put out the fires. And while they thus waste their time and energy, the flames spread and in many places the damage is already irreversible. The church is the house of God (I Tim. 3:15) and it is being threatened by the fires of change. If it were your home, would you welcome all firefighters to try to save it, or would you refuse to allow some of them to help? Jesus said, "the sons of this world are for their own generation, wiser than the sons of the light" (Luke 16:8).

137. THOSE NEGATIVE FIREFIGHTERS

Have you ever considered just how negative the life and work of firefighters is? Their entire work day is spent waiting for and looking for bad news . . . for fires. Their job exists to fight against something evil. They prevent destructive people from having their way. They spoil the fun of arsonists. Their job is dangerous and dirty. Even though all of the above is obviously true, no one other than arsonists is critical of firefighters. None think they are unneeded. They serve a useful and beneficial role in every community. Thinking people thank God for them and the work they do.

In the kingdom of Christ there is also a need for firefighters. The tongues of some folks are set on fire of hell (Jas. 3:6). Such is true of false prophets (I John 4:1) and factious souls who are able to bring destruction upon a congregation (Tit. 3:10-11). Thus the Holy Spirit charges preachers to "Preach the word, reprove, rebuke and exhort" (II Tim. 4:1-2). They are to "put the brethren in mind of these things" (I Tim. 4:6). Some must be rebuked sharply (Tit. 1:13). Warnings must be issued when dangerous men are threatening the welfare of congregations (Acts 20:28-30). Spiritual fires are just as destructive as house fires. Those who have lived long have witnessed both individual Christians and even congregations lost in such fires. Some have been fortunate enough that when the fire of error broke out, a seasoned, experienced gospel preacher was able to come to the rescue and douse the flames of error and save those who were endangered. Others, not so fortunate suffered great harm or even perished.

No godly preacher enjoys having to fight against the fires of error. It is unpleasant and generally an unappreciated task. Yet if no one steps forward to do so, great and often irreparable damage is done to the Cause of Christ. Just as you appreciate your local firemen, you should appreciate the man of God who is vigilant in spotting devil-inspired fires and extinguishing them. Be grateful for him and thank the Lord for his ability to douse the flames of error and save those threatened thereby. This lesson is especially timely as arsonists promoting destructive changes circulate among our churches. The man who warns and works to put out the flames is not the enemy, he is your friend and benefactor. Lend him your support and encouragement.

138. PARABLE OF JACK THE FIREFIGHTER

Jack's dream and ambition were to become a fire-fighter. He wanted to save homes and lives. But there was something about those powerful red trucks, racing though town with their sirens wailing that thrilled his soul. After much study and several attempts he was able to pass the exam and land the job of his dreams. He was now a firefighter at Engine Company 11 in Churchville.

Jack was no slacker, he volunteered right away to keep the engines washed and polished. No speck of mud or tar was allowed to spoil their shiny finish. While other units washed and wax their equipment every week, Jack did theirs every day. In fact, he became so accomplished at his task that he wrote a handbook on how to keep your fire engine sparkling. Even when the crew was called out to a fire, Jack was sometimes seen lagging back with a rag in hand, wiping away the water and smudges from the engine.

On one occasion, the crew was sent to a serious fire. Every man was put to the test to bring it under control. The captain looked about for Jack. He was needed to help man a hose but could not be spotted. Then word came, that he was back at the engine, rubbing away some of the dirt and water that had settled on it.

The captain was furious. Good men were fighting an inferno. Those men searching the building were at risk and Jack was trying to keep his engine clean and shiny. The irate captain, dressed Jack down and reminded him that there is a time and place for everything. "Now is the time to fight this fire! That's what you are paid for!" Jack was humiliated. All his co-workers agreed with the captain. He was ashamed to be with his comrades as they sat around the table for supper. He had allowed an important thing to get in the way of something far more important.

Many gospel preachers are like Jack. They love their jobs. They went to great lengths to prepare themselves for preaching. But like

Jack they have gotten so wrapped up in good things that they are neglecting more important matters. For some it is endless hours of study. For others it is mission work. For some it is a favorite benevolent program. For others it is building up their local congregation. Some love visiting the sick and elderly. Others love counseling. All of these things are vital aspects of a preacher's work, but there is yet another that cannot be neglected. We who preach are expected to be good soldiers of Christ Jesus (II Tim. 2:2). We are to contend earnestly for the faith (Jude 3). We are to be set for the defense of the gospel (Phil. 1:16). We are to fight the good fight of the faith (I Tim. 6:12). Today the church is under a widespread and aggressive attack by a body of men who march under the banner of change. They see the church of Christ as flawed and unable to cope in the Postmodern world, so they have an agenda of change they are seeking to impose upon her congregations. This is no local skirmish. It is raging in virtually every large city in the nation and even in some of our mission fields abroad. Christ needs thousands of courageous volunteers to step forward and protect his church from those who would harm her. Unfortunately, like Jack the firemen, many of our soldiers are too busy polishing their engine. They are too busy with their study, their projects, their special interests to be bothered with a shield of faith and the sword of the Spirit and doing battle with a deadly enemy. How tragic! They have forgotten a vital part of their duty as a preacher.

The captain will not be pleased when he finds them, away from the line of combat, even though they are busy doing something quite good in itself. Those who are supported to preach God's Word, I urge to think on the lesson of this parable.

139. PARABLE OF THE BIRDS

This morning while out for my bike ride, I came upon a fascinating scene. A group of ten or so black birds were in hot pursuit of a barn owl. The owl was as large as all ten of his pursuers. Taking them one at a time he could easily overpower, defeat and devour any one of them. But when faced with ten determined black birds, he could only flee, and that he did. Owls are carnivores. They like to raid the nests of other, weaker birds. Left unchallenged, the nestlings will be his meal. Parent birds have a natural instinct to protect their nest and its precious contents. Those who do not, lose their little ones to the predator.

So it is in the kingdom of Christ. Satan is the great predator. Like a roaring lion he walks about seeking whom he may devour (I Pet. 5:8). Look as you may, you won't see an actual lion or the typical artist's image of Satan. Peter uses a simile (*as* a roaring lion). Today Satan is sending his agents into congregations of God's people across the land to capture them or at least to snatch out those they can (Matt. 7:15).

The preachers of the change movement are like the big birds that prey on the nestlings. Many of them occupy stations in large, wealthy and influential churches. They use this advantage to influence and lead away those who are young, immature and untaught in the fundamentals of the faith. Also professors in those Christian universities that have embraced the change agenda are like the predator birds. They capture the hearts and minds of young students whom unsuspecting parents send their way. They send them home to spread the change message in the churches

The little birds are the hundreds of ordinary preachers who spend their days toiling in the vineyard of their local congregation. They have neither wealth, power nor high credentials but they love the church and God's people. They cannot sit idly and watch while the predators sweep in and snatch their brethren away from the simplicity and purity of the gospel (II Cor. 11:3). Alone, one small preacher might not be able to accomplish much, but working together with others, they can have enough force and influence to put to flight those who would harm the church.

I urge every man among us, be he young or old, whether he be plain or polished, to rise up to defend the church of the Lord Jesus. If we do nothing, great harm will surely follow. If we choose to act alone, we will find the odds insurmountable. But working together with and with God's help we can put an army of aliens to flight (Heb. 11:34).

"Dear Lord in heaven, please help us to be as wise as the lowly blackbirds which you have made. Give us the courage to resist those who would harm the bride of your Son. In Jesus' name."

140. THE PARABLE OF THE MOSQUITO

Just recently I visited an old friend who is confined to a convalescence home. Just 65, Bill was still strong and healthy. He owned his own business and was flourishing. Then one night a tiny mosquito landed on him and bit him. When he felt the sting, he brushed it away and thought nothing of it. But in the seconds that the creature was on him, it injected him with a terrible virus. A few days later he experienced fever, chills and headaches. Three days later his brother found him on the floor of his home, in a deep coma. His diagnosis was viral encephalitis. Physically he recovered, but he suffered irreversible brain damage. Today he is much like a stroke victim, all because of a tiny mosquito carrying an invisible virus.

This poor fellow's unfortunate experience reminds me of a terrible spiritual virus that is being spread among churches of Christ. There are men circulating among us like that mosquito. They look and seem harmless enough. Many brethren don't care for the ideas they are promoting, but they mistakenly view them more as an annoyance than a deadly threat. The disease they are carrying is called "Change." The carriers of this disease are a band of preachers and university teachers who have taken it upon themselves to introduce revolutionary changes into the faith, worship and life of our congregations. They have successfully infected a large number of young men while they were attending Christian Universities. They have gone forth and sought out positions in our churches . . . and begun to spread their deadly ideas. Scores of churches are already infected.

So drastic are the changes proposed that any congregation that embraces and follows them to their logical end will no longer be a church of Christ. The symptoms are easily discerned: a loss of respect for the authority of the Bible in the life of the church; especially a refusal to recognized the law of silence that forbids us to go beyond what is written (I Cor. 4:6). Victims are restless and bored with the worship Christ ordained and crave entertainment and sensual excitement. They tend to experience a marked change in their attitude toward fellow-Christians, past and present, who do not embrace their program of change. They feel a strong urge to reach out and fellowship denominational people and their activities. Singing praises to God with the sacred hymns of the past is unpleasant for victims. They demand new songs and instrumental music to accompany them. Their spiritual appetite for the Lord's Supper flags and they find it necessary to turn it into a common meal for their bellies.

The virus affects their ability to read Scripture. When God says, "I permit not a woman to teach, nor to have authority over a man" (I Tim. 2:12), to their jaundiced eyes it seems to say it is all right for women to do just that. When the Book of God says, "by works a man is justified and not by faith only" (Jas. 2:24), the words are scrambled in their minds and come out "a man is justified by faith alone without works." The change in their spiritual personality is pronounced. They dislike their own spiritual ancestors and embrace those who despise the church of which they are members. They often feel ashamed of whom they are and try to disguise their places of worship, by calling them "Community Churches" or some other non-Biblical name.

This viral infection has reached epidemic proportions among our people. It can only be brought under control by isolating those infected and not allowing the carriers into the pulpits and classrooms of congregations. Students should shun schools where this disease is breeding, lest they too be infected. Any coming from a church or school that is infected should be carefully examined before being accepted into the fellowship of a congregation. Behold what terrible damage that one small mosquito did to my friend Bill. Be warned what one promoter of change can do to your congregation.

141. PARABLE OF THE DINOSAUR DOG

Recently I saw a dog dressed in a dinosaur costume. The color and outward appearance resembled a dinosaur, but underneath the costume it was still a dog. When the creature uttered a sound, it was obviously that of a canine, not a reptile. While one could pretend that it was a prehistoric creature, sooner or later the costume had to come off and the true nature of the beast was revealed.

Among churches of Christ today there are numerous men that present themselves as **gospel preachers** but their true identity is otherwise. True, they have diplomas from Christian schools, and they carry Bibles into their pulpits. They claim membership in the church of Christ. To the untrained eye they appear to be gospel preachers doing the work God gave preachers to do. But like the dog described above these men are only wearing the outer costumes of gospel preachers. Beneath the outer facade they are something altogether different. Their doctrine of salvation is that of the Baptist Church or some other denominational body. The worship they promote resembles that of Pentecostals. Their view of Bible authority is that of Protestantism. Their concept of the church is that of a denominational body. The churches they lead soon bear little resemblance to the church revealed in the Scripture and to the vast majority of churches of Christ around them. In fact, observing their conduct and considering their teaching, one must conclude that they are only pretending to be gospel preachers of churches of Christ.

Beneath the outer cloak, they are just denominational teachers who by accident of birth, marriage or education have found themselves in the fellowship of churches of Christ. When they open their mouth and speak one hears a message such as he would expect to hear in a Christian Church, a Baptist Church or some other similar body.

It was downright funny to see that dog prancing about, pretending to be a dinosaur. It is downright disgusting to see men standing before congregations of God's people pretending to be faithful gospel preachers and members of the Lord's church when in reality they are not. They are sent among us by the great enemy of truth to disrupt and destroy the church for which Jesus died.

142. PARABLE OF THE CHANGED CAR

The champions of change prefer stories to biblical preaching. I have a story to share with you and them. Many years ago a young friend bought a hotrod car. The previous owner, whom we will call Lynn, started with a Henry J. (Young folks may never have heard of that one, but it was a real brand, on the market in the 50s). When the owner wanted a hotrod to use for racing he began to modify and change his Henry J. First he removed the fenders. Then he removed the seats and installed bucket seats in the front. Roll bars were added. Special springs and shocks were placed on the back to elevate it and large oversize racing tires were installed. The Henry J motor was replaced with a powerful Cadillac engine, the transmission and drive chain with that of an Oldsmobile. The differential was also exchanged for a racing type. The mufflers were stripped away.

Now my question is, when did Lynn's car cease to be a Henry J and become the creation of Lynn. When I saw this machine, it did not look like, drive like, sound like or in any way resemble the Henry J designed by and produced by Kaiser-Frazier Motor Company. It was, at that point, a car that had been totally changed by Lynn and its original design marred and destroyed.

Another Lynn and lots of his friends are busily at work among churches of Christ attempting to redesign and change our churches into a new model that meets their personal interests and needs. The original model was designed by Christ and set in motion by his apostles. The blueprint and design are clearly recorded in the New Testament. The following changes have already been made in many places:

* The name. It seems the change agents are uncomfortable with the name church of Christ (Rom. 16:16) and prefer most any other designation.
* The communion. Rather than a sacred memorial in an hour of worship (I Cor. 11:17-34), they prefer a setting with a common meal (See John Mark Hicks, **Come to the Table**).
* The congregational, acappella singing(Eph. 5:19), they would replace with choirs, soloists and instrumental music.
* The proclamation of the gospel by men of God (I Cor. 1:21), they would replace with story telling, drama and interpretative dances.
* The ancient way of Salvation by grace through faith repentance and baptism (Acts 2:38) they would replace with "grace only" or "faith only." (See Max Lucado and Rubel Shelly's pronouncements).
* The New Testament as an authoritative pattern for the church to follow (Heb. 8:5; II Tim. 1:13) they would replace with "love letter" and personal illumination of the Holy Spirit.
* The one unique church purchased by the blood of Christ, built by the Savior, loved by the Savior as his bride and to be saved by Him, they would replace with a denomination founded by Alexander Campbell and Barton Stone.
* The church as the one and only family of God to which He adds all the saved, they would change to a denomination of the same value as the twelve hundred others in our world.
* The male leadership God ordained for his church (I Cor. 14:34), they would change to a leadership made up of both men and

women.
* The decent and orderly worship of the New Covenant (I Cor. 14:40), they would exchange for a boisterous service or hand-clapping and emotional display.
* The church that is always looking back to the original pattern set forth by Christ and attempting to be like it, they would change for a church that is open to new ideas and ways of doing things.

I am sure there are other modifications that these designing brothers are working on, but these suffice for my point. We asked when did Kaiser-Frazier's Henry J cease to be their product and become Lynn's? Now when does a church that is being so radically changed ceased to be Christ's and become Lynn's or Royce's or Rubel's? When the church in Ephesus left her first love, Christ warned them, "Remember therefore whence thou art fallen, and repent and do the first works; or else I come . . . and will move thy candlestick out of its place . . . " (Rev. 2:5).

143. PARABLE OF THE "VINCIBLE" ARMY OF CHRIST

Once upon a time a noble and righteous kingdom found itself under siege and in danger of an overthrow by an army of rebels. Though few in number, the rebels were united in both plan and purpose. They were determined to wrest control of the territories of the king.

Within the ranks of the king's men were sufficient soldiers to easily rout the rebels and drive them out in defeat. Unfortunately, they could not reach agreement on who should bear arms for their king.
* Some insisted that only perfect specimens of manhood be allowed to serve, no men with wounds or scars were allowed in the ranks.
* Others insisted that all meet the same physical standards, that they be 5'10" and weigh 185 pounds, not more nor less, before they could be trusted in arms.
* Some said all had to be trained in the same camp as they were.

* Others insisted that all should be armed exclusively with Browning weapons, while others demanded that the weapons be Remingtons.
* Some demanded that all rifles be 30.06 calibers but others wanted 30.30 calibers.
* Some were trained as infantry and had no use nor place for cavalry, air or naval forces. Special teams such as intelligence planners they despised and rejected.
* One group was resentful of those trained in Officer Candidate Schools and the other insisted that all had to be thus trained.
* Large numbers of the men wanted to be recognized as high ranking officers even though the king had not thus appointed them. They refused to serve in lesser positions.
* Each of the contending parties was so sure of their position that they were highly suspicious of and contemned those who did not agree with their point of view.

For days, weeks, and months the quarreling and debating continued. Fights broke out between various factions. Each sought to persuade the citizens to support their demands. The various groups refused to fight along side of the others. Eventually many of the soldiers grew weary and discouraged. Multitudes dropped out and returned to their old occupations. The citizens were bewildered and confused about what was going on.

Each day the rebels grew stronger and bolder. One by one they occupied the villages, towns and cities of the kingdom. Eventually the kingdom fell into their hands with but a few sporadic shots being fired.

The surviving soldiers were forced to flee to a distant place and tried to rebuild a new kingdom for their Lord. But even there they could not agree to disagree on their cherished points and the contention continued. Eventually they all died out and soon were forgotten.

When the teacher was asked to explain his parable, he said, The king is the Lord Jesus. The kingdom is his church. The rebels were known as change agents. The quarrelsome soldiers were preachers of the king's church. The once invincible army had become quite "vincible." The war, we are in even today.

He that hath ears to hear, let him hear what the Spirit saith to the churches: "Every city or house divided against itself shall not stand" (Matt. 12:25); "But if ye bite and devour one another, take heed that ye be not consumed on of another" (Gal. 5:15).

144. A LESSON FROM NATURE IN A DAY OF CHANGE

King Solomon found it useful to draw illustrations from nature to teach his moral lessons. Ants teach diligence, locusts team work, lizards audacity and conies wise planning (Prov. 30:25-28). Nature also provides Christian leaders useful lessons in this day when liberal proponents of change are surfacing throughout our brotherhood.

As **termites** delight to feed on the foundations of fine old homes and eventually bring them to ruin, so the liberal preacher or disciple loves to eat away at the foundations of a congregation. Termites do their destructive work secretly and quietly. The unsuspecting owner never realizes their presence until serious damage is done. So the liberal does his work in a congregation. Many an unsuspecting eldership has labored under the false impression that they had a great servant of God in their midst. Thinking he was building up the body of Christ, they discovered later he had undermined their authority and subverted their leadership. Consequently the congregation fell into the hands of those who had abandoned the faith of Christ for a new gospel (Gal. 1:6-7).

As the **chameleon** can change his colors to match his environment, so the liberal can put on various faces as the occasion demands. If asked point-blank if he is teaching error, he can easily deny it or couch his answer in slippery words designed to fool his questioner.

He can affect an air of being crushed that anyone would doubt his loyalty to the old Biblical ways. In the presence of strong conservatives he can appear to be one of them. But with a fellow liberal he can take on his hue. He is capable of preaching good sermons that have the ring of the old "Jerusalem gospel" but he can go into a home and cast doubt on the foundational truths of the religion of Christ. Speaking for a liberal church he can give them just what they wish to hear, and then do the same for a conservative congregation. To a liberal, truth is a malleable, subjective thing. He does not believe it to be hard and fast. Also he tends to believe that his agenda for changing the church justifies his being like the chameleon to achieve his goal.

Just as **mice** never wait for an invitation, so liberals will insinuate themselves into a congregation and begin to make it their own. They rarely wait to be invited to come and change a church. They take it upon themselves to do so. Just as no thinking person wants mice in his home, no spiritual minded elder wants to have a liberal at work in the congregation he leads. Once ensconced, they are hard to get rid of and they are destructive.

In delivering his lessons from nature, Solomon said, "Go to the ant . . . Consider her ways and be wise" (Prov. 6:6). Wise leaders will remember the termite, the chameleon and the mouse and be wise.

XIV.
SOME BASIC TRUTHS THAT NEED TO BE REEMPHASIZED

(The following lessons were first published in gospel papers of our local newspaper. For generations these doctrinal points were held by all of those who claimed membership in churches of Christ and were boldly preached by her ministers. All of these are now challenged by the leaders of the change movement.)

145. KNOWING AND DOING GOD'S WILL IN OUR POSTMODERN AGE

Christ expects those who preach his word and lead his people to teach converts to "observe all things whatsoever . . . (he) commanded" (Matt. 28:20). His holy Word will judge us and all of humanity in the last day (John 12:48). He describes his Word as a "pattern" to which we are to conform (II Tim. 1:13). He expects us, as he did Moses, to build his church according to the pattern shown us (Heb. 8:5). Preachers are intrusted with the responsibility to preach "the word" (II Tim. 4:1-2), not just any word, but that sacred word delivered to us by the Spirit of God (John 16:13). To respect God's Word is to respect God who spoke it. To disregard His Word is to disregard Him.

Having given us a written revelation of His will, God expects us to honor it as our only standard for our faith and practice as Christians. God's Word takes precedence over culture, tradition, popularity, public opinion, majority opinion or the pronouncements of scholars. It does not allow for adjustments to new generational interests such as Baby Boomers, Generation Xers etc.

Lip service to the authority of the Bible is inadequate (Matt. 7:21).

So is partial respect that honors only those precepts and principles that please us or are convenient. God demands that His Word be preached and honored "in season and out of season" (II Tim. 4:2).

The message of the Bible is the same for our post-Christian age as it was for those in apostolic times. His Word will never pass away (Matt. 24:34). God's Word is as changeless as is He (I Jehovah change not) This basic, primary lesson needs to be instilled in the heart and mind of every young preacher (and older ones as well) and proclaimed in every congregation of the church of Christ in America, not just once, but repeatedly until every member knows that our faith is governed by, restricted by and regulated by the Word of God and that alone. We must be reminded that we may not add to nor take away from the Word either by tampering with the written message or in our response to it. We must obey its precepts. We must respect its silence. To do more or less is to fail to respect the authority of His Word.

146. ATTRIBUTES OF CHRIST'S CHURCH

Near the city of Caesarea Philippi, Jesus promised his apostles: "Upon this rock I will build my church; and the gates of Hades shall not prevail against it" (Matt. 16:18). Even his death at the hands of Jews and Romans did not deter him from keeping his word. On the third day he arose triumphantly from the tomb and some 47 days later his glorious church came into existence. The birth date of Christ's church was Pentecost Sunday in the 33rd year of his life. The place was Jerusalem. The event is recorded in the Acts of the Apostles, Chapter 2.

The apostles were gathered together. The Holy Spirit which Christ had promised them (Acts 1:5, 8) came with a sound of a rushing mighty wind and filled all the house where they were sitting. "And they were all filled with the Holy Spirit and began to speak with other tongues as the Spirit gave them utterance" (Acts 2:1-4).

Guided by God's Spirit, the apostles preached the good news of the resurrected Christ. They showed Jesus to be the fulfillment of the ancient messianic prophecies. Three-thousand Jews were convicted of their sins and driven to cry out, "what shall we do?" Peter answered them, "Repent ye, and be baptized every one of you in the name of Jesus Christ unto the remission of your sins . . . " (Acts 2:38). All who gladly received his word were baptized and the Lord added unto them about three-thousand souls (Acts 2:41). From that day forth the church is spoken of as an existing reality (See Acts 2:47 KJV, 5:11, etc.).

This was no denomination or sect founded by a sinful man, it was the kingdom of God upon the earth. It was not just another great religion that would take its place beside Buddhism, Hinduism and others. This was the strait and narrow way that leads to life (Matt. 7:14). This was God's family of saved children destined to live with him in eternity (Eph. 5:23-28).

The Church of Christ is Divine in Origin

It was God's plan from eternity to make his will known to men through the church (Eph. 2:10-11). It was predicted by the Hebrew prophets that his church would be established in the last days of the Jewish state, in Jerusalem (Is. 2:2-4).

Daniel foresaw a kingdom not made with human hands (i.e., divine in origin) that would become great and fill the whole earth (Dan. 2:34-35, 44-45). Christ made preparation for his church while on the earth. In his death on the cross, he purchased the church with his blood (Acts 20:28). Through his chosen apostles he established it. God appointed his Son "to be head over all things to the church . . . " (Eph. 1:22). Today he reigns as both Lord and Christ (Acts 2:36) over his church kingdom. He has all authority in heaven and on earth (Matt. 28:18).

Christ's Church is Universal in its Outreach

In Daniel's vision the kingdom of heaven, which began as a little stone, became a great mountain that filled the whole earth (Daniel 2:34-35). God did not ordain different churches for different nations such as the Church of England and Church of Scotland. Rather he planned a church that all nations would flow into (Is. 2:2).

On the cross, the Savior "abolished the enmity . . . that he might create in himself of the two (races: Jews and Gentile) one new man, so making peace and might reconcile them both in one body unto God through the cross . . . " (Eph. 2:15-16). Now, in Christ's church there must be no social, racial or national distinctions. "There can be neither Jew nor Greek . . . bond nor free . . . no male and female; for ye are all one man in Christ Jesus" (Gal. 3:28). In his great commission Jesus sent the apostles into "all the world" to "preach the gospel to every creature" (Mark 16:15). It is the mission of God's people to tear down the walls of separation, and never to be guilty of building them.

The Lord's Church is Eternal in Duration

Daniel wrote that "the God of heaven (shall) set up a kingdom which shall never be destroyed . . . " (Dan. 2:44). Earthly kingdoms founded by men bear the seeds of their own demise. They live a few hundred years at best, and then fall. The kingdom of heaven will stand till Jesus comes and delivers it up to God his Father (I Cor. 15:24). The church revealed in the New Testament is as relevant, vibrant and valid today as in its infancy. Its meaning, message and ministry are as needed today as in that first century. The world is yet lost and in need of salvation. It is her task to take the message of salvation to every creature (Mark 16:15-16). The poor are still with us in great numbers and its ministry is "to visit the fatherless and widows in their affliction" (Jas. 1:27). The world today languishes in ignorance, error and superstition as it did two-thousand years ago. The church is God's beacon light in the world, holding forth the word of life and hope (Phil. 2:15-16). As long as sin-cursed men inhabit planet earth, so long will there be a need for the church of Christ to enlighten their minds, soften their hearts, refine their conduct, bring them salvation and prepare them for eternity.

The Church is Two-Dimensional

Many folks have been turned off toward the church because of a bad experience with some of her members. This reminds us that the church has two distinctly different sides, the divine and the human. The former is all perfection, without spot or blemish, being the product of the Divine mind. The latter is as weak and fallible as the material of which it is made. A local group of Christians is no better than the sum of its members. While on earth's side of eternity, none of us reach perfection. Even of God's people it is true that all sin and fall short of his glory (Rom. 3:23). We are but sinners saved by his grace (Eph. 2:8-9). It is, therefore, impossible to find a perfect congregation. If we should, we would surely spoil it by our imperfect presence.

The church planned by God and established by Christ is perfect in its structure, doctrine and duties. We dare not lift a hand to change one practice or precept (Rev. 22:18-19). We must, like Moses, "make all things according to the pattern that was showed" us (Heb. 8:5). Thus, while we are militant to follow exactly that divinely given blueprint for the church, we will be patient with brethren who are struggling to live up to the Christian ideal in their lives and worship. What a marvelous privilege it is to be invited to be members of "the church of the first born who are enrolled in heaven" (Heb. 12:23). May we never cause offence to the church of God (I Cor. 10:32) but rather give Him "the glory in the church: unto all generations" (Eph. 3:20).

147. MUST I BE IN THE CHURCH TO BE SAVED?

Christ saves the lost (Luke 19:10). But is the church essential to our salvation? Many feel the church is good but not essential. If one is speaking of membership in church which men have founded, he is right; you need not be a member of any of them. In fact, membership in such religious groups will jeopardize one's hope of heaven. Jesus said speaking of such religious bodies, "Every planting which my heavenly Father hath not planted shall be rooted up (Matt. 15:13). If one contemplates the church Jesus established (Matt. 16:18), he will get a different answer.

You cannot be saved outside of Christ's one true church! The Lord adds the saved to the church (Acts 2:47). Christ is savior of the body (Eph. 5:23), which is the church (Eph. 1:22). Jesus purchased the church with his blood (Acts 20:28). If one can be saved without the church, he can be saved without the blood of Christ.

Saul persecuted the church (I Cor. 15:9). Jesus said to him, "Saul, why persecutest thou me?" (Acts 9:4). The church is so related to Christ that to harm it is to hurt Him.

"Salvation is in Christ" (II Tim. 2:10). But one is "baptized into Christ" (Gal. 3:27). Baptism also puts one into the one body or church (I Cor. 12:13). Therefore, when one is baptized into Christ, he is saved and added to the church.

The church is not a building, institution or organization in the usual meaning of those words. The church is God's saved people. The word "church" is a translation of the Greek word, *ekklesia*. It means "a called out people." Its New Testament meaning is, Christians are called out of a life of sin into a life of fellowship with Christ. Those who are not members of the called out church are not among the saved! Are you a member of that one true church you can read of in your Bible?

148. WHAT THE CHURCH IS AND IS NOT

It is enlightening to contemplate what the church is and is not. First, **what she is not:**

* It may come as a shock to you to learn that the church is not a human organization run by a hierarchy of officials to promote their own ideas and opinions.
* It is not a social agency to meet the needs and demands of the community.
* It is not a community social hall where folks can be married or have their funeral services.
* It not a religious social club where people of like mind gather for fun and fellowship.
* It is not a cathedral made of bricks, mortar and stained glass.

The church is:
* **The body of Christ** (I Cor. 12:27), with Christ as head and each disciple a functioning organ of that spiritual body.
* It is **the kingdom of Christ** (Col. 1:13). It is not a worldly political kingdom (John 18:36). It has no geographical territory. Rather it is composed of citizens from around the world who have pledged their lives to Christ (Matt. 28:19-20). Regardless of where they live the kingdom of God is within them (Luke 17:21).
* It is **the bride of Christ** (Eph. 5:22-27). This speaks of the loving relationship of Christ and his people and of their loving submission to him as their Lord.
* The church is **the family of God** (I Tim. 3:15). We all have a common Father in heaven. We wear a common name, Christian (Acts 11:26). We are all brothers and sisters in Christ (Matt. 23:8). We have a common love and concern for each other as brothers and sisters should (Gal. 6:1-2).
* The church is **a spiritual temple** composed of all Christians who are likened to living stones built upon Christ, the divine foundation (I Pet. 2:5; Eph. 2:19-22).

If you would like to know more about Christ's church, visit the **Church of Christ** in your community.

149. THINGS NOT FOUND IN CHURCHES OF CHRIST

Churches of Christ are a distinctive body of people. They seek to restore in this present age, the pure and simple Christianity of the first century. They recognize Christ as the only head of the church (Eph. 1:22) and His New Testament as the only guide in faith and practice. Since only those things are accepted that find their authority in the New Testament, there are many common religious beliefs and practices not found in their faith, worship and practice.

* No sacred images are found in churches of Christ for God says, "thou shalt not make unto thee a graven image, nor any likeness of any thing . . . " (Ex. 20:4).
* No ministers are called "Father" in churches of Christ, for Christ said, "call no man your father on earth: for one is your Father, even he who is in heaven" (Matt. 23:8).
* No women preachers are found in them since Paul said, "let the women keep silence in the churches: for it is not permitted unto them to speak" (I Cor. 14:34).
* No unmarried bishops are found therein inasmuch as the Bible says "the bishop therefore **must** be . . . the husband of one wife" (I Tim. 3:2).
* One finds no holy water, prayer beads, candles or incense in these churches since they were totally unknown in the church of the New Testament.
* Instrumental music is not seen in their worship. This is because Jesus said, "Teach them to observe all things whatsoever I commanded you" (Matt. 28:20). Paul plainly tells us to sing and make melody with our heart" (Eph. 5:19).
* Sprinkling and pouring for baptism are not found in churches of Christ since Bible baptism is a burial (Rom. 6:4) and is symbolic of Christ's death, burial and resurrection (Rom. 6:5).

Do you say those "churches of Christ are surely different?" You are right. Different in faith and practice from those who base their practice on the traditions and precepts of men (Matt. 15:6-9). Learn more about the religion of Christ by visiting a **Church of Christ** near you.

150. THE CHURCH AND DENOMINATIONALISM

The denominationalism prevailing in contemporary Christendom is in sharp contrast with the church which Christ established. Consider the following:

* Christ founded his church (Matt. 16:18), but mortal men and women founded denominations.
* Christ's church was founded in Jerusalem in 33 A.D. but all denominations were founded long afterwards, in other places.
* Christ's church wears his holy name. Paul wrote, "All the churches of Christ salute you" (Rom. 16:16). Denominations wear their own distinguishing names that honor men, doctrines or practices.
* Christ is the only head of his church (Eph. 1:22), but men are chosen to head denominations.
* Each congregation of Christ's church is overseen by its own elders (Acts 14:23). Denominations are ruled by governing bodies.
* Christ's church follows only the Bible (Matt. 28:20). Denominations are guided by creedal books written by uninspired men.
* The church that Christ built worships as he ordered in his word (John 4:24). Denominations change worship to suit the wishes of their members and leaders.
* Christ's church teaches people to be saved as Christ ordained. They must hear the gospel preached, believe it and be baptized to be saved (Mark 16:15-16). Denominations teach other ways of salvation. Some offer salvation by faith alone which Scripture clearly denies (Jas. 2:24). Others demand a Holy Spirit baptism, but the Bible knows only "one baptism" (Eph. 4:5). Some posit salvation on works of human merit. Paul plainly declares, that it

is "not by works of righteous which we have done" (Eph. 2:8-9).
* Christ loves, blesses and saves his church (Eph. 5:22-25). But denominationalism is contrary to his will (I Cor. 1:10-13). Those who promote denominationalism stand condemned by Him. We are told to "mark them that are causing the divisions and occasions of stumbling, contrary to the doctrine which ye learned: and turn away from them. For they that are such serve not our Lord Christ . . . " (Rom. 16:17-18). Denominational division thwarts the dying prayer of Jesus for the unity of his people (John 17:11).

151. CHRIST'S CHURCH AND MEN'S CHURCHES

Christ built his church (Matt. 16:18). In dying on the cross, He purchased his church with his life's blood (Acts 20:28). God appointed Christ to be head over all things to his church (Eph. 1:22). He adds all who are saved to his church (Acts 2:47). He is the savior of his church (Eph. 5:23). Christ built only one church (I Cor. 12:12,20) His dying prayer was that all his disciples be united in his one church, even as he and the Father are (John 17:20-21). In the early years, all Christians were united as he desired. Paul rebuked certain Christians at Corinth because they were divided and denominating themselves as disciples of Paul, Cephas, Apollos (I Cor. 1:10).

The present situation in the Christian world, with more than a thousand different kinds of churches, stands in stark contrast with the one church of the Lord revealed in Scripture. Anyone can start his own church, but Christ is under no obligation to claim it or bless it. He has his own church that he will bless and take with him to heaven. Christ's church has no human head. It has no earthly headquarters; no human legislative body. It has no man-made creed nor human traditions to obey. It wears no human names.

Consider this: If you had to choose between my church and Christ's church, which would you pick? I did not die for your sins. I have not been resurrected, nor do I have the power to raise you from the dead. I do not have all power in heaven or on earth. I cannot save you, bless you, or reward you. I cannot plead your case before the Father on judgment day. But Christ can. That's why you need to be a member of his church! It would be a terrible mistake to seek salvation in my church.

152. IS ONE CHURCH GOOD AS ANOTHER?

This is a valid question that millions of folks have pondered. To help put it in focus ask yourself: Is one medicine as good as another? Or one doctor? Is one car as good as another? Or one airline? When you are traveling, is one direction as good as another? When balancing your checking account is one answer as good as another? Is one political candidate as good as another? Is one school as good as another? Is a counterfeit bill as good as a genuine piece of currency? Or a forged check of equal value with a good one? Of course the answer to all of these question is no. One is not necessarily as good as the other; in many cases one is downright inferior or even worthless.

Only in the realm of religion would we even considered such a statement to have any merit. In any other area, to affirm that one thing is as good as another would cause us to be laughed off the platform. Christ purchased a church (Acts 20:28); he built a church (Matt. 16:18); he is savior of a church (Eph. 5:23); he is head of a church (Eph. 1:22). That church is undisputedly of ultimate value and benefit to all who become members of it. New Testament writers speak of it as an exclusive, unitary church. They call it "the" church. They tell us there is one body or church (Eph. 4:4-5). Across the centuries, men and women have established hundreds of churches of their own design and making. Who would say that any one of them is of equal value with that church which Christ built? Christ's church existed long before any human denomination, sect or cult was created. Our eternal destiny depends on our being members of the church which is God's saved family (Eph. 5:23). It behooves us therefore to be members of that church which Christ built. Paul referred to this body when writing to the Romans, saying, "All the churches (i.e., congregations) of Christ salute you" (Rom. 16:16). No other church is equal in value to that of Christ.

153. RESTORING A THING OF VALUE

Lovely works of art are often marred by accumulations of dirt and grime. Specialists are employed to restore them to their original beauty. They carefully remove the foreign matter than obscures their true nature. Fine furniture can become worn and damaged. Its beauty is hidden by tattered upholstery and layers of paint. To see it as it came from the hands of the artisan it needs to be restored by a skilled workman. The paint and ragged upholstery needs to be stripped away.

Christianity is two thousand years old. Its modern appearance is greatly marred and distorted by the accumulation of human doctrines and practices imposed upon it over the ages. A careful reading of the New Testament provides one with an accurate picture of Christianity as it came from the hands of Jesus. A comparison of that with modern denominational versions of Christianity reveals a stark difference. Hardly a single teaching or practice of the original faith has been untouched. Human hands have defiled and marred its beauty with their changes.

But as with the work of art or the fine furniture, we can restore the church to its original simplicity and beauty. First we look to the New Testament of Christ to determine just how he intended the church to be; what she was to believe; how she was to worship. We then resolve that we will follow those guidelines faithfully. Each item of faith and practice must be examined carefully in light of Christ's word. Anything not as old as the New Testament must be discarded.

Anything that has been left out or neglected must be put back in its proper place. We must be willing to endure the complaints, criticisms and ridicule of those who love their human traditions more than they do the original faith of Christ. We must be prepared to be a minority because Jesus said "Many are called but few are chosen" (Matt. 22:14). We must resolve to hold fast to that which we find to be true lest we let it slip from us (Heb. 2:1).

The labor will be intense, the cost will be high, but when you have done the necessary work of restoring you will possess the pure and holy church of Christ which he purchased with his own blood (Acts 20:28). You will have found the way that is right, which cannot be wrong. The restoration of New Testament Christianity is the goal and commitment of faithful Christians around the world.

154. BACK TO THE FOUNTAIN HEAD

Many years ago I visited the little mountain town of Elijay, GA. An elderly gentleman gave me a tour of the area. Our drive took us to a spot high on Appalachian mountain. Parking the car, he led me to a bubbling spring that gushed from the rocky ground. Taking a small cup from his pocket, he filled it with the crystal water and said "Have a drink from the Tennessee River." That pure water not only quenched my thirst, it provided me an illustration I have used hundreds of times since. No one in his right mind would drink the water from the great Tennessee River that flows through the valleys on its way to the Mississippi. Sewerage systems, chemical plants, industrial waste, agricultural and road run-off foul its water, making it unsafe to drink without purification. But if one makes his way back to the source, it is pure, clean and wholesome.

This aptly illustrates the situation in modern Christianity. In the beginning, when the Word of the Lord went forth from Jerusalem, it was pure sweet and wholesome, bringing only the richest blessings to those who partook of it. As years passed and the gospel spread across the face of the earth, changes began to creep in. There is something about the human mind that leaves us unsatisfied with what has come from the past. We are always trying to improve on such things. Men thought they could improve on the religion of Christ. For some that meant creating a governing body to control the life of the church and her members. Others sought to improve the worship, by incorporating practices and customs popular with the newly converted masses. Still others felt the need to enhance the church's power by moving her into the political realm. Some found the original doctrinal basis of the church too simplistic. They sought to make it more philosophical. In time there came the splintering of the church into hundreds of competing bodies, some large, some small. The current situation in the world of Christendom is like that polluted river.

When one reads his New Testament, he sees Christianity as it was in the beginning; pure, undiluted. One marvels at the simplicity and beauty of the message: a message of personal salvation; of encouragement to live the Christlike life and avoid those things that will alienate one from God. There he finds a church without all the modern accouterments: no political power, no wealth, no real estate, no social standing, no entertainment. There we see the church in her true glory as the family of God, the bride of Christ, the kingdom of God, the body of Christ. In the Book of Christ we discover the real power of the Christian message to change the world for good. It is addressed to the individual. Like leaven, the heavenly message goes from life to life changing people's hearts into the likeness of Christ. No physical force is ever used, no political or legal coercion is found. The servants of the Lord go forth with a message and seek to win the hearts and minds of humanity.

Today with our Bibles in hand, we can make our way back to the fountain head of Christianity. Leaving behind the foreign items accumulated over the ages, we can learn for ourselves and practice the pure, undiluted religion of the Son of God. Clear and clean, wholesome and pure, it will truly be a blessing to our souls.

155. A NAME OF WHICH WE SHOULD NEVER BE ASHAMED

To the Christians in Rome Paul wrote, "All the churches of Christ salute you" (Rom. 16:16). Other names are also ascribed to the Lord's church. In I Corinthians it is called "the church of God" (1:2). Paul also called it "the church of the Lord" (Acts 20:28). Sometimes it was simply called the church. This shows us that Christ did not appoint a single, exclusive name for his church. Since in heaven's plan there only one church, there was no need for a specific name to distinguish it from other religious bodies.

In a world of over 2,000 denominations, all claiming to be Christ's church, we identify ourselves as **Churches of Christ**. We do so because it is clearly a biblical name that God approves of. It tells the world to whom we belong. It gives the glory to our founder and savior. While not the only name that a body of Christians can scripturally use, it is highly appropriate for many reasons.

* Christ established the church (Matt. 16:18).
* He called it "my church" (Matt. 16:18).
* He gave himself for the church, dying for her (Eph. 5:25).
* In his death on Calvary, he purchased the church with his shed blood (Acts 20:28).
* The church is his spiritual body, of which he is head (Eph. 1:22-23).
* He is the chief cornerstone of the church (Eph. 2:20).
* It is his house (Heb. 3:6).
* The church is his bride (II Cor. 11:2).
* He is the savior of the church (Eph. 5:23).
* He adds to his church all who are saved (Acts 2:47).
* The church is his family (Eph. 3:15).

Given all of these facts, it seems entirely reasonable that we call the church "the church of Christ." This holy name gives our Lord recognition for his role in giving us the church, preserving and protecting her. It acknowledges our dependance upon him. It expresses our love for him who saved us. It glorifies him as head of the church.

Paul declared that he was not ashamed of the gospel of Christ (Rom. 1:16), nor should we ever be ashamed of, embarrassed by, or apologetic for this holy name we wear.

156. DOES IT MAKE ANY DIFFERENCE?

Does it matter that preachers teach things that are not as the Bible teaches? Is accuracy in one's religious beliefs and practice important? Most people seem to think that sincerity and faith in God are the only things necessary for pleasing God. This is reflected in the theory that "one church is as good as another," or "it's not what you believe it's what you feel," or "we are all heading for the same place, just traveling different roads."

It is only in religion that men would make such ridiculous statements. In what other field is it true "That it doesn't make any difference what you believe as long as you are sincere?" Should your doctor prescribe a medicine for you, would you tolerate a druggist who filled prescriptions on the principle that it makes no difference which ingredients are used so long as the pharmacist is sincere?

What if a carpenter built your house on this theory? Does it really matter how one measures the pieces, fits the joints or levels theories floor, just as long as he is sincere? Believe it who will.

What space scientist would argue that one need not be concerned about details? What astronaut would risk his life under the supervision of such a thinker?
The illustrations could be multiplied a thousand times. **It does matter** that we be absolutely right in our religion.

Do we have a choice? Paul tells us in Ephesians 4:4-5 that there are a number of things in Christianity about which there can be no difference of opinion. He says that there is:

1. **One body** which is the one church (Eph. 1:22). It is the church of Christ (Rom. 16:16), for he built it (Matt. 16:18), and purchased it with his blood (Acts 20:28). You have no more choice of which church to be a member of than of which God to believe in.
2. **One Spirit** that dwells in the heart of every saved person (Rom. 8:13).
3. **One hope**. The same hope is held before all men. It is heaven and eternal life therein (John 14:1-3). Do we really have a choice? There is only one way to heaven (John 14:6). Our only choice is to accept Christ and obey his commands, or refuse him, thus choosing hell.
4. **One Lord Jesus Christ**. He alone can save you!
5. **One faith** or system of doctrine that must be accepted, believed and followed. This faith is the Word of God which is able to save our souls (Jas. 1:21). There is but one source of the one faith. It is the Bible (Rom. 10:17). Hence there can not be different creeds and beliefs to choose between. We must accept the Scripture as the only authority in Christianity.
6. **One baptism** which is a burial in water (Rom. 6:3-4, John 3:23), for the remission of sins (Acts 2:38). There being **only one baptism**, then we cannot choose between sprinkling or pouring or Holy Spirit baptism.
7. **One God**. You must believe in Him exclusively.

It does make a difference what we believe and practice in religion. If not, why would the Lord warn us so often against error in religion? "Though we or an angel from heaven should preach unto you any gospel other than that which we preached unto you, let him be anathema..." (Gal. 1:8-9).

Be sure of your faith. Demand Bible, book, chapter and verse for that which you are asked to accept and practice! It does make a difference. Your being right with God now will determine where you will spend eternity.

157. "AND THIS IS HOW THOU SHALT MAKE IT"

When God found it necessary to destroy with a flood, the wicked race of Noah's day, he made provision to save righteous Noah and his family. The means by which they would be saved was to build an ark suitable to lift them and a remnant of animal life safely above the overwhelming deluge. God did not leave Noah to figure out how to construct the ark. He said to Noah, "and this is how thou shalt make it" (Gen. 6:15). He then gave him detailed plans which included the type of wood, the dimensions, and all other necessary information for construction. Noah and his family set to work to build that massive life boat, undaunted by magnitude of the task or the time it would take to complete it. While all others perished, they were saved without loss from the flood waters because, "thus did Noah according to all that God command him" (Gen. 6:22).

From this great story we can draw some valuable lessons. Our wicked world will one day be destroyed by God (II Pet. 3:10). But God has made provision for our safe escape from that cataclysmic event. Rather than an ark, he has given us salvation in Christ. In clear and certain terms he has told us "this is how thou shalt do it." We must believe on Jesus as our Savior (John 8:24). We must repent of our sins (Luke 13:3). We must confess our faith in Christ as Lord (Rom. 10:9-10). We must be immersed in water for the forgiveness of our sins (Acts 2:38; 22:16).

Would Noah have been safe had he built his ark differently than God instructed him? Will you be safe if you fail to prepare your soul precisely as God has told you?

This same lesson can be applied to the way we organize our church; the way we worship in our singing, our communion, our giving and every other aspect of the Christian life.

God is not willing that you should perish (II Pet. 3:9). He has given you a safe plan of escape. Be like Noah and do according to all that God commands you.

158. WOMEN AND LEADERSHIP

We live in the midst of the Feminist Revolution. The champions of this social/political movement have challenged every traditional concept about the role of women in the home, society and the church. Without doubt some of the old ideas needed challenging. Some of the changes have been wholesome and beneficial. In two areas however, the goals of the feminists are in direct conflict with the will of God as revealed in the Bible. This poses no problem for most feminists since many of them reject God and Christ, and refuse to recognize the Scriptures as having any authority in their lives. However, to those women who fear God and follow Jesus; who order their lives by the New Testament and hope to spend eternity in heaven, their liberties must conform to the divine plan.

In the realm of the family: God ordained that "wives be in subjection unto (their) own husbands, as unto the Lord. For the husband is the head of the wife, as Christ also is the head of the church . . . " (Eph. 5:22-23). Husbands are expected to "love (their) wives, even as Christ loved the church and gave himself up for it."

For the church God declares: "As in all the churches of the saints, let the women keep silence in the churches; for it is not permitted unto them to speak; but let them be in subjection, as also saith the law" (I Cor. 14:33-34). "Let a woman learn in quietness with all subjection. But I permit not a woman to teach, nor to have dominion over a man, but to be in quietness" (I Tim. 2:11-12).

From these injunctions we learn that women are not allowed to fill leadership roles over men in the administration and public teaching of the church. Men are to be selected as elders(I Tim. 3:1-2). Men are to be the preachers, evangelists and teachers of the congregation.

This does not means that women have no role to fill in the life and teaching of the church. A woman can teach women and children (Tit. 2:4-5). She can be a leader among the women in their activities. But mixed classes of men and women are taught by men and public worship is conducted by men. In rare cases where no men are present, then women could do anything that needed to be done since they would not be exercising authority over men by so doing.

Such doctrine is anathema to committed feminists, but to women of God, it is truth and righteousness and must be accepted. Tragically, most of the denominations about us have capitulated to the noisy demands of the feminists. May God grant all of us the courage to stand faithful to his revealed will, even if the whole world rejects it.

159. THE FINE ART OF WORSHIP

What a marvelous privilege it is that we, the work of His hands, are invited to worship the Almighty Creator. In one sense we worship God as we live for Him and serve Him in daily life (Rom. 12:1-2), in deeds of kindness to others (Gal. 6:10). We are also expecteded to worship him in the company of fellow-Christian when we assemble as his church (Acts 20:7). We sing, we pray, we present our gifts, we commune, we listen to His words for us.

Just to worship is not enough. We must worship God in the way that He ordained. Neither is it enough to do just the correct things.

* Our worship must be in spirit and in truth (John 4:24).
* It must be with the spirit and the understanding (I Cor. 14:15).
* It must be from a heart of undivided love (Matt. 22:37-38).
* It must be to the glory of God rather than for man's glory (I Cor. 10:31).

* It must be according to the divine pattern he has shown us in Christ (Heb. 8:5; II Tim. 1:13).
* It must be offered to God through Jesus, the one and only mediator he will accept (I Tim. 2:5).
* It must be offered from a pure and sincere heart (Jas. 4:8).
* It must be accompanied by holy living (Rom. 12:1-2)
* It must be accompanied by a willingness to forgive those who sin against us (Matt. 6:15).

As our worship is offered up to Jehovah, it also blesses all of those present as it edifies their hearts and directs them toward the Father, His divine will and our eternal home. With David we should always be glad when they say to us, "Let us go unto the house of Jehovah . . . " (Ps. 122:1).

160. WORSHIP IS NOT ENTERTAINMENT

Syndicated religious writer, Richard Ostling, recently wrote, *"Much of Evangelical worship has degenerated into showmanship, with applause and canned orchestra music–a naked (and rather successful) quest for popularity in a media culture."* In this the writer is right on target. One need only look at many of the televised religious services to see his point in living color.

Those who love and honor Christ must continually resist the temptation to join the mad rush away from the simplicity of New Testament Christianity to the paltry substitute of entertainment. To be faithful Christians we must ever keep our eyes on the Bible as our only standard and guide in worship, faith and practice. As the writer of Hebrews says, "See saith he, that thou make all things according to the pattern that was showed thee" (Heb. 8:5). The Apostle Paul made it clear that we must not go beyond the things that are written (I Corinthians 4:6 ASV).

Those who perceive of worship as a time for entertainment need to ponder how their "show time" exercises (I cannot call such worship), would resonate in those early days when Christians risked their all to assemble for worship to their crucified and resurrected Lord; when they saw their brethren dragged away to a horrid death before a screaming mob. The entertainment crew would be so ashamed they would hang their heads and slink away in embarrassment for the insults they had offered to God and the harm done to his church.

The earliest Christians communed in sacred "remembrance of Christ" (I Cor. 11:25). They sang and prayed with the spirit and understanding (I Cor. 14:15). They heard preaching that glorified, not an entertainer, but "Christ Jesus as Lord" (II Cor. 4:5). They gratefully gave their gifts and offerings as an act of worship (II Cor. 9:7,12), not to see the hottest show in town.

It is true that some things grow obsolete and need to be discarded for newer inventions or versions, but it is sheer presumption for finite man to think that he can improve on the worship designed and ordained by the God of heaven. When we come to worship the Living God; like fine wine, the old time approach is better than the latest classy entertainment.

161. UNACCEPTABLE WORSHIP

Not all worship offered is acceptable to God. It is a commonly held error that He is obliged to accept any crumb man chooses to toss Him. Consider the following:

*A wicked lifestyle makes worship unacceptable. "The sacrifice of the wicked is an abomination" (Prov. 21:27).
* A lack of sympathy for the poor and unfortunate renders worship unacceptable. "Pure religion and undefiled before our God and Father is . . . to visit the fatherless and widows in their affliction . . . "(Jas. 1:27).

* A lack of respect for God's law nullifies ones worship; no matter how formal, elaborate and beautiful it may be. "He that turneth away his ear from hearing the law, even his prayer is an abomination" (Prov. 28:9).
* Unconfessed sin negates worship. "He that covereth his transgression shall not prosper; but whoso confesseth and forsaketh them shall obtain mercy" (Prov. 28:13).
* Worship based on traditions of men rather than the Word of God is offered in vain (Matt. 15:6,9).
* "Will-worship" is of no value (Col. 2:23). Will-worship is based upon a foundation of "I wish; I think; I believe; I feel" rather than upon the law of God (Matt. 7:21).
* Worship that seeks to approach God through images, angels or men is not acceptable. "Thou shalt not make unto thee a graven image" (Ex. 20:14). Peter forbade Cornelius to worship him (Acts 10:25-26) and God's angel forbade John's worship of him (Rev. 22:8-9). There is only "one mediator between God and man . . . Christ Jesus" (I Tim. 2:5).
* Only worship offered to God in spirit and truth will bring the desired blessing (John 4:24).

162. SACRED MUSIC 101

Just as today's school kids know little or nothing about history, Western Civilization and America's illustrious past, so many in the church (including preachers) seem to know little about the history of the religion of Christ and of our attempts to restore the faith and worship He instituted. From the great **Cyclopedia of Biblical, Theological and Ecclesiastical Literature** by McClintock and Strong (Vol. 6, pp. 757-759), we offer the following basic introduction to the worship of the early Christians.

It was the practice of the early Christians to praise God with congregational singing. **Pliny** in his letter to Trajan (103-104 A.D.) observed that Christians would "meet before day to offer praise to

Christ). **Tertullian** (160-220 A.D.) and **Eusebius** (260-340 A.D.) described the praise worship of the church in their day thusly, "Arising at the dawn of the morning, they sang hymns to Christ as God" (**Eccle. Hist.** 3:32). Justin Martyr (100-165 A.D.) wrote, "We manifest our gratitude to him by worshiping him in spiritual songs and hymns, praising him for our birth, for our health, for the vicissitudes of the seasons, and for the hope of immortality" (**Apology**, 5:28). "Their psalmody was the joint act of the whole assembly in unison," according to **Hilary** (A.D. 355). **Chrysostom** (347-407 A.D.) wrote, "It was the ancient custom, as it is still with us, for all to come together, and unitedly to join in singing ... all join in one song ... " (**Hom.** 9: Vol. 12, p. 349). McClintock and Strong then conclude, "Such was the character of the psalmody of the early church ... "

Under a section appropriately headed "**Innovations**" the authors note, "The appointment of singers as a distinct class of officers in the Church for this part of religious worship, and the consequent introduction of profane music into the church, marks another alteration in the psalmody of the church. These innovations were first made in the 4th century; and though the people continued for a century or more to enjoy their ancient privilege of all singing together, it is conceivable that it gradually was forced to die, as a promiscuous assembly could not well unite in theatrical music which required in its performers a degree of skill altogether superior to that which all the members of a congregation could be expected to possess. An artificial theatrical style of music, having no affinity with the worship of God, soon began to take the place of those solemn airs which before had inspired the devotions of his people. The music of the theater was transferred to the church, which accordingly became the scene of theatrical pomp and display rather than the house of prayer and of praise, to inspire by its appropriate and solemn rites the spiritual worship of God."

The church historian **J. A. Neander** wrote, "We have to regret that both in the Eastern and the Western Church their sacred music had already assumed an artificial and theatrical character, and was so far removed from its original simplicity that even in the 4th century the abbot **Pambo of Egypt** complained that heathen melodies (Accompanied as it seems with the action of the hands and the feet) had been introduced into their Church psalmody"

Jerome (342-420 A.D.), in remarking upon Eph. 5:19, says: "May all hear it whose business it is to sing in the church. Not with the voice, but with the heart, we sing praises to God. Not like the comedians should they raise their sweet and liquid notes to entertain the assembly with theatrical songs and melodies in the church, but the fire of godly piety and the knowledge of the Scriptures should inspire our songs . . . "

The Roman Catholic Council of Trent (1545-1563) "arranged the choral service on a proper footing, freeing it from all extraneous matters, gave choral music also a sanction which it had hitherto wanted. From that time the Church of Rome began to display that profound veneration for choral music which it has continued to manifest down to the present day" The same spirit that worked to introduce the choirs and solos in ancient times is still at work and is seen in our agents of change.

In section III, under **Use of Instruments in the Church,** McClintock & Strong continue, "The Greeks as well as the Jews were wont to use instruments as accompaniments in their sacred songs. The converts to Christianity accordingly must have been familiar with this mode of singing; yet it is generally believed that the primitive Christians failed to adopt the use of instrumental music in their religious worship." "...the general introduction of instrumental music can certainly not be assigned to a date earlier than the 5th or 6th centuries; yea, even Gregory the Great, who toward the end of the 6th century added greatly to the existing Church music, absolutely prohibited the use of instruments. Several centuries later the introduction of the organ in sacred services gave a place to instruments as accompaniments for Christian songs, and from that time to this they have been freely used with few exceptions. The first organ is believed to have been used in Church service in the 13th century.

Although our position is presently a minority view such was not always the case. Notable scholars from various religious bodies understood the Bible's teaching just as we do.

Charles Spurgeon, the greatest Baptist preacher of the 19th century England, refused to allow instruments of music in his Metropolitan Tabernacle.

Adam Clark, the brilliant Methodist Bible commentator wrote, "the whole spirit, soul and genius of the Christian religion are against this (instrumental music); and those who know the Church of God best, and what constitutes its genuine spiritual state, know that these things have been introduced as a substitute for the life and power of religion; and that where they prevail most, there is least of the power of Christianity. Away with such portentous baubles from the worship of the infinite Spirit who requires his followers to worship in spirt and in truth" (**Commentary**, Vol. IV, p. 684). He continued, "I am an old man, and an old minister; and I here declare that I never knew them (instruments) productive of any good in the worship of God; and have had reason to believe they were productive of much evil . . . instruments of music in the house of God I abominate and abhor."

John Wesley, founder of Methodism is quoted by Clarke as saying, "I have no objection to instruments of music in our chapels, provided they are neither HEARD nor SEEN."

John Calvin, founder of Presbyterianism wrote "Musical instruments in celebrating the praises of God would be no more suitable than the burning of incense, the lighting of lamps and the restoration of the other shadows of the law. The Papists (Catholics) therefore, have foolishly borrowed these, as well as many other things from the Jews. Men who are fond of outward pomp may delight in that noise, but the simplicity which God recommends to us by the apostles is far more pleasing." **(Commentary on Psalm 33)**.

Thomas Aquinas Roman Catholic theologian wrote, "instrumental music as well as singing is mentioned in the Old Testament, but the church has accepted only singing on account of its ethical value" . . . Therefore their use is unwise, and consequently the Church refrains from music instruments" **(Summa Theologica**, Question 91, Article II).

Alexander Campbell great preacher and scholar of our Restoration Movement wrote, "That all persons who have no spiritual meditations, consolation and sympathies of renewed hearts, should call for such aids is but natural. Pure water from the flinty rock has no attraction for the mere toper or wine bibber. A little alcohol, or genuine Cognac bandy, or good old Madeira is essential to the beverage to make it truly refreshing. So to those who have no real devotion or spirituality in them and whose animal nature flags under the oppression of church service, I think that instrumental music would no only be a desideratum, but an essential prerequisite to fire up their souls to even animal devotion. But I presume to all spiritual-minded Christians, such aid would be as a cowbell in a concert" **(Millennial Harbinger**, Series 4, Vol. 1. p. 581). (These quotes as cited by James Tolle in his excellent tract, **Instrumental Music in Worship**.)

Keep this information safely stored and when the sirens of change seek to convince you that our congregational *acappella* singing is only our tradition, share it with them; for they obviously know not the Scripture or the past history of the church.

163. SING AND BE HAPPY

Imagine, a church with no choir, no soloist, no piano or organ performance, no band to entertain; just a congregation of Christians singing heartfelt praises to God. "How quaint," you may say. You may feel pity that they cannot afford an organ or organist to perform for them. But to view it thusly is to misunderstand.

Churches of Christ **sing** psalms, hymns and spiritual songs without instrumental accompaniment because that is the way the earliest Christians worshipped. Our goal is to worship as they did without addition or subtraction. Such unaccompanied singing is called **acappella,** which means "as in the church," and refers to the ancient practice of the Christians.

Jesus' final charge was that his disciples "observe all things whatsoever (he) commanded" (Matt. 28:20). Should you take the time to read the New Testament of Christ through, you would discover that no command or example exists for Christians to worship God with instruments of music. We are told to sing and make melody in our hearts (Eph. 5:19). The closing words of the Bible warn against adding to or taking away from what is written (Rev. 22:18-19). When we sing to God, we neither add to nor take from his holy will. Since we are not under the Old Testament (Heb. 8:7-13), there is no value in looking there to justify the use of instrumental music.

If you are weary of choirs, soloists and musical performances and long to lift your voice up to God in songs of worship and praise, visit a congregation of the **Church of Christ** near you.

164. EASTER: DID YOU KNOW?

To most people Easter is an integral part of Christianity. They may not know where to look, but they are sure it is in the Bible. Consider the following quotations regarding this ancient Holy Day. "There is no trace of Easter Celebration in the New Testament" **(International Standard Bible Ency. Vol. II, p. 889)**. "In any case ... it must be admitted that ... there is no conclusive evidence in the first century or more of the keeping of the Pasch (Easter) ... "

(**Catholic Ency. Vol. V, p. 229**). "The Apostolic Fathers (earliest Christian writers) do not mention it" (**Ibid. p.224**). "At the end of the second century, the celebration of Easter as the feast of the resurrection of Christ was general among the Christians" (**Ency. Of Religion by Ferm, p. 239**). The Bible does not mention an Easter celebration. The church of the first century did not observe it. True, the King James Bible has the word Easter in Acts 12:4. The original Greek term is pascha, rendered in all other places "Passover." All later versions so translate it.

Where then did Easter come from? It is a convergence of three traditions. (1) **Pagan**: The word is derived from the Norse Ostara or Eostre, meaning the festival of spring at the vernal equinox when nature is in resurrection after winter. (2) **Hebrew**: The Jewish Passover is celebrated at approximately the same season as Easter. (3) **Christian**: Jesus' resurrection from the dead (**Americana Ency. Vol. 9, p. 506**). The first yearly festivals among the Christians originated with Jewish converts who "retained . . . all the Jewish festivals, although gradually they ascribed to them such Christian import as might naturally present itself... among Gentile Christians, there were probably from the first, no yearly festivals whatever . . . " (**History of the Christian Religion and Church, Neander, Vol. 1, p. 297**).

The Bible teaches that Christ died and was resurrected. The first Christians commemorated his death and resurrection each first day of the week (Acts 20:7). The highest authority for the Easter holy season is human tradition. Our commitment is to follow Jesus in all things. He says, teach them to observe all things I have commanded you (Matt. 28:20). Again, he says, "In vain do they worship me teaching as their doctrines the precepts of men" (Matt. 15:9). To those Christians observing other special days, Paul wrote, "I am afraid of you lest I have bestowed upon you, labor in vain" (Gal. 4:11).

165. THE LANGUAGE OF SALVATION

When Jehovah chose to reveal his great salvation to humanity he directed his inspired spokesmen to describe it by illustrations from their everyday life so the most humble soul could easily understand it. The many illustrations utilized are much like the various acts of a play or verses of a song, in that they are saying essentially the same thing. In all of them we see man separated from God by an impassable barrier called sin (Isaiah 59:1-2), then we see how God saves man from his predicament through his holy Son, Jesus.

Justification

Our first illustration is drawn from the law courts. This metaphor pictures the sinner before God, his judge. He is a guilty, condemned lawbreaker. Because of his guilt, he can only look forward to an awful punishment in hell. But when all hope is gone, Christ, the innocent one, steps forward to pay the penalty of death for the sinner. "For while we were yet weak ... Christ died for the ungodly ... much more then being now **justified** by his blood, shall we be saved from the wrath of God ... " (Rom. 5:6-9). The condemned sinner is "justified by faith" in his Savior (Rom. 5:1). He is no longer condemned (Rom. 8:1). He is a sinner but now God treats him as though he were innocent. Because of Christ and his trust in him, God deals with the sinner "just as if he had never left." When asked how he would reward the South for their rebellion, President Lincoln said, "I am going to treat them as though they had never left." This too is the lesson of the way the loving father received his prodigal son (Luke 15:20-24). Condemned ones are justified through faith in Christ, not by the works of the law of Moses (Gal. 2:16).

Reconciliation

Our next example is from the social realm and has to do with friendship. Here we see man pictured as an enemy of God. "...while we were enemies, we were reconciled to God through the death of

His Son..." (Rom. 5:10). Sinners are alienated and enemies in their minds and in their evil works (Col. 1:21). In this plight, separated from God by our foolish actions, we are lost. We need to make friends with our God and thus be reconciled. But we sinners have no suitable gift to bring to our Lord against whom we have sinned. What can we do? God meets our need. "For it was the good pleasure of the Father... through Christ to reconcile all things unto himself..." (Col. 1:19-20). Peace was effected "through the blood of the cross" (Col. 1:20) and we were "reconciled in the body of his flesh through death" (Col. 1:22). The reconciliation of all men is realized in the "one body" of Christ (Eph. 2:16). But what is this one body? This favorite expression of Paul is defined in Ephesians 1:22. God gave Christ "to be head over all things **to the church, which is his body**..." So we are reconciled to God in the one true church of Christ.

Remission

From the business world we have our next illustration. Man is represented as standing before God with an impossible debt to pay, i.e., his sins. This is seen in the parable in Matt.18:23-27. The servant owes his king over a million dollars. In a day when workers earned some 15 cents per day, this was a debt he could never pay. By right, the king could have inflicted great punishment upon him, but he forgave the debt. In Christ we have our debt of sin canceled or paid in full. God calls it **remission of sins**. No money or good works can achieve this, for "apart from shedding of blood there is no remission" (Heb. 9:22). The blood of bulls and goats could never take away sins (Heb. 10:4). But the apostles taught, "that through his name, every one that believeth on him shall receive remission of sins" (Acts 10:43). When does this occur? Hear Peter, "Repent ye, and be baptized every one of you in the name of Jesus Christ unto (for) the remission of sins..." (Acts 2:38). Without water baptism no one can enjoy remission of sins, i.e., have his great debt of sin marked paid in full by the Lord.

Redemption

In the Roman world, over half the population was in bondage. Slavery was a very real and everyday fact of life. Every slave longed for the day when he could be redeemed from his master and set free. It was usually through the kindness and generosity of some benefactor that a slave's price was paid and he was set free. Every man is enslaved to the tyrant Sin, with no way to free himself. "Everyone that commiteth sin is the bond-servant of sin" (John 8:34). God, through Christ, redeemed us. "Ye were bought with a price" (I Cor. 6:20). "Ye were redeemed, not with corruptible things, with silver or gold, from your vain manner of life... but with precious blood, as of a lamb without blemish... even the blood of Christ" (I Pet. 1:18-19). We have our redemption **in Christ** (Col. 1:13-14). How then may we get **into Christ**? Paul says we are baptized into Christ (Gal. 3:27). Thus only those who are properly baptized into Christ are redeemed from the bondage of sin by his precious blood.

Conclusion

Space fails us to deal with all of God's terms that describe our glorious salvation but perhaps these will suffice to show the honest soul that his only hope of salvation is through faith in God's Son, baptism in water according to his gospel and fellowship in the church which bears his name. Will you accept the salvation God offers today?

166. HOW DOES GOD JUSTIFY SINNERS?

Justification has been called "the supreme paradox of he gospel." It means that the just God accepts the sinner as just. It seems more rational to say that God being just must therefore condemn a sinner as a criminal. But the paradox is that even though He is just, God somehow, in his remarkable and miraculous grace, revealed in Jesus, accepts we sinners, not as criminals, but as beloved children.

Imputation

The explanation of how God can justify sinners is found in **the great doctrine of imputation**. The prophet Isaiah foresaw the Messiah who "was wounded for our transgressions . . . bruised for our iniquities; the chastisement of our peace was upon him; and with his stripes we are healed . . . and Jehovah laid on him the iniquity of us all." God would see the travail of his soul and be satisfied and the righteous servant would justify many (Is. 53:5-6, 11). Our sins were imputed or charged to Christ who paid the penalty for us. Peter writes that "Christ suffered for you . . . who his own self bare our sins in his body upon the tree, that we, having died unto sins, might live unto righteousness: by whose stripes ye were healed" (I Pet. 2:21, 24). Similarly, Christ's righteousness is imputed to us. Paul tells us, "Him who knew no sin he made to be sin (bearer) on our behalf; that we might become the righteousness of God in him (II Cor. 5:21).

Again, Paul exalts this grand truth in Philippians 3:8-9: "that I may gain Christ, and be found in him, not having a righteousness so my own, even that which is of the law, but that which is through faith in Christ, the righteousness which is from God by faith. We see a beautiful illustration of imputation in Paul's message to Philemon. He writes about a runaway slave named Onesimus, who was guilty of numerous offenses. The apostle was willing to assume full responsibility for his slave-friend's obligations. He writes, "But if he hath wronged thee at all, or oweth thee aught, put that to mine account; I Paul write it with mine own hand, I will repay it" (Phile. 18-19).

This too, is the typical lesson of Azazel, the scapegoat of the ritual of the Day of Atonement. The high priest laid his hands on the head of the living goat and confessed over him all the iniquities of the children of Israel. "And the goat shall bear upon him all their iniquities unto a solitary land; and he shall let go the goat in the wilderness" (Lev. 16:21-22). Thus Jesus bore the sins of humanity, symbolized by his cross, outside the gates to the place of death.

Our sins were imputed to Christ, but not so as to make him a sinner. Likewise, his righteousness is imputed to us, but it does not make us personally and actually worthy of God's favor. Jesus assumed our legal responsibility and was treated just as if he had been the sinner. We have received his righteousness in our justification and are treated just as if we were righteous altogether.

With David, we praise God for his marvelous grace. "Blessed is the man, unto whom God reckoneth righteousness apart from works . . . Blessed are they whose iniquities are forgiven, and whose sins are covered. Blessed is the man to whom the Lord will not reckon sin" (Rom. 4:6-8).

In the Gospels we see Jesus treating sinners as if they were the men and women they had the potential to become. The Jews treated Zacchaeus as a sinner, hopelessly lost. The Lord treated him as a potential saint. The same was true of the woman taken in adultery (John 8:1-11).

The Corinthians were justified when they were washed and sanctified (I Cor. 6:11). The washing occurred when they were baptized to wash away their sins (Acts 22:16). So today when in faith we are baptized into Christ, the great God of the universe justifies us and makes us his beloved children (Rom. 5:1).

167. SAVING FAITH

Faith is the bed rock of a Christian's relationship with God and his Son, Jesus. "Without faith it is impossible to be well-pleasing unto God; for him cometh unto God must believe that he is . . . " (Heb. 11:6). Jesus said, "except ye believe that I am he, ye shall die in your sins . . . " (John 8:24). "Faith is being sure of what we hope for and certain of what we do not see" (Heb. 11:1 NIV). The faith that is essential for salvation "comes from hearing the word of Christ" (Rom. 10:17). Apart from the truth revealed in the New Testament one cannot have saving faith. Thus Jesus said, "Go . . . preach the gospel to every creature. He that believeth . . . " (Mark 16:15-16).

Contrary to popular opinion, saving faith is not just an acceptance of the fact that God and Christ exist and a warm feeling of trust in them. God's word speaks of the "obedience of faith" (Rom. 1:5). The eleventh chapter of Hebrews presents a collage of biographical sketches that illustrate the meaning faith. Able offered his sacrifice; Enoch walked with God; Noah built his ark; Abraham offered his son; Moses chose to suffer with God's people rather than remain in Egypt. James devotes the second chapter of his epistle to clarifying the meaning of faith. "What doth it profit my brethren, if a man say he hath faith, but have not works? Can that faith save him?" (2:1). The answer is no. Again he says, "show me thy faith apart from thy works and I by my works will show thee my faith" (2:18). "Faith without works is barren" (2:20). "Ye see that by works a man is justified, and not only by faith" (2:24). " As the body apart from the spirit is dead, even so faith apart from works is dead." (2:26). In every example of conversion mentioned in the Acts of Apostles, those who believed obeyed Christ by being baptized (Compare Acts 2:41; 8:12; 18:8; 22:16). If you really believe on the Lord and want to enjoy his wonderful salvation you will do just as those disciples did. That's why Jesus said, "He that believeth and is baptized shall be saved" (Mk. 16:16).

168. YOUR FREE GIFT FROM GOD

"The free gift of God is eternal life in Christ Jesus" (Rom. 6:23). "Not by works done in righteousness, which we did ourselves, but according to his mercy he saved us . . . " (Tit. 3:5). Jesus said, "He that will, let him drink of the water of life freely" (Rev. 22:17). Because salvation is the free gift of God's grace, some mistakenly assume there is nothing to be done to receive it.

Our local radio station routinely gives away vacation trips and other nice gifts. While these gifts are completely free, to receive and enjoy them, the recipients must travel across to town to the station's office and claim their prize. Those who fail to go and claim them never get them. This illustrates an important aspect of salvation. Because of my personal sins, I am hopelessly lost (Is. 59:1-2). Nothing I can give or do has the power to wash away my sins. That, only the blood of Christ can do (I John 1:7). The question is, how can I receive my free gift of salvation? God, the giver of the gift, has set certain conditions that must be met in order to receive it. Consider the following verses.

* "Preach the gospel to every creature, he that believeth and is baptized shall be saved" (Mk. 16:16).
* When the Jews that had crucified Jesus heard the gospel preached and realized their horrible mistake, they asked what they must do? Peter, guided by the Holy Spirit, responded, "Repent ye and be baptized, every one of you in the name of Jesus Christ for the remission of your sins and ye shall receive the gift of the Holy Spirit (Acts 2:38). Those who gladly received his word were baptized (Act 2:41).

This free gift is yours to have, but you must fulfill the conditions God has set forth in his Word. Have you done that? To learn more about salvation, visit the **Church of Christ** in your neighborhood.

169. THE DAY YOU WERE BAPTIZED

* That was the day you confessed your faith in Christ as your Lord and Savior (Mark 16:15; Rom. 10:9-10).
* It was the day when you resolved to turn away from sin and follow Jesus. God calls that repentance (Acts 2:38).
* It was the day when a man of God gently immersed your body in a watery grave in the likeness of Jesus' burial (Rom. 6:3-4).
* In that experience the redeeming blood of Christ washed away your sins (Acts 22:16).

* Coming forth from the water was like a new birth for you (John 3:3-5). It marked the first day of your new life in Christ (II Cor. 5:17).
* On that day God gave you a special gift, his Holy Spirit, as an earnest of your home in heaven (Acts 2:38; Eph. 1:13-14).
* It was the day when God translated you out of the power of darkness (Satan's domain) and translated you into the kingdom or church of his dear Son (Col. 1:13; Acts 2:47; I Cor. 12:13).
* That was the day you took up your cross to follow Christ wherever he might lead you (Matt. 16:24).

Nothing could be more important than that blessed day; that life-changing day. We should always remember it, cherish it and be loyal to the commitment we made. If you were baptized as an infant and cannot remember that day, you need to consider the fact that Christ expects baptism only of those old enough to make their own choice and decision. That infants cannot do. Acceptable baptism is a decision only the recipient can make.

170. IS BAPTISM A WORK OF MAN?

Some folks label baptism as "a work." Since the Bible says, "for by grace have ye been saved through faith; and that not of yourselves, it is the gift of God; not of works . . . " (Eph. 2:8-9), they conclude, if baptism is a work it eliminates the need for God's grace. In this they are mistaken:

The Bible mentions three different kinds of works in connection with our religion:
1. **There are works of God that we must do.** Jesus said, "We must work the works of him that sent me . . . " (John 9:4). "This is the work of God that ye believe on him whom he hath sent" (John 6:28-29). Peter said, "he that feareth him, and worketh righteousness, is acceptable to him" (Acts 10:35). Paul wrote, "For in Christ Jesus neither circumcision availeth anything, nor

uncircumcision; but faith working through love" (Gal. 5:6).
2. **There are works of the law of Moses** which are of no avail now that Christ has come. Paul wrote, "by the works of the law shall no flesh be justified." (Gal. 2:16). Thus "we are justified by faith apart from the works of the law (of Moses)" (Rom. 3:28).
3. **There are works of man's own righteousness.** "Not by works done in righteousness, which we did ourselves, but according to his mercy he saved us . . . " (Tit. 3:5). Such works of man's righteousness are cited in I Cor. 13:3. "If I bestow all my goods to feed the poor, and if I give my body to be burned, but have not love, it profiteth me nothing." No matter how good or how many, such things cannot save us from sin. Only the blood of Christ washes away sins (I John 1:7-9).

Remember; while works of the law of Moses and works of our own righteousness are of no value for salvation, the works that God ordained and appointed for us are. Scripture says clearly, "Ye see that by works a man is justified, and not only by faith" (Jas. 2:24). Baptism was ordained by God as the appointed time and place where he would save us from our sins. We do not believe in water salvation. We believe we are saved by the blood of Jesus when in faith we obey his command to be baptized (Acts 10:48).

171. WHAT BAPTISM IS NOT

Viewing a thing from the negative standpoint helps us see it clearer. Consider what Christian Baptism is not:
* **Baptism is not merely a physical act**. It is a gesture of the heart (Rom. 6:3-4; 17-18).
* **Baptism is not to cleanse the body**. It "is the answer of a good conscience toward God" (I Pet. 3:21). In baptism the soul is cleansed from the guilt of sin (Acts 22:16).
* **Baptism is not a church ordinance**. It is a command of the Lord Jesus (Mark 16:15-16; Matt. 28-19-20).
* **Baptism is not a christening ordinance for infants**. It is a

condition of becoming a Christian (Gal. 3:26-27).
* **Baptism is not a work of man's righteousness**. It is a portion of God's righteousness (Tit. 3:5; Acts 10:48).
* **Baptism is not an outward sign of an inward grace**. It is an act of obedience wherein Christ washes away our sins (Acts 22:16).
* **Baptism is not an act performed to show the world that we are saved**. It is an act of obedience complied with in order to receive salvation (Acts 2:38).
* **Baptism is not by sprinkling or pouring of water on the head**. It is a burial and resurrection like that of Christ (Col. 2:12; Rom. 6:4-5).
* **Baptism is not just to join a denomination**. It is to be born again (John 3:3-5).

To be properly baptized, we must:
* **Do so with the right attitude**; with genuine faith and repentance and submission to Christ (Heb.ll:6; Acts 17:30; Matt. 7:21).
* **Do so in the right way**; by immersion in water (Rom. 6:3-4; Acts 8:37-38).
* **Do so for the right purpose**; to receive forgiveness (Acts 22:16) and to be united with Christ and his church (Gal. 3:26-27; I Cor. 12:13).

Have you complied with Christ's will in baptism? If you wish to know more about God's plan for your life, contact a **Church of Christ** near you.

172. BLESSINGS OF THE HOLY SPIRIT

When a believing person is baptized into Christ he is given "the gift of the Holy Spirit" (Acts 2:38).

* The Spirit is the seal of our acceptance. Christians are "sealed with the Holy Spirit of promise" (Eph. 1:13). Ancient kings had their personal signets or seals by which they identified their possessions and documents. For us to be thus sealed means that

we are God's possession.
* The Spirit is the "earnest of our inheritance" (Eph. 1:14). An earnest is a down payment on a purchase that secures it for the one making it. In salvation God gives us his own earnest, the Holy Spirit.
* We are strengthened with power in the inward man by the Spirit (Eph. 3:16).
* "The Spirit also helpeth our infirmity and when we do not know how to pray as we ought, "the Spirit . . . maketh intercession for us . . . according to the will of God" (Rom. 8:26-27).
* The love of God is shed abroad in our hearts through the Holy Spirit was given unto us" (Rom. 5:5).

The reception of these divine gifts is tied to the sacred Word of God which the Holy Spirit caused to be written (I Pet. 1:20-21). Without the Scriptures we would be like those men of Ephesus who did not even know the Spirit had been given (Acts 19:2). God's Word is the sword of the Spirit (Eph. 6:17). The implanted Word, given by the Spirit, is able to save our souls (Jas. 1:21).

God in his mercy saves us, "through the washing of regeneration (baptism) and the renewing of the Holy Spirit," which he pours out upon us richly through Jesus . . . " (Tit. 3:5-6). Have you claimed your gift of the Holy Spirit?

XV.
WHAT THE FUTURE HOLDS

173. IMAGINE THE FUTURE OF THE CHURCH

Futurists tell us what the future of our society will likely be. A numerous band of preachers and professors have taken it upon themselves to "change" the faith, worship and practice of churches of Christ. Already they control two of our major universities and have a foothold in some others. They have been able to capture congregations in every section of the country, including some of our largest.

Having recently read a dozen books written by prominent spokesmen of the change movement, we can reasonably predict what churches embracing this movement will be like, given time to reach the full extent of their transformation.

* They will have renounced the concept of restoring the faith and practice New Testament Christianity. Many of the leading spokesmen have done already this.
* They will have dropped the name "Church of Christ" from their congregations. Already several congregations have done this and others are being encouraged to do so. They find such names as Community Church more appealing to them.
* They will not view the Bible as the final and absolute authority of their faith and practice. They will deny that it is a pattern for them to follow. This is a cardinal doctrine of the change agents.
* They will have women in all areas of leadership, including the pulpit. Already a few have ventured thus far. The advocates are busy preparing the way for this change.
* They will use instruments of music in their worship. When they first begin their transition they all deny such will ever happen. But they argue that our objection to instruments is not a Biblical

injunction, just our opinion and tradition. The use of them they will not condemn as sinful. They already are willing to allow the use of instruments on some occasions such as in Bible classes, youth programs and special services. Like their older brothers in the Christian Churches/Disciples of Christ, who said and did the same thing, they will eventually have them.
* They will use choirs and soloists to sing in their worship services. Some already have introduced these changes. Others are insisting such is acceptable to God. Such is a vital part of the entertainment approach to worship.
* They will have transformed their communion service. Some are advocating and some have already begun to observe it as part of a common meal. Some insist that the day of observance is not limited to the first day of the week.
* They will be openly fellowshipping denominational bodies. Many are already doing so. Some are even inviting leaders of other religious bodies to come and speak at their services. Some are already participating in interdenominational campaigns such as the Billy Graham Crusades.
* They will not think of themselves as the Lord's one true church. Rather they will openly present themselves a denominational body; one of the hundreds of similar bodies, all of the same worth and value.
* They will be claiming Alexander Campbell and Barton W. Stone as their founder. Many of their "historians" are already doing so.
* They will have demonstrative, charismatic/pentecostal type of worship services, strong on emotionalism and excitement and extremely short on Bible.
* They will prefer storytelling and drama instead of old-fashioned Bible preaching. This trend is well along even now.

Such megatrends in churches tend to take one or more generations to reach full flower. Major shifts always trigger a reaction from those not inclined to embrace such radical departures from the faith and worship they hold dear. This tells us there will almost certainly be an open rupture in the brotherhood of our churches. While it may take 20 or more years to happen, absent some major deliverance, it will occur. The extent of the damage the church will suffer is dependent on the response of those who prefer the old paths of primitive Christianity to the broad paths of denominationalism. If, like Rip Van Winkle, we sleep the next twenty years, we run the risk of losing the great majority of our congregations, schools and people to the change movement. If, by God's grace, faithful brethren can be stirred to action, we may hold our losses to a minimum. How does the future of the Lord's Cause look from where you stand? Will you sleep or take your place on the walls?

174. LOOKING AHEAD TO THE YEAR 2050

Futurists study the past and present and tell us what the future might possibly be. They analyze trends and predict future changes, for good or bad. Wise businessmen consider such projections when investing for the future of their companies. I am no prophet, but I invite you to make an imaginary trip to a large American city in the year 2050. Our purpose will be to visit a Church of Christ and worship with them. Given current trends and projections at work among our brethren here are some things you might possibly find.

You may find a woman teaching the adult Bible class, preaching or even serving as an elder. Already professors are telling us that we have misunderstood the verses that seem to forbid such. They tell us we have too long denied our Christian ladies the privilege to use their talents to the glory of God. A few trendsetter congregations already have their women teachers and preachers.

The minister or ministeress may well be adorned in a lovely clerical robe. Our objections to such practices will likely have been determined by change agents to be based only on our rural, frontier heritage and our narrow, unscholarly approach to interpreting the Bible. The preacher may well be identified as pastor of the church and have "Rev." affixed to his or her name. They would argue that such matters are our traditions and too trivial to dispute about.

There might even be a guest speaker from the Catholic, Baptist or Pentecostal church. They no will longer think of the church as an exclusive body. To them all denominations are equally pleasing to God.

You may well find the service to be unfamiliar in tone and content. There could be a dramatic presentation, and possibly even an "interpretive spiritual dance." The service would likely be demonstrative with bodily gyrations, shouting and applause. The music likely will be "contemporary" and may well include instrumental accompaniment from a piano or organ and possibly a rock band. Rather than join in congregational singing, you will be expected to sit quietly and listen as the soloist or praise team present their performance. The choir will then sing their selection and finally the congregation will be invited to join in a hymn or two. Such features are already being discussed and rationalized and some are already implementing some or all of them.

The lesson of the hour may well consist of a brief story or parable related by a clergyman or woman. Little emphasis will be placed on the Bible, as "proof-texting" will have long ago been rejected. Nothing will be presented as absolutely right or wrong. Postmodern thinking will not allow such utterances. Doctrine will have no place in the lesson. Promoters of change concluded that doctrine doesn't matter and that it is doctrine that makes people disagree and divide. The story will come to a close with a call for those who want a relationship with Jesus to come and be saved by grace through faith. Baptism will no longer be considered as essential to salvation since they have concluded that obedience plays no part in salvation. It may however possibly be retained for church membership.

Communion may possibly be observed following dismissal. It will be offered in the fellowship hall, during the pot luck meal. It will be a joyful and festive celebration of the good life they have in Christ.

This is already being advocated by some. There may also be a Saturday evening service with Communion for those who do not wish to assemble on the Lord's Day. The leading lights of our change movement have rejected the idea of a Biblical pattern that must be followed. They have concluded that Communion can be observed on other occasions than the first day of the week. The prevailing thinking in that element of the church is that we must give the people what they want if we expect to get them into our churches. Since other religious bodies are doing this with success, we would be foolish not to follow their suit.

Bible classes will offer alternatives for every taste. There well may be a class devoted to reviewing contemporary books, or perhaps classic literature with relevant themes. Others may offer physical fitness for Christians, or the challenges of aging. There could be an armchair travelers' class which views travel logs. A class could study classic movies and television shows. There could be arts and crafts. A course in social activism will cover such topics as ecology, AIDS ministry, money management, the challenges of leisure time and other timely subjects. It will truly be a "felt needs" program. For those who are elderly and traditional in their thinking they will still have a few classes that study the Bible.

If you are currently 50 or older, and a faithful Christian, very likely you are totally revulsed at the idea of such an incredible situation. Your blood pressure would rise and your stomach would churn. You probably would get up and walk out. I would! Such a group would be a church of Christ in name only, even if they were directly descended from a faithful church of today. If you searched hard enough, you likely could find a congregation that would still worship and serve in the way you are familiar with. It probably would be small in size and likely on the outskirts of town or in a rural setting.

You may be wagging your head and saying "You are crazy! Such is so farfetched as to be insane." But my dear friend, the things I am seeing as future possibilities are already being done here and there by those who are clamoring for change. The section on the Bible classes is straight from the bulletins of local denominational churches. Our change agents are following these churches in all other areas and it is only reasonable to think they will embrace such programs as well.

As in all futuristic projects factors may arise that will nullify the prediction. For example if our brethren should wake up and realize just how wrong and destructive the change movement is; if they should show the promoters of change the door; if they should repent and turn back to God with humble and obedient hearts; we might well see Christ's church, as we have known her, surviving and flourishing in that distant day. May God grant that this be the case.

XVI.
OUR PLEA AND PRAYER FOR OUR DEPARTING BRETHREN

175. RETURN O BACKSLIDING ISRAEL

As we are confronted with the sweeping waves of apostasy that we call the "change movement," we find ourselves locked in a battle for the survival of the church. We must never forget that those who are arrayed in the army of the change movement are our own brethren. They are God's children, even though they are alienated, estranged and hostile to the family of their spiritual birth. While we must oppose their destructive efforts and protect the church from their incursions, we still have a duty toward them. God "is not wishing that any should perish, but that all should come to repentance" (II Pet. 3:9). That certainly includes his own children whom Satan has deceived and turned against their Savior's Way.

* The prophets of ancient Israel never ceased to appeal to their backsliding brethren to repent and return to God's ways. God sent Jeremiah to say to his brethren, "Return, thou backsliding Israel, saith Jehovah . . . return and I will heal your backslidings" (Jer. 3:12, 22). With this in mind consider the following thoughts when you pray:
* We must fervently pray that they will realize the error of their ways. With Elisha we must pray, "Lord open (their) eyes that (they) may see" (II King 6:17). A multitude of young, impressionable preachers have been indoctrinated with the doctrines of the change movement by their Bible professors while attending schools they thought were faithful to Christ. Others have been deceived by the smooth and fair speech of false teachers who can make the good look bad and the bad appear to be good (Rom. 16:17-18). If they can be helped to see the doctrines of change in the clear light of God's Word maybe some

of them will be salvaged.
* We must pray that they will cease from troubling Christ's church. Men who are unhappy with the simple gospel and the simple worship of the New Testament should resign their positions as preachers and seek employment elsewhere. If they no longer love the church, they should leave it rather than sow discord and division by trying to impose unapproved changes upon her. God hates those who do this (Prov. 6:16-19).
* We must pray that they will renounce the false teaching they have embraced and be content to walk in the old paths of Scripture truth. No matter how glamorous or successful in gaining numbers, if a method or message is contrary to God Will it is deadly and must be renounced.
* We must pray that they will seek God's mercy and forgiveness for the harm they have done to his family.
* Pray that they may once again be useful servants in the Master's service. Some of these men have great talent and ability that are needed to build up the kingdom and save the lost. Pray that they will not be lost to a false way.
* Pray that they will build up that which they have damaged. May they be sorrowful and ashamed for their past behavior and determined to repair the breaches and spend the balance of their days contributing to her well-being.
* We must pray that if they cannot and will not do the above, they will be honest and honorable enough to leave and go to their own place. To do otherwise is dishonorable.
* Not only should we pray, but when presented with the opportunity, we should say to these misguided brethren, "Return O backsliding brother to the church you once served, to the kingdom of God's dear Son, to the household of faith, while the opportunity is yours."

176 A PRAYER FOR CHRIST'S CHURCH

In a day when Christ's precious church is being ravaged and torn by agents of change who reject his authority and rebel at his prohibitions, we offer up the following prayer. Please join us in daily prayer for the welfare of the Lord's church.

Holy Father: We pray that you will bless **the men who stand before your congregations as preachers** of your gospel. May they take seriously their privilege and duty to represent You to your people. May they preach "the whole counsel of God," taking no liberties with it and omitting nothing that is needful for your people. Give them the courage to be faithful even in the face of opposition. Please raise up a new generation of young men who love your church, your Word and your Son.

We ask that you bless **the elders who lead your people**. That they will lead wisely, seeing that your flock is properly fed and protected from those who would do them harm. Give them wisdom and discernment that no one be able slip into their fold and steal away the hearts of your people. May their congregations grow strong and flourish under their supervision and guidance. May they not be intimidated into compromise by those who clamor to be like the world about them.

Please bless **those who teach our classes**. May they understand the importance of indoctrinating your people in the truth, showing their students the right way to serve you and pointing out the dangers of the wrong.

Be with **those who work with our young people**. There are tremendous allurements to draw them away from faithful Word to the allusions of entertainment and emotionalism. Please help them be faithful stewards looking after their charges. May they fill their young disciples with love for Christ and his Church and an appetite for the knowledge of your Word. May they lead them to understand that discipleship in Christ means service to God and humanity, taking the gospel to the lost and not just having fun.

Please bless **our sisters in Christ**. They are under tremendous pressure by the world to embrace the ideas and lifestyle of the Feminist Movement. While we are grateful that they have opportunities in higher education and the business and professional world, may they not seek to bring the standards of the world into your church. Please help them to be content with the role you have prescribed for them in your holy Word. Help them to understand, that great will be their reward in heaven if they are faithful to your standards.

Father, we pray for **those who lead and teach in our Christian schools**. We are truly grateful for the many contributions they have made to the progress of your kingdom in days past. It appears that some of them have forgotten their proper role as helpers to your church. Please Father, help them to reject those who seek to use them to impose harmful changes to your spiritual family. May they be faithful in teaching the ancient truths of the gospel and in strengthening the faith of our young people and preacher students.

Dear Lord, we pray that you will **protect your people** from those who have embraced the doctrines of men and are seeking to interject them into your church. Please Father, defeat those who would destroy your people by their false teachings. Confound their schemes and projects. We pray that they will repent and return to the safe boundaries of your Holy Word and once again be true soldiers of Christ. But if they refuse to do so, please dash and destroy their plans to change your church into a church of their own design.

Please bless your people, one and all, that they will awaken to the dangers before us and rise up to defend the walls of Zion against her enemies. May every preacher be willing to take his place in the battle lines. May every elder be a strong leader of the home-guard. May every member shout "No with an emphatic voice when false teachers seek to lead them astray.

Help us Holy Father to be strong in evangelism, benevolent to everyone in need and determined to maintain the unity of the Sprit in the bonds of peace. May we please you in all ways and in all things is our prayer,

Through our Lord Jesus, Amen.

XVII.
ARE YOU WILLING TO HELP?

177. NEEDED 1,000 FAITHFUL HELPERS

We need a thousand faithful Christians who love the Lord and his church and are willing to get seriously involved in this endeavor to stem the tide of apostasy. We must establish a network of helpers who will stand together in the defense of the faith once delivered (Jude 3), and then coordinate our efforts for maximum success. A thousand helpers, strategically placed across the nation, could effectively block the advances of the promoters of change and contain those pockets already under their influence. The 1000 helpers we need can be men or women, young or old, preachers or not. They just need to be willing to work with us in praying for God's intervention and help, for others who will help us and for those who are struggling with the enemy in their local congregations. Just today we received an e-mail from a brother in Nevada whose congregation is bring torn to pieces by this problem. He is distraught and discouraged. He needs our prayers and encouragement to keep on keeping on.

As to specific ways to help:
* A helper could duplicate copies of **Christianity: Then and Now** and distribute them within his congregation and mail them to the other congregations in his area. That could be a city, county, region or state, depending on his resources and the number of congregations involved. A copy shop can duplicate the paper for something like .20 per copy or maybe less. It could be done on a copy machine owned by the congregation or by some businessman who wants to help.
* The helper could provide the funds and we would mail the churches from here. It costs us $ .50 per month to mail two copies to each church . . . addressed to Minister/Elders. We can

tell you how many congregations are in a given city or state and furnish the addresses. Several brethren already provide the funds so we can mail churches in their area.
* The helper could persuade his congregation to underwrite the cost of the mailing to their city, county or state . . . or some other state.
* He or she might persuade the ladies' Bible class to take this as a project or recruit several individuals to pitch in and help on a regular basis so we could blanket a chosen area.
* The helper could assemble his own monthly packet of materials from various sources and mail them to the preachers and elders of his area. One brother in Ft. Worth area and another in New York do this.
* The helper could talk to individual Christians and persuade them to pitch in and help us mail the paper from here.
* There are some tracts that need to be written and printed. The helper could assist us in providing the funds to print one or more titles. We need a tract to cover every aspect of the change movement.

The author has taken it upon himself to read and review the books written by the change agents and those of our brethren who are responding. When the reviews are written they are sent out to those who are helping. Eventually they are used in the paper and on the website. These you can share as you wish. Perhaps you can send them to your web contacts, fellow-Christians and preachers.

Among the projects that need attention is sending **Christianity Then and Now** to our overseas missionaries. This is important because historically, false teachers always make a run for mission outposts. New converts, with no depth of knowledge and experience are easy targets for them.

We need to get the paper to all our churches in Canada. Probably we have no more than 200-250 there. If you know of a good preacher or congregation up there, we could work through them since postage from the US to Canada is quite high.

We need to be able to send the paper to preacher students in our colleges and schools of preaching.

Since the change movement seems to flow from our Christian Schools, we need to make sure we send it to every church in the vicinity of those schools. For example we are now mailing all of the churches in Nashville, Memphis, Oklahoma City, Abilene, Nebraska, Oregon, Los Angeles, Lubbock, Montgomery, Florence, AL, Parkersburg, WV and Searcy, AR. You might wish to help us with the cost of these mailings. This is not to say that all of the schools in those cities are promoting the change agenda, but we are trying to practice preventive medicine to stop the spread of a deadly contagion. We need to vaccinate even healthy people.

Another project that needs attention is to include pertinent tracts and inserts in our mailings. Using the bulk mailing permit, we can have up to 3 1/2 oz. in each piece we mail. We have already included a tract, a sermon and a Strategy sheet. The idea is, if we can put into the hands of preachers and elders such material it will help them fortify their members' faith. We encourage them to order quantities to give to each family. For example, Bro. Wayne Jackson has an excellent tract on Choirs and Solos in Worship. We could send that along with each set of papers mailed for .30, the cost of the tract. A thousand tracts would cost us $300 plus postage. Other good tracts need to be sent from time to time.

For your information, We are now mailing to the leaders of approximately 4,400 churches. We cover all the congregations in 37 states . . . primarily in the mission states. Many others receive the paper in the other states, but not every church gets it. We could add all the congregations in Kentucky or Arkansas for approximately $250 each per month. The change problem is at work in many of the congregations in the large cities over the nation. It is essential that we act quickly and decisively.

Would you be interested in being one of a thousand sentries that will be set for the defense of the gospel? (Phil. 1:16)? If so please contact us at once. We stress again that we do not want to form any kind of organization. We just want to find sound and faithful Christians who will work together for the common good of the kingdom of Christ. Each will answer to his own elders and Christ. We will help each other, keep each other informed and plan our efforts for the best results. We have no interest in forming a clique or faction or building a fiefdom for ourselves and I am sure you feel the same. May God bless and use us to his honor and glory. May it be that when we finish our course on this earth, the church will be stronger and larger than when we first became members of it.

John Waddey
12630 W. Foxfire Dr.
Sun City West, AZ 85375
Ph. (623) 214-3715
e-mail: johnwaddey@aol.com

OTHER BOOKS BY JOHN WADDEY

An Album of Bible Characters (paper) $ 6.00
The Anatomy of Sin (cloth) $ 6.00
Character Cameos From the Bible (paper) $ 4.00
A Child of the King (cloth) $ 6.00
Declaring God's Righteousness (cloth) $ 8.00
An Exposition of Ecclesiastes and Song of Solomon (paper) $ 7.00
Family Living in Christ (paper) $ 5.00
Fighting the Good Fight of Faith (cloth) $ 7.00
Following Jesus (paper) $ 8.00
The Great Commission and You (paper) $ 3.00
Growing in the Grace and Knowledge of Christ (paper) $ 3.00
The Great Inheritance (paper) $ 8.00
Churches of Christ of East Tennessee, a history (paper) $12.00
Churches of Christ of East Tennessee, a history (cloth) $16.00
Introducing the Church of Christ (paper) $ 4.95
Liberalism, Deadly Enemy of the Church (cloth) $ 7.00
Life and Lessons of H. Leo Boles (paper) $ 6.00
Life and Sermons of J. W. McGarvey (paper) $ 8.00
Pen Portraits of Bible Characters (paper) $ 6.00
Preaching to Preachers About Preaching (cloth) $ 6.00
Searching the Scriptures (cloth) $ 8.00
Outlined Introduction to the Old Testament Vol. 1 (cloth) $10.00
Outlined Introduction to the Old Testament Vol. 2 (paper) $10.00
Outlined Introduction to the New Testament (cloth) $45.00
Tennessee School for the Blind: the First 150 Years (cloth) $40.00
Does God Exist? Correspondence with an Atheist (paper) $ 4.00
Two Points of View: An Exchange With an Atheist (paper) $ 4.00
Christianity Then and Now, Vol. I (paper) $ 6.50
Christianity Then and Now, Vol. II (paper) $ 6.50
Christianity Then and Now, Vol. III (paper) $ 6.50

* Plus Shipping and handling.

Books may be ordered from the author at
12630 W. Foxfire Dr.
Sun City West, AZ 85375
johnwaddey@aol.com